CW01528528

COLERIDGE AND THE PSYCHOLOGY OF ROMANTICISM

Coleridge and the Psychology of Romanticism

Feeling and Thought

David Vallins
Research Fellow in English
University of Hong Kong

First published in Great Britain 2000 by
MACMILLAN PRESS LTD
Houndmills, Basingstoke, Hampshire RG21 6XS and London
Companies and representatives throughout the world

A catalogue record for this book is available from the British Library.

ISBN 0–333–73745–8

First published in the United States of America 2000 by
ST. MARTIN'S PRESS, INC.,
Scholarly and Reference Division,
175 Fifth Avenue, New York, N.Y. 10010

ISBN 0–312–21579–7

Library of Congress Cataloging-in-Publication Data
Vallins, David.
Coleridge and the psychology of Romanticism : feeling and thought / David Vallins.
p. cm.
Includes bibliographical references and index.
ISBN 0–312–21579–7 (cloth)
1. Coleridge, Samuel Taylor, 1772–1834—Knowledge—Psychology. 2. Coleridge, Samuel Taylor, 1772–1834—Philosophy. 3. Poetry––Psychological aspects. 4. Emotions and cognition. 5. Thought and thinking. 6. Romanticism—England. 7. Consciousness. I. Title.
PR4487.P8V35 1999
821'.7—dc21 99–15388
CIP

This book is printed on paper suitable for recycling and made from fully managed and sustained forest sources.

10 9 8 7 6 5 4 3 2 1
09 08 07 06 05 04 03 02 01 00

Printed and bound in Great Britain by
Antony Rowe Ltd, Chippenham, Wiltshire

It is the dire epidemic of man in the social state to forget the substance in the appearance, the essence in the form.

(Say, 1: 77)

As every faculty, with every the minutest organ of our nature, owes its whole reality and comprehensibility to an existence incomprehensible and groundless, because the ground of all comprehension: not without the union of all that is essential in all the functions of our spirit, not without an emotion tranquil from its very intensity, shall we worthily contemplate in the magnitude and integrity of the world that life-ebullient stream which breaks through every momentary embankment, again, indeed, and evermore to embank itself, but within no banks to stagnate or be imprisoned.

(Friend, 1: 519)

Contents

Acknowledgements

Thanks are particularly due to Roy Park, for great generosity with his time, advice, enthusiasm and encouragement both as supervisor of the thesis in which much of this book originated, and on numerous more recent occasions; to the British Academy and the University of Hong Kong, for the Research Studentship and Research Fellowship during which most of the book was written; to the Committee on Research and Conference Grants of the University of Hong Kong, for generous assistance with research-funding; to Nicholas Roe, James Engell, and Thomas McFarland, for advice and encouragement; and to Charmian Hearne and Julian Honer, for advice and practical assistance in preparing the manuscript for the press. Others who have commented on parts of the text at various stages include Paul Hamilton, Jerome Christensen, John Beer, A. D. Nuttall, and Nicholas Reid, as well as several anonymous readers for journals and publishers. I am also grateful to Rick Tomlinson for providing me with a transcript of Coleridge's Opus Maximum manuscripts. The last part of Chapter 2 is based on a paper presented at the 1996 Coleridge Summer Conference; an earlier version of parts of Chapters 3 and 4 has appeared in *ELH* (© 1997 by the Johns Hopkins University Press), and parts of Chapters 5 and 6 have appeared in *Prose Studies* (reprinted by permission from *Prose Studies*, Vol. 19, No. 1, published by Frank Cass Publishers, 900 Eastern Avenue, Ilford IG2 7HH, Essex, England), and *Modern Philology* (© 1996 by the University of Chicago. All rights reserved), respectively. Material from *Collected Letters of Samuel Taylor Coleridge*, ed. E. L. Griggs, 6 vols. (OUP, 1956–71) is reprinted by permission of Oxford University Press, and material from S. T. Coleridge, *The Friend*, ed. Barbara E. Rooke, 2 vols (copyright © 1969 by Routledge & Kegan Paul Ltd.), and S. T. Coleridge, *Biographia Literaria*, ed. James Engell and W. Jackson Bate, 2 vols (copyright © 1983 by Princeton University Press) is reprinted by permission of Routledge & Kegan Paul Ltd. and Princeton University Press.

Symbols and Abbreviations

SYMBOLS

~~*word*~~	Text struck out thus indicates a deletion in Coleridge's manuscript.
< >	Indicates an insertion between the lines in Coleridge's manuscript.

ABBREVIATIONS

AR	S. T. Coleridge. *Aids to Reflection*. Ed. John Beer. *Collected Works*, Vol. 9. Princeton, NJ: Princeton UP, 1993.
BL	*Biographia Literaria*. Eds James Engell and W. Jackson Bate. *Collected Works*, Vol. 7. Princeton, NJ: Princeton UP, 1983.
CJ	Immanuel Kant. *The Critique of Judgement*. Trans. J. C. Meredith. Oxford: Clarendon, 1928; 1952.
CL	*Collected Letters of Samuel Taylor Coleridge*. Ed. E.L. Griggs, 6 vols. Oxford: Clarendon, 1956–71.
CM	S. T. Coleridge. *Marginalia*. Ed. George Whalley. *Collected Works*, Vol. 12. Princeton, NJ: Princeton UP, 1980–.
CN	*The Notebooks of Samuel Taylor Coleridge*. Ed. Kathleen Coburn. New York: Routledge, 1957–.
CPR	Immanuel Kant, *Critique of Pure Reason*. Trans. Norman Kemp Smith. London: Macmillan, 1929.
CPW	S. T. Coleridge, *Poetical Works*. Ed. E. H. Coleridge, 2 vols. Oxford: Clarendon, 1912.
C&S	S. T. Coleridge. *On the Constitution of the Church and State*. Ed. John Colmer. Collected Works, Vol. 10. Princeton, NJ: Princeton UP, 1976.
C17thC	*Coleridge on the Seventeenth Century*. Ed. R. F. Brinkley. Durham, NC: Duke UP, 1955.
ELH	*English Literary History*
EOT	S. T. Coleridge. *Essays on His Times in 'The Morning Post' and 'The Courier'*. Ed. David V. Erdman, 3 vols.

	Collected Works, Vol. 3. Princeton, NJ: Princeton UP, 1977.
Friend	S. T. Coleridge. *The Friend*. Ed. Barbara E. Rooke, 2 vols. *Collected Works*, Vol. 4. Princeton, NJ: Princeton UP, 1969.
JAAC	*Journal of Aesthetics and Art Criticism*
JHI	*Journal of the History of Ideas*
Lects 1795	S. T. Coleridge. *Lectures (1795) On Politics and Religion*. Eds Lewis Patton and Peter Mann. *Collected Works*, Vol. 1. Princeton, NJ: Princeton UP, 1971.
Lects 1808–19	S. T. Coleridge. *Lectures 1808–19 On Literature*. Ed. R. A. Foakes, 2 vols. *Collected Works*, Vol. 5. Princeton, NJ: Princeton UP, 1987.
LS	S. T. Coleridge. *Lay Sermons*. Ed. R. J. White. *Collected Works*, Vol. 6. Princeton, NJ: Princeton UP, 1972.
Monboddo	James Burnet, Lord Monboddo. *Of the Origin and Progress of Language*, 6 vols. Edinburgh, 1773–92.
MP	*Modern Philology*
OED	*Oxford English Dictionary*
OM	David Hartley. *Observations on Man*, 2 vols. London, 1749.
PLects	*The Philosophical Lectures of Samuel Taylor Coleridge*. Ed. Kathleen Coburn. London: Pilot, 1949.
PMLA	*Publications of the Modern Language Association of America*
Say	Victoria College Library, MS 29 (numbering of volumes follows that in the manuscripts).
SR	*Studies in Romanticism*
STI	F. W. J. Schelling. *System of Transcendental Idealism*. Trans. Peter Heath. Charlottesville, VA.: University Press of Virginia, 1978.
SWF	S. T. Coleridge. *Shorter Works and Fragments*. Eds H. J. Jackson and J. R. de J. Jackson. *Collected Works*, Vol. 11. Princeton, NJ: Princeton UP, 1995.
TT	S. T. Coleridge. *Table Talk*. Ed. Carl Woodring. *Collected Works*, Vol. 14. Princeton, NJ: Princeton UP, 1990.
UTQ	*University of Toronto Quarterly*

WProse — *The Prose Works of William Wordsworth*. Eds W. J. B. Owen and J.W. Smyser, 2 vols. Oxford: Clarendon, 1974.

WPW — *The Poetical Works of William Wordsworth*. Eds E. de Selincourt and Helen Darbishire, 5 vols. Oxford: Clarendon, 1940–9.

Introduction

Coleridge is unique among British Romantics in the extent to which a fascination with psychology – or 'the science of the nature, functions, and phenomena of the human soul or mind' (as *The Oxford English Dictionary* puts it)[1] – dominates his writings in diverse genres and on superficially unrelated topics. What chiefly distinguishes his poems from those of his contemporaries, indeed, is their degree of introspection or self-reflexiveness, and especially their tendency to explore the relationships between various aspects of consciousness or mental functioning.[2] Wordsworth's evocations of the connections between environment and imagination or past and present consciousness, for example, place far more emphasis on a world conceived as existing independently of the mind, and informing or shaping our responses to it.[3] Though Blake's visions of political and spiritual liberation are among the most powerful externalizations of desire in Romantic literature, moreover, the political and social realities underlying his quest for transcendence are far more prominent than in most of Coleridge's poems.[4] Though sometimes indirectly expressed, Shelley's ideals of political liberation and scientific enlightenment consistently play a more central role in his writing than explorations of personal psychology *per se*, let alone the combinations of psychology with metaphysics and epistemology which, as we shall see, Coleridge's idealist theories enabled him to develop. Keats's evocations of a yearning to transcend the quotidian perhaps come closer than any other Romantic lyrics to paralleling Coleridge's own ambiguous combination of idealism (whether political or philosophical) with reflection on its psychological causes. Yet the fleeting nature of such speculative or imaginative liberations is itself so prominent a theme in Keats as repeatedly to shift his view of reality towards the practical limitations in which they originate, rather than maintaining the subjective and idealist emphasis which – despite their ambiguities – characterizes most of Coleridge's poems.[5] Whether they explore the relationships between emotion, imagination, and philosophical reflection (as in 'Dejection' and the Conversation Poems), or between the conscious and unconscious mind (as in 'Kubla Khan', 'Christabel', and 'The Pains of Sleep'); whether they give external and dramatic form to states of emotion (as in 'Limbo' and 'Ne Plus Ultra'), or combine the drama of emotions with that of ideas and of religious faith (as in 'The Ancient Mariner'), Coleridge's poems are remarkable for the extent to which subjective experience rather than any aspect of external reality forms their principal topic.

Not only this introspective quality, but also the analytical tendency prominent in many of his poems, is no less evident in Coleridge's critical theory, whose celebrity is due primarily to its attempt to establish how literary and artistic creation relate to other mental processes such as perception and philosophical inquiry. His emphasis on the internal or subjective, indeed, is reflected in his adoption of Schelling's theory of a single productive process underlying all aspects of consciousness, whereby the act of perception is explained as an earlier or lower form of the imaginative power expressed in works of philosophy and art. Through this theory, the external world which Wordsworth describes as largely determining not only his own creative consciousness, but also the ideas and language of the rustic characters depicted in *Lyrical Ballads*,[6] becomes merely another aspect of subjective experience, and the deterministic theories of empiricists such as Locke and Hartley are replaced with a vision of purely internal dynamics, effectively combining psychology with metaphysics and epistemology.

This reduction of the seemingly external to an aspect of our own self-consciousness (or of a process which transcends the distinctions of 'self' and 'other') has the advantage of theoretically liberating the self from the merely passive role accorded to it by empiricism, and at the same time rendering emotion a matter of no less fundamental importance than physical processes or other supposedly external realities. By defining externality as nothing more than an appearance, indeed, Coleridge's theory represents not only emotional life, but also imaginative and intellectual activity, as in a sense more immediately real than the external world, and at the same time exempts both the poet and the speculative philosopher from the merely secondary roles to which a 'scientific' or empirical outlook is liable to reduce them.

Hence not only Coleridge's poetry, but also his philosophy and critical theory assert the overwhelming importance of subjective experience as against the objective worlds described by natural science and empiricist philosophy.[7] In so doing, however, they also express with unusual intensity a characteristically Romantic sense of alienation, and an associated desire to rediscover a sense of unity between the self and its social or physical environment. Coleridge's emphasis on the unity of thought and perception, that is, arises not merely from a desire to celebrate the self as distinct from the external world, nor merely from an interest in tracing the relationships between different aspects of consciousness, but also from a desire to transcend alienation by achieving a conviction of the unity of self and other.[8]

That the flight from alienation into ideals of unity plays so central a part in Coleridge's writing, indeed, is among the factors which make it particularly representative of the psychological patterns that characterize Romanticism more generally. If there is a single factor which distinguishes the Romantics from writers of other periods or movements, I would argue, it is their fascination with a process of transcendence whereby the uncertainties and dissatisfactions of the phenomenal world are replaced by visions of ideal unity and fulfilment.[9] This pattern, indeed, is no less prominent in those female Romantics who, as Mellor argues, highlight experiences of sympathy between individuals rather than a solitary sense of unity with the physical 'other'.[10] Even in male Romantics, moreover, transcendence is by no means always associated with the idealist theories which Coleridge uses to explain the unity of what appears to be divided – whether this be the conflicting mass of individual selves, or the apparently discrete and separate entities of self and other or subject and object. In Blake, for example, it is expressed primarily in visions of liberation from the deadening constraints of contemporary society and of empirical or scientific knowledge. In Shelley, it emerges principally in visions of social, political, and scientific progress unified and governed by the sympathetic imagination;[11] and in Byron, in the ideal of a transcendent individual forging his own values in opposition to all moral or political constraints.[12] In each case, however, the perfect alternative to reality implies the very real imperfections of the world from which these visions of transcendence arose – a world, above all, of political repression in Britain coupled with a faltering revolution on the continent, in which the youthful aspirations of poets from Blake to Shelley were destined to be thwarted, while Wordsworth and Coleridge abandoned their quest for social and political progress in favour of less tangible ideals.[13]

The experience of negation is thus fundamental to the desire for transcendence expressed equally in Blake's or Shelley's visions of political liberation and in the idealized unity of self and other which Coleridge repeatedly evokes. This dualism is also prominent in Mary Shelley, whose visions of the disappointment of various

Romantic ideals are unusual mainly for the persistence with which she gazes into the abyss of isolation and despair.[14] Though implicitly criticizing the Romantic quest for transcendence, indeed, Shelley's visions of negation have much in common with those of Coleridge's poems which focus on the loss of faith, the absence of hope, and the impossibility of envisaging any unity with others or with God.[15]

It is in the complex of ideas and emotions associated with transcendence, however, that the interaction of feelings and ideas described by Coleridge is most vividly and frequently demonstrated. The feeling of the sublime, he suggests, not only enables us to recognize those truths which intellect alone is unable to grasp, but also arises from our efforts to grasp them.[16] The emotions of elevation and excitement generated by such confrontations with the inexplicable, however, are not only used by Coleridge to justify the insights he claims to possess into the nature of perception and of consciousness in general, but also conceptualized in his evocations of the forces underlying these phenomena. His frequent descriptions of an upward progression through various classes or stages of consciousness towards a sublime awareness of the infinite are clearly informed by emotions generated in the process of thinking, and these emotions are themselves described by Coleridge as liberating him from the dejected states of mind produced by practical and personal disappointment.

Hence the role of the sublime in Coleridge is essentially complementary to that of dejection, or the emotions he associates with an absence of intellectual activity and a consequent sense of being the passive victim of events. Coleridge's writing shuttles between these two polarities of emotion, and the effort involved in articulating his ideas is the bridge from the negative emotions of loss, exclusion, and despair to the positive feelings of elevation, enthusiasm, and excitement which he associates with the discovery or contemplation of fundamental truths.

In referring to these contrasted feelings of alienation and transcendence – whether in Coleridge or his contemporaries – however, we are faced with precisely the difficulty of distinguishing feelings from ideas and vice versa which Coleridge himself indicates when discussing the relationships between emotion and thought. The sense of alienation expressed in much of his writing is at once an intensely painful emotion, and a rational perception of the failure of the external world to satisfy internal desire, and of the fragmentation and conflict involved in everyday experience and social relationships. Similarly at the opposite pole of Romantic consciousness, transcendence is at once a feeling of elevation or sublimity, and a process of contemplating, explaining, or evoking the unity of phenomena which in other states of consciousness appear to be divided. As Coleridge himself pointed out, emotions are often indistinguishable from ideas, and this is never more clearly the case than in the experience of the sublime, which consists in a conviction (or feeling) of truths which have little specific content apart from the idea of their inexpressibleness.[17]

In subtitling this book 'Feeling and Thought', therefore, I refer primarily to the common-sense distinction between the non-rational and the rational – or between sensation, perception, and emotion on the one hand, and thought or rational activity on the other – which is the starting-point not only for Coleridge's analyses of mental functioning, but also for those of contemporary empiricist and idealist philosophers alike. Both Hartley and Schelling (the idols respectively of Coleridge's earliest thought and that of his middle period) argue that sensation and perception (or more generally, those mental processes which appear to be passive) are more closely related to thought or reasoning than they immediately appear to be; but whereas Hartley explains mental processes as in fact being merely physical ones, Schelling explains both mental and physical phenomena as arising from a single productive process. Fundamentally, their objective is the same: namely to explain how mind and matter are related, or how consciousness of objects can arise.[18] This very problem, however, only occurs because of the appearance of a difference between passive and active forms of consciousness, or what (for convenience) I have referred to as 'feeling' and 'thought'.

Certain aspects of experience, however, do not fit neatly into these parallel oppositions of active and passive or mental and physical. Emotions, for example, are often ambiguously situated between the mental and the physical. At the same time, however, they appear to be passive rather than active forms of consciousness, or in other words to arise involuntarily, rather than sharing the deliberate and voluntary qualities of 'thought'.[19] Similarly in the case of 'intuition', something is felt or believed without rational cause or voluntary activity, yet the feeling or belief is clearly at least partly mental, though possibly including physical elements as well. All of these experiences, of course, are explained in Coleridge's later philosophy as arising from a single productive process which transcends the categories of 'mental' and 'physical'. In appearing to be passive, however, 'emotion' and 'intuition' (in the common-sense uses of those terms) are clearly more akin to 'feeling' than to 'thought'.

In using these terms to refer to aspects of experience, however, it is important to note that several of them also have specific technical uses in the works of individual thinkers. 'Intuition', for example, is used by Kant to refer to the source of our knowledge of an external world, though he also considers the possibility of an 'intellectual intuition' which would provide knowledge of essential reality.[20] In Schelling, however, not only consciousness of an external world, but also intellectual and creative activity are forms of 'productive intuition', since both arise from a single dialectical process underlying all forms of consciousness.[21] 'Reason', on the other hand, is used by both Kant and Coleridge to refer to the source of our ideas about essential reality (both metaphysical and moral), which both thinkers describe as deriving not from analytical reflection, but from a form of spontaneous intuition (in the common-sense use of that term).[22] In several places, moreover, Kant decribes such ideas as accompanied by specific forms of 'feeling', such as the feeling of the sublime, and the feeling of reverence for the law.[23] Clearly, therefore, the technical uses of these terms often differ from the non-technical ones, just as the explanations of experience given by both idealist and empiricist philosophers contrast with immediate appearances (for example, in Hartley's theory that thought is governed by the association of ideas).

The central thesis of this book, however, is that feeling and thought are not easily separable or distinguishable, that what claim to be rational arguments are often dependent on sensation, emotion, and intuition, and that the process of articulating concepts or arguments itself influences these non-rational elements in the thinker, resulting in a continuum of feelings and ideas which is revealed with particular clarity in Coleridge's writing. Hence, I argue, the 'common-sense' distinctions between rational and irrational, mental and physical, thought and feeling, etc., tend to break down under analysis, much as they do in Schelling's and Coleridge's theories of the unity of mind and matter. Hence also, Coleridge's work reveals how both philosophy and poetry involve an attempt to articulate intuition or emotion, and thus gives substance to his (and other Romantics') theories of the unity of intellectual and creative activity.[24]

Coleridge, then, is at once an instance – perhaps the supremely vivid instance – of the patterns of negation and transcendence which dominate Romantic consciousness, and unique in the detail and incisiveness with which he documents and analyses those patterns. In other words he is at once poet, psychologist, and philosopher in the highest degree: exemplifying the patterns of experience and desire which dominate Romanticism in general, documenting and analysing those patterns in poems, notebooks, letters, and other writings, and interpreting and seeking to unify them into a complete philosophical system in his best-known prose works. He combines the roles of poet and philosopher, however, not merely in the sense of performing each of these roles alternately, but also in the extent to which emotion informs his theories and vice versa. While analysing his own sensations and emotions, that is, Coleridge is also demonstrating the patterns of thought and feeling – and above all of the flight from alienation into visions of sublime unity – which these very analyses describe.[25]

Most importantly, perhaps, this unity or inseparableness of feeling and thought is demonstrated in Coleridge's transformation of the feelings which accompany intellectual activity into his evocations of the universal process underlying phenomena. Paradoxically, this process is described most clearly by Hume – a thinker whom Coleridge rarely referred to in any but the most negative terms.[26] Both in his *Treatise of Human Nature* and in the *Enquiry Concerning Human Understanding,* Hume suggests that a particularly 'strong' or 'lively' idea – one, that is, which the mind is particularly active in contemplating – can acquire the force of an impression or sensation, whose qualities are then attributed to the object of our contemplation. Hume's chief example is the idea of that 'Force, Power, Energy, &c.' which according to empiricism facilitates the connections between cause and effect. Far from understanding these connections, he argues, 'we consider only the constant experienced conjunction of the events; and as we *feel* a customary connection between the ideas, we transfer that feeling to the objects; as nothing is more usual than to apply to external bodies every internal sensation, which they occasion.'[27] Despite the fact that the context of his discussion is empiricist thought, Hume thus describes with impressive clarity precisely the process whereby Coleridge moves from the excitement or activity of thinking to the objectification of that excitement in his evocations of an energetic, upwardly aspiring universe whose consummation consists in the mind's recognition of its own powers.[28] Yet we must add to Hume's analysis that the indefinable 'quality, with which the mind reflects' on its liveliest ideas includes in Coleridge's case – and, I would argue, in that of many other Romantics – not merely the action of the mind in connecting its ideas, but also the emotions which that action engenders or suppresses.[29] Coleridge's thought, in other words, seems not only to have been the source of sensations which it objectifies in metaphysical concepts, but also to have been at least partly determined by its ability to influence his state of emotion, and especially to replace feelings of dejection and alienation with a sense of sublime activity and energy.

Hume's discussion of how (as Pinch phrases it) 'empiricism ... is set in motion when we take that "je-ne-scai-quoi" of the mind's own motions, give it the names of life – vivacity, liveliness, energy, force – and project it out into the world' thus also assists us in explaining how feeling can be deduced from the purely textual evidences of Coleridge's writings and those of his contemporaries.[30] Coleridge's works, that is, are among the most vivid illustrations of how the processes of thinking and writing can themselves determine the emotions they express, and this circular relationship of thought and feeling, or of feeling and expression, removes certain of the theoretical problems which my discussions of emotion in Coleridge might otherwise seem to involve.[31] That Coleridge frequently had the experience of striving to express feelings or convictions which resisted expression, however, is – I would argue – no less evident than the suffering he experienced in the absence of such creative and intellectual effort. Moreover, the moods of isolation and despair which he escaped through these activities cannot reasonably be regarded purely as effects of his writing, however much they are transformed and formalized in the process of composition.[32] The essentialism implicit in my reference to these emotions, however, can be at least partly reconciled with the scepticism of poststructuralist approaches through a dichotomy which is among Coleridge's own central themes – namely the distinction between mental passivity (or mere receptivity to external determinants) and that creative or intellectual activity which liberates us from such forces. Coleridge, that is, often describes how an empirical or scientific outlook tends to represent individual consciousness as a mere effect of external influences, and how in failing to subject these and other popular attitudes to our own rigorous inquiry we in fact become their victims, seeing both ourselves and others in terms which are unnecessarily reductive.[33] Hence his moods of alienation can in fact be seen as arising from forces which in a broad sense are textual – that is, from popular modes of thought which have not been subjected to the rigorous critique through which he transcends their influence. Though I postulate a reality of emotion underlying his ideas, therefore, I do envisage textual forces as influencing many aspects of the emotions he expresses, and my analysis thus coincides in certain respects both with historico-biographical and with poststructuralist approaches to Romanticism.

In order to treat this complex pattern of ideas and emotions systematically, however, I have – as noted above – provisionally divided it in terms of 'feeling' and 'thought', or on the one hand that combination of emotions, intuitions and sensations which Coleridge and Schelling describe as being experienced in a predominantly passive mode, and on the other, those processes of intellectual or imaginative creativity which they describe as involving an active interpretation or reorganization of the materials of perception and sensation. This distinction is, of course, problematic to the extent that (as many Romantics noted) poetic or artistic creativity involves a combination of active and passive elements, through which spontaneous feeling is unified with the products of reflection.[34] Even Romantic philosophy, indeed, is often an attempt to give rational form to intuition or emotion; yet only through a detailed comparison of the patterns of consciousness revealed in each of these contexts can we understand either the development of Coleridge's writing or the unifying features of Romanticism more generally.

Hence I have begun this study with an exploration of how ideas and emotions interact in the various modes of writing which Coleridge adopted at different stages of his career. I then examine his view of thought as involving an attempt to give verbal and logical form to intuition or emotion, and his associated view of knowledge as depending on a feeling which no words can adequately express. Chapter 3 discusses his attempts to distinguish the feelings associated with knowledge from those accompanying the delusions which he attributed to his literary and philosophical opponents. Chapter 4 explores the ways in which his contemplation of the sublime or inexpressible facilitated a transition from negative to positive emotions, and his attempts to justify this liberation by interpreting truth as a process rather than a fixed form of knowledge, and by arguing that the activity of thinking brings us as close as possible to the divine. Chapter 5 shows how the feelings

produced by intellectual activity are reflected in his numerous theories of an ascent of being whose significance is not only intellectual and emotional, but also metaphysical and moral – a relationship which demonstrates particularly clearly the circular and mutual influence of thought and emotion in his writing. Chapter 6 examines his attempts to rationalize his feelings of the sublime and of the underlying unity of phenomena, showing how the impossibility of explaining the origin of consciousness parallels the difficulty of encapsulating the mental processes underlying our ideas. These analogous difficulties, I argue, repeatedly lead Coleridge to associate the process of thinking with divine creativity, and are reflected in his adoption of a prose style which encourages reverence both for the thinking it expresses and for the sublime objects it refers to.

The extent to which Coleridge's work highlights the most important elements of Romantic aesthetics will doubtless remain a matter of controversy; yet as this study seeks to demonstrate, the patterns of thought and emotion involved in Coleridge's varied evocations of a sublime unity underlying the diversity and conflict of phenomena reveal a flight from the limitations of quotidian experience into ideals of unity, progress and freedom which characterizes a much wider range of Romantic writers than merely those who shared Coleridge's political and philosophical opinions, or indeed his gender. In seeking liberation from static definitions of reality into an experience of its indefinableness whose energetic process of self-criticism reflects the elusiveness of its object, Coleridge particularly exemplifies a form of Romantic consciousness which links him not only with Fichte, Schelling, and their Neoplatonic antecedents, but also with Emerson, Nietzsche, and such varied twentieth-century authors as Wallace Stevens and Jacques Derrida.[35] Beyond this specific train of thought, however, the passionate intensity with which he illustrates not only Romantic melancholy but also Romantic optimism, not only the loftiest extremes of the sublime but also the depths of quasi-Schopenhauerian pessimism,[36] not only the most vividly spontaneous expressions of the subconscious in Romantic poetry, but also the most intellectualizing explorations of his own mental functioning, and together with these, the diverse visions of an alternative reality – whether an improved society, or a higher world of faith, love, and unity with the divine – which traditionally distinguish the 'Romantic' of all periods, makes Coleridge the ultimate exemplar of Romantic psychology in most important senses we can give to that expression.

1

On Poetry and Philosophy: Romantic Feeling and Theory in Coleridge and Schelling

If there is a single feature of Coleridge's writing by which (at least in academic circles) he is most often distinguished from other English Romantics, it is his intellectualism. Though Keats's criticism of his inability to remain 'content with half-knowledge' has undergone numerous modifications in succeeding centuries, indeed, the Romantic philosophical tendencies which (among other qualities) Coleridge's work exemplifies are still not infrequently the target of critical deprecation.[1] T. S. Eliot's remark that *Biographia* shows 'the disastrous effects of long dissipation and stupefaction of his powers in transcendental metaphysics' is perhaps the most absurd of twentieth-century assessments; yet it is chiefly feminist critics who now most energetically deprecate Coleridge's intellectualism, especially as exemplifying the pursuit of individual power by which Mellor, in particular, characterizes the work of male Romantics.[2] Despite the prestige which his literary theories (in particular) have enjoyed since the Victorian period, moreover, many are in doubt as to the relationship between the extremes of abstraction which characterize much of his later thought, and the vigour and concreteness of his language and imagery in poems such as 'Kubla Khan' and 'The Ancient Mariner'. Some reconciliation of these polarities has been achieved by critics, such as Kathleen Wheeler, who explore the dramatization of his philosophy in the earlier and best-known poems;[3] yet beyond demonstrating this continuity in his ideas, the question of what unifies his poetic and philosophical writings, and especially of how their experiential functions and significance might be related, has rarely (if ever) been satisfactorily answered. Among the reasons for this, clearly, is the sometimes intimidating influence which poststructuralist assumptions as to the inaccessibleness of any author's experience or motivations have exercised over studies of Romanticism as of every other literary field.[4] Hence, in recent years, studies of Coleridge's thought have tended to emphasize ideas almost to the exclusion of their experiential context – a trend which it is among the aims of this book to reverse.[5]

Rather than showing how Coleridge's philosophy is reflected in his poetry, therefore, this chapter will illustrate certain of the ways in which his writings in both poetry and prose reflect a single – though continually evolving – set of emotional forces. As noted in my Introduction, Coleridge often highlights the ways in which his thought-processes not only give verbal and logical expression to non-rational aspects of consciousness, but themselves influence his emotions in a mutually determining cycle. What – I will argue – connects his poetry with his philosophy, and with his more spontaneous and personal reflections in notebooks, marginalia, and letters, therefore, is chiefly the pleasure or consolation which they both express and seek to sustain, whether through belief in the unity of human beings with each other, with God, and with the natural world, or through faith in the redemptive power of religious devotion, or through the elevated emotions produced by striving to evoke the spirit underlying human consciousness and creativity.

Firstly, I explore the subtly differing ways in which his early poetry and the evolving philosophy of his middle and later periods reveal the pursuit of ideals of unity between God, man, and nature whose elevating and consoling effects are continually highlighted by Coleridge himself. His early poetry, I argue, primarily expresses a spontaneous intuition of such unity, though also exploring topics such as the nature of creative genius and the incomprehensible nature of ultimate truth. The philosophy of his middle period (approximately from 1802 to 1818), however, increasingly seeks to define the ground or source of this unity – an objective which, because that source can only be known through intuition, is strictly unattainable, yet the pursuit of which itself intensifies his conviction of its unifying power. In his philosophical writings after 1818, however, Coleridge increasingly develops a system of symbols for the unity of what appears to be divided, combining Schelling's dialectic with Trinitarian thought primarily in order to express the faith in God's mysterious creative and redemptive power which he believed was indispensable to his spiritual salvation.

The second section examines the varied ways in which Coleridge's early poems express his enduring preoccupation with the unity of self and other, showing how his evocation, in the Conversation Poems, of an idealized unification of the individual with God and physical nature is paralleled, firstly, by his confident descriptions, in 'Religious Musings', of an upward progression of being towards unity with the divine, and secondly, by his attempts to give external and dramatic form to subconscious or prelinguistic emotion in 'Kubla Khan' and 'The Ancient Mariner'. In combining conscious with unconscious and the rational with the intuitive through dramatizations of his imaginative quest for a consoling or redeeming unity, I argue, Coleridge seeks to achieve a reconciliation of individual emotion with its alienated 'other' analogous to that which he idealizes in the Conversation Poems. Hence 'Kubla Khan' and 'The Ancient Mariner' illustrate particularly clearly the function which he attributed to imagination – namely to unify those 'opposite or discordant qualities' which arise from the experiential division of self and other or the intuitive and the rational.[6]

1. THE QUEST FOR UNITY

Coleridge's reputation as the most philosophical of English poets has often obscured the extent to which not only his poems, but also his prose writings on philosophical, religious, and other topics are expressions of intuition or emotion. Whether his poems are explicitly philosophical ('Religious Musings' and the principal Conversation Poems are the best-known examples), or implied to be so by the nature of the puzzles and challenges to interpretation with which their reader is presented (as in 'The Ancient Mariner'),[7] whether they blend the spontaneous and dreamlike with the speculative and intellectual (as in 'Kubla Khan'), or evoke the dominance of perception and creativity by a force of emotion which only philosophical reflection can overcome (as in 'Dejection'), it is consistently the emotional or intuitive – that which ultimately has no justification or support except the poet's word itself and the real or imagined experience to which it refers us – that forms the basis of his argument.[8] To describe any of Coleridge's poems as philosophical, indeed, is to use the word 'philosophical' only in one of its lesser senses – namely as denoting the presentation or suggestion of a theory about the nature of reality, rather than an argument for or an attempt to justify that theory. The central metaphor of 'The Eolian Harp', together with the apologetic self-descriptions which surround and seek to explain (if not to justify) the most philosophical passage of the poem (itself presented as a rhetorical question) may render this speculative quality more overt than usual.[9] Yet it is repeatedly as such 'flitting phantasies' provoked in an 'indolent and passive brain' by the interaction of empirical perception with a non-rational element which somehow bridges the gap between the sensuous and the intellectual that the philosophical content of the Conversation Poems is presented.[10] The 'Voice of Adoration' which 'rouses' the poet of 'Religious Musings' to his adoring certainties, moreover, is scarcely less explicit in its emphasis on the non-rational, albeit that Coleridge's voluntary meditation on 'manifest Godhead' is claimed itself to contribute to the idealized unity of God and man which it describes.[11]

This may, perhaps, be little more than to say that Coleridge's poems demonstrate what he himself described as 'imagination' – according to his definition in *Biographia* (as to Schelling's in the *System of Transcendental Idealism*) the power *par excellence* which bridges the gap between the sensuous and the intellectual, being in one form the origin of the perceptual world, and in another that of works of art or philosophy.[12] In case this seems to involve too precipitate an acceptance of Coleridge's and Schelling's theories, their descriptions of the practical functioning of imagination in producing works of art are no less suggestive. That 'reconciliation of opposite or discordant qualities' which *Biographia* describes as characterizing poetry can clearly be seen as reflecting the tendency of Coleridge's 'idling Spirit' repeatedly to seek an 'Echo or mirror ... of itself', and in so doing to connect the world of sense with that of speculation or interpretation.[13] Similarly in Schelling, it is the 'intuition of art' which finally overcomes the opposition between subject and object, free and not-free, resolving contradictions which intellect alone can never surmount.[14]

Such attempts to represent either metaphysical speculation or works of art as arising from the unity of mind and nature which they describe, however, are obviously problematic in philosophical terms. Schelling's argument, no less than Coleridge's, is clearly self-serving, and reminds us that according to both thinkers, the overarching theory which interprets art and philosophy as being intrinsically united with perception is itself among the products of 'secondary imagination', and thus implicitly of the same order as

Coleridge's 'flitting phantasies'.[15] Schelling's invocation of art as the only means of grasping that which intellect cannot explain, indeed, attributes so much importance to artistic imagination that his philosophical arguments seem helpless without it, and the truth with which he claims to present us has no more solid underpinning than the (supposedly self-fulfilling) faith which Coleridge expresses in 'Religious Musings'.

In such an age of metaphysics, therefore, philosophy was as much dependent as poetry on that power – be it 'imagination' or some form of emotional need – which enabled, or even forced, Coleridge to seek analogies in the perceptual world for his own mental functioning, and to move from these analogies to a theory of underlying unity. This tendency in the Conversation Poems, indeed, has so much in common with the structure of Schelling's *System* (albeit Schelling begins with the theory, and then explains its dependence on the power of imagination) that Coleridge's claim to have arrived at his opinions by 'genial coincidence' derives substantial credibility from the comparison.[16]

To describe the capacity or tendency to construct such analogies and seek justifications for them as 'imagination', however, would clearly be to risk obscuring the issue by ignoring the argument implicit in Coleridge's terminology. To the extent that thought and perception *do* arise from this single power, its speculative or fantastic productions in Coleridge's poetry and thought would be at least substantially validated. Such theories, however, were clearly never susceptible of any proof; and though the practical qualities which Coleridge attributes to imagination are clearly evident in much of his verse and prose, his claim as to its identity with perception has no more solid basis than the frequently 'organic' nature of the products of one and the contents of the other.[17] If there is a single conclusion which can be drawn from Coleridge's or Schelling's tendency to construct and theorize such analogies, indeed, it is that this tendency is irrational, belonging to the realm of feeling, intuition, or emotion rather than that of scientific or (strictly) philosophical inquiry. Clearly, this tendency gave rise to theories of as intensely intellectual or ratiocinative a character as any before or since – though in Coleridge's case at least, I will suggest, this ratiocination was motivated at least as much by the pleasure he derived from such thinking as by the need to find arguments which would support belief.[18] What he reflects on, however, remains remarkably consistent from the poems of 1795 to his latest speculations on the *logos* and the Trinity: namely analogies between the physical world and the products of the mind, and between mind itself and that which engenders or underlies the physical. Increasingly in his later thought, these analogies are mediated by the idea of 'logos', or that 'divine Word' which miraculously unites the theories of the philosopher with knowledge and objective being.[19] Coleridge's later tendency to connect the Christian Trinity with the 'trichotomy' which arises when a 'higher principle' is introduced as 'the source and unity of all thesis and antithesis relations' similarly reveals his enthusiasm for invoking the mysteries of religion, with all their cargo of legitimacy, to support his theories of 'ideal realism', and effectively to stand in for the feeling or emotion which in fact governs his analogizing tendency.[20] By constructing this further analogy between Trinity and trichotomy, Coleridge seeks to mysticize the resolution of oppositions which both he and Schelling postulate in the idea of a single origin for objective and subjective phenomena. The role of reaching beyond the immediacy of thought to finally unify it with its products and discover the indemonstrable basis of transcendental idealism is thus shifted from the analogizing imagination of the Romantic philosopher to the sublimely self-justifying certainties of faith.[21] Whether we attribute this unification to God or to the 'intuition of art', however, its origin remains firmly in the realm of the intuitive and emotional – that is, of the nebulous 'feeling' with which we started.

Coleridge's increasing tendency to connect his own dialectical reflections with the functioning of *logos*, the nature of the Trinity, or similar religious mysteries, however, does more than merely add a further stage of mysticism and complexity to his own construction of analogies or the desire for a sense of 'oneness' which, from many of his self-descriptions, seems to underlie it.[22] What these parallel frameworks (all, ultimately, reflecting his original effort to overcome the opposition between mind and matter, or the inward and the outward) appear to reveal is an increasing desire to stabilize the resolution of dialectical conflict – that is, to escape from the 'infinite series' which both Schelling and Coleridge (most notably in *Biographia*) recognized would result from abandoning that presupposition of the continuity of consciousness which is implied in all reflection.[23] It was, indeed, only the earlier willingness of both these authors to challenge the principle of self-consciousness, and ask what grounds there were for identifying the thinking subject with that which it observed in self-reflection, that allowed the dialectical process of self-questioning – so similar, in many respects, to Derrida's repeated movement 'from ground to ground', gesturing in the direction of an infinite series – to arise in the first place. Had the continuity of consciousness been assumed in the way that both authors saw was *implicit* in all reflection, the sequence of displacements which results from the impossibility of simultaneously thinking and describing that thinking would never have become so important a metaphor and focus for the ubiquitous Romantic concern with connecting the inward and the outward or the self and the other.[24]

What changes, then, in Coleridge's later meditations on *logos*, the Trinity, and (perhaps the supremely mystical illustration of his search for unity) the 'Pythagorean tetractys', is that the self-questioning diminishes, and the dialectical movement through a potentially infinite series of attempts at self-objectification slows down or even ceases, so that subject and object become solidified in an increasingly static system of relationships.[25] As Perkins suggests, we cannot easily say what relation obtains between the Trinity and trichotomy, unless it is one of resemblance, similarity, or identity.[26] Again, we cannot say *how* logos unites consciousness with external objective being, but only that it is said to do so, by analogy with the 'mystery solving all mysteries' – the 'idea of the eternal Tetractys or the Trinity'.[27]

It seems, in other words, that the dialectical pursuit of self-objectification (albeit always tinged with the reassuring religious certainties of the 'infinite I AM')[28] which characterizes the middle period of Coleridge's writing has been replaced by a search for mere models of unity, or analogies for an assumed unity – as if the process of transcendental inquiry has been abandoned in favour of analogies for what it strove but failed to discover, namely an intellectual justification for Coleridge's intuition of or desire for a universal oneness. Faith, that is, has become central at the end of Coleridge's life, displacing the search for intellectual reassurance.

How, then, does this movement from the unfulfilled inquiry of *The Friend* and *Biographia* to the 'Trinitarian Resolution' of the 'Logosophia' relate to the early poetry for which, to this day, Coleridge remains far better known and more greatly admired?[29] Summarized briefly, Coleridge's work seems to progress from an intuitive conviction of the unity of self and other, first to an intellectualizing pursuit of that *ground* of unity which, however, can never be fully understood, and then to a more stable conception of unity involving sophisticated and arcane analogies between Christianity and idealism, and largely freed from the hesitancy or anxiety about his speculations which Coleridge highlights in 'The Eolian Harp' and 'Frost at Midnight'. The enthusiasm of youthful speculation, that is, gives way first to an exploratory and rationalizing tendency (albeit that the mystical 'one' continues to be the inexplicable conclusion of Coleridge's researches), and then to a stable and almost mantra-like repetition of the framework of mysterious unities which he constructs around *logos* and the Trinity. At each of these stages, of course, Coleridge emphasizes the sublimely incomprehensible nature of the divine or of the unifying ground of being. Yet whereas in his middle period – that of *The Friend* and *Biographia* – the locus of the sublime is primarily the forward-moving process of reflection (so much so that he repeatedly attaches more importance to this process than to the truths which it discovers),[30] the richest evocations of sublime feeling in his early poetry coincide not with a progressive movement of thought, but with a spontaneous emphasis on the unity of self and other or the presence of God in nature; and this relatively static form of reflection is repeated and sustained more consistently (albeit through a different system of concepts) in the projections for his *Logosophia*.[31]

In broad terms, then, Coleridge's creative and intellectual career represents a movement from an originally well-defined (if, in the earliest instances, sometimes hesitantly expressed) sense of unity, through a period of relative disruption and intense dialectical activity, to a period in which this dialectical movement is stabilized and the previously irresolvable contradictions between subject and object seem (albeit only in terms of Coleridge's subjective feeling about them) to be overcome through his repeated contemplation of religious mysteries. Sublime feeling is central to Coleridge's thought at each of these stages; but in the first this feeling is associated primarily with enlightenment (or at least with a *sense* of enlightenment), in the second with the incomprehensibility of ultimate reality, and in the third with peaceful certainty and tranquillity. In the first phase Coleridge speculates on the unity of man, nature, and God; in the second he inquires into the relations between them, and in the third he abandons the pursuit of truth in favour of a circling system of related symbols which stands in for the knowledge he has found to be unattainable. Each stage, additionally, is accompanied by its subtly distinctive mode of feeling: the first by an excited sense of undiscovered, unprobed possibilities; the second by an intense confrontation with the infinite and with unanswerable questions; the third by a hypnotic quality seeming to correspond to the state which he characterized in 1809 as 'blessedness' or 'the Peace of God that passeth all understanding'.[32] Following Coleridge's example, we may perhaps be justified in saying that his career itself thus resembles a form of dialectic, in which the initial excited sense of unity is first actively probed and questioned, before both speculation and inquiry are transcended by the third term of pure religious conviction. Such a pattern, indeed, contains an obvious analogy with that of Schelling's *System of Transcendental Idealism*, in which it is an inexplicable artistic 'intuition' that finally cuts the Gordian knot of that dialectical inquiry which elaborates and tests the initial theory of the original identity of all forms of consciousness in terms of an undifferentiated Absolute.[33] This pattern, indeed, was also reflected in Schelling's own career, in which (as the theologian Franz von Baader remarked) 'His early philosophy of nature was a generous tasty steak', but his later thought resembled 'a ragout with Christian spices'.[34] At the same time, however, we must acknowledge that Coleridge's consistent interest in the identity of opposites is reflected in the development of his own thought and writing, and that there is as much continuity in his career as individuation in its stages.[35]

We have, then, already seen that to speak of Coleridge's 'thought' is often problematic. Ratiocination is present at each stage of his career, though in differing forms; but the truth which he either seeks or presumes himself to have discovered always either depends on feeling, or has no other existence than in the realm of feeling. None of his confrontations with the ground of being has any rational substance; each – however much it arises from intellectually *seeking* that ground – is defined by sensation or emotion. Coleridge's thought begins and ends in the non-rational – a fact he made explicit in *The Friend*, stating that 'In *wonder* ... does philosophy begin: and in astoundment ... does all true philosophy *finish*.'[36]

2. POETRY: THE ACT OF UNIFYING

The much-debated question of why Coleridge's poetic production diminished so sharply after 1802 may therefore already have been answered. It seems, that is, that his initial speculative expressions of an emotional intuition of unity eventually ceased to satisfy his intellect as he not only sought much firmer grounds for belief than those hesitantly (though enthusiastically) put forward in the Conversation Poems, but also sought to reconcile pantheism with Christianity.[37] What primarily distinguishes his poetic from his prose reflections is that the philosophical or speculative content of his poems is primarily an expression of the emotions which continue to be their central subject-matter, whereas his prose pursues the philosophical implications of these emotions – seeking, for example, to reconcile the sense of a divine presence in the physical world with the necessity of conceiving God as beyond the phenomenal.[38] At the same time, however, his prose continually expresses the same sense of infinite unity as emerges less philosophically in his early poetry; and in its repeated emphasis on confronting the limits of human knowledge, both reflects and seeks to promote that 'sense of something far more deeply interfused' which defines Coleridge's aesthetic and intellectual values even more than those of Wordsworth or any of their British contemporaries.[39] Coleridge's evocations of the incomprehensible ground of being, indeed, often seem to be informed chiefly by an awareness of the excitement with which he contemplates these otherwise indescribable mysteries, and the cumulative style of his prose no less than his poetry is explicitly designed partly to evoke and encourage belief in such objects.[40]

Not all of Coleridge's early poems, however, have the quality of spontaneous speculation displayed by the Conversation Poems. 'Religious Musings', for example, differs from this model in several obvious ways: firstly in the directness with which it expresses the optimistic faith which Coleridge suggests will bring its own fulfilment; secondly in the central role played by the combination of Christian and Neoplatonic theories which Coleridge derived from Hartley and Priestley;[41] and thirdly in terms of the far greater sense of certainty (at least compared with 'The Eolian Harp' and 'Frost at Midnight') which these more overtly Christian ideas permit. The poem's evocation of humankind's upward progression towards union with the deity, however, involves ideas and emotions which throughout Coleridge's work are associated with analogies between his own experience of meditation and the productive process underlying both mental and physical phenomena.[42] His theories and imagery in the poem, that is, seem to be as much informed by emotional elevation as those of the Conversation Poems or many passages in *The Friend* and *Biographia*; and the optimistic faith which the poem expresses is itself a central part of its subject-matter, being described as the principal cause of the progression he envisages.[43]

'Kubla Khan' clearly differs more sharply from the Conversation Poems in seeming not to be meditative but rather to be a spontaneous product of its author's subconscious.[44] Coleridge's claim that the images and language of the poem 'rose up before him... without any sensation or consciousness of effort', that is, appears to be confirmed both by the notorious difficulty of interpreting its images as purely allegorical, and by their obvious sexual connotations, which contrast sharply with Coleridge's habitual reticence on such topics.[45] The passage of the poem connecting the music of the 'Abyssinian maid' with the narrator's potential to reconstruct the 'pleasure-dome', however, suggests an interpretation coinciding with his later view of imagination as being involved in ordinary perception as much as in consciously creative or intellectual activity.[46] The idea that what we dream of or 'imagine' (in the ordinary sense of that word) might also be able, through the power of music or of poetry, to be as 'real' as anything that we perceive, that is, implies the interchangeableness of ideal and real in terms of their mutual dependence on a single productive power or activity.[47]

The poem's concluding image of the visionary discoverer of imagination being regarded with 'holy dread' by all who meet him suggests a further coincidence with Coleridge's later thought in terms of the profound sense of intellectual alienation from most of his contemporaries which is evident in much of his later prose, and which he theorized in the distinction between 'genius' and 'talent'.[48] His definition of genius as 'originality in intellectual construction', and distinction of this from 'the comparative skill of acquiring, arranging, and applying the stock furnished by others' was not original.[49] But his additional statement that the 'character and privilege of genius' consists in its ability 'To carry on the feelings of childhood into the powers of manhood' and to rescue 'the most admitted truths from the impotence caused by the very circumstance of their universal admission' reveals that Coleridge's 'genius' in fact has very much the same characteristic of reconciling opposite or discordant qualities as he elsewhere attributes to 'imagination' – a point in which he again coincides with Schelling, who writes that 'Genius is... marked off from everything that consists in mere talent or skill by the fact that through it a contradiction is resolved'.[50]

What Coleridge calls 'genius', therefore, seems also to be the intellectual tendency which chiefly distinguishes his own thought, namely that search for a unification of opposites which, as Perkins has shown, becomes almost obsessive in his later work.[51] As both an aficionado of 'imagination' or 'genius', and a drinker at the 'deep well' of the subconscious or intuitive,[52] Coleridge thus seems very much to coincide with the feared and isolated visionary described at the end of 'Kubla Khan'. The poem's fantastical dramatization of a confrontation between the 'genius' of the isolated individual and the 'talent' of the majority, indeed, shares much of the tone of Coleridge's description of the dramatist Nathaniel Lee in *Biographia*, albeit that the latter's supposed sense of frustration at the popular incomprehension with which his works or views were greeted also emphasizes the more negative side of Coleridge's confrontation with popular attitudes.[53]

The chief question raised by 'Kubla Khan', therefore, seems to concern the relationship between the discovery of 'imagination' (or the power of giving objective reality to the products of the mind), and that spontaneous production of ideas from the subconscious which the preface describes it as recording, and which – as we have seen – various aspects of the poem itself appear to demonstrate. The answer to this question, however, seems to lie in the fact that the poem presents these ideas through an image or evocation of a dramatic situation, rather than by means of theoretical inquiry or analysis. The prevalence of the issue of genius and talent in Coleridge's later theoretical writings, that is, suggests that the concluding image of the poem may have been as much a spontaneous expression of subjective feeling as the description of the sacred river. Coleridge, in other words, may be as 'uncensored', and in a sense as unintellectual, in this image of the isolated genius, as in any of those which precede it. And in revealing both his subconscious and the most enduringly important aspect of (at least) his intellectual relationships, the poem effectively combines conscious and unconscious in the way that, Schelling argued, 'imagination' alone could do. In thus combining the philosophical with the spontaneous, indeed, 'Kubla Khan' is perhaps the best illustration in Coleridge's work of that artistic 'intuition' which, according to Schelling's and his own later writings, overcomes the division between subject and object. A further refinement of this interpretation is suggested by a passage from Schelling's discussion – published two years after the composition of 'Kubla Khan' – of how artistic 'genius' reconciles the free with the not-free and conscious with unconscious production. 'Just as the man of destiny does not execute what he wishes or intends, but rather what he is obliged to execute by an inscrutable fate which governs him', Schelling writes,

> ... so the artist, however deliberate he may be, seems nonetheless to be governed, in regard to what is truly objective in his creation, by a power which separates him from all other men, and compels him to say or depict things which he does not fully understand himself, and whose meaning is infinite.
>
> (*STI*, 223)[54]

Not only the poem's apparently spontaneous dramatization of ideas which Coleridge later expresses theoretically, but also the sense of an isolation or alienation arising from his greater insight which is expressed both in this poem and in his later prose, thus corresponds closely to Schelling's analysis of 'genius'. Schelling's theory, indeed, encourages the view that what caused Coleridge's isolation was precisely that capacity for uniting the spontaneous with the voluntary and the subconscious with the intellectual which is evident in 'Kubla Khan'. The poem's exemplification of the qualities which Coleridge defined as those of genius and imagination, and as producing the characteristic isolation of the artist, thus makes 'Kubla Khan' among the strongest pieces of evidence that Coleridge not only arrived at his opinions by 'genial coincidence', but as a result of the nature of creative imagination itself.[55]

Coleridge's poems, however, are notably diverse in their styles and techniques, seeming to reveal a wide variety of creative processes. 'The Ancient Mariner', for example, differs from 'Kubla Khan' in having an obvious allegorical content, yet combines its dramatization of a process of religious enlightenment with stylistic and formal eccentricities which challenge the interpretative skills of the reader, implying the necessity of individual thought and questioning if traditional beliefs are to have any meaning or significance for us. The same point is emphasized by the long Latin epigraph (a quotation from the seventeenth-century theologian Thomas Burnet) added to the poem in 1817, which focuses directly on the importance of pursuing truth and knowledge for ourselves, rather than merely accepting established beliefs, if we are to acquire any sense of ultimate realities or of the limits of our understanding.[56] This parallelism between the implications of plot, form, style, and epigraph, however, again involves a unification of the idea with the image, and (at least for the reader) of the spontaneous with the intellectual, albeit that the spontaneity of Coleridge's own creative process seems less demonstrable here than in 'Kubla Khan'. More importantly, however, the poem's emphasis on the importance of acknowledging religious mysteries once the limits of human knowledge have been tested closely parallels the dominant patterns of Coleridge's later thought and career, in which, despite his search for intellectual justifications of a primary intuition of oneness, the feeling of a confrontation with incomprehensible truths is ultimately most powerful.

The patterns of thought and emotion in Coleridge's later poems, and the ways in which they relate both to his early poetry and to his later prose writings, are among the topics examined in Chapter 4. The examples discussed above, however, show that his early poetry repeatedly expresses ideas and values which are central to his later prose, but differs from the latter both in emphasizing the emotion which underlies his later thought, and in combining ideas with images and the intellectual with the emotional in ways which closely parallel not only the effects of artistic 'intuition' described by Schelling, but also the qualities which Coleridge attributes to poetic imagination.[57] Though – as we shall see – poetry continued to serve important functions for Coleridge until the end of his career, moreover, the hesitancy and indirectness with which certain of his most enduring themes are expressed in his early poems suggests that a desire to give these the form of rational arguments rather than of poetic 'phantasies' was latent in his writing even in the 1790s, and that the evocation of feelings, perceptions, dream-experiences, or other elements of what Schelling called 'unconscious production', needed to be welded to intellectual arguments in order effectively to express or sustain Coleridge's conviction of the inexpressible. At the same time, however, much of Coleridge's writing suggests that his interest in sustaining this conviction arose from a need to escape from negative states of emotion by replacing them with the pleasurable feelings to be derived from creative and intellectual activity.[58] As I will show, moreover, the feeling he most consistently sought and derived from intellectual effort was essentially that of the sublime – a combination (as Kant observed) of elevation with a sense of the underlying unity of self and other in terms of an infinite creative power.[59] The chapters which follow will explore the various functions and manifestations of this feeling in Coleridge's work, and the ways in which it governs and is the implicit subject-matter even of his most demandingly intellectual writings.

2

Feeling into Thought

Coleridge's thought has often been divided into an initial phase of support for Hartley's or Priestley's emphasis on material processes determining consciousness and gradually increasing the perfection of mankind, and a later period of enthusiasm for idealist theories describing an ascent of consciousness whose origin precedes the distinction of 'mental' and 'physical'.[1] The formal resemblances between these two sets of theories, and the ways in which their imagery of ascent or elevation reflects the emotional value which Coleridge found in the experience of thinking (and particularly in contemplating or developing these theories themselves), form the principal topics of Chapter 5. What I wish to demonstrate here is the extent to which his later idealist theories of the unity of mental and physical are prefigured in his early response to Hartley's materialist explanation of the origins of our ideas. Rather than describing thought as arising from physical processes of which we are unconscious, Coleridge's early discussions of Hartley suggest that thought involves an attempt to articulate intuition or emotion, and that these non-rational aspects of consciousness are also responsible for the association of ideas. Consciousness, he suggests, is neither purely physical, nor purely mental, but combines articulable concepts with affective or sensuous elements in a process which is irreducible to either. Hence his Hartleian or 'necessitarian' period not only shares the emphasis on a gradual ascent or elevation of consciousness which is central to his later interest in Schelling, but also highlights a sense of the inseparableness of thought and feeling, and of mental and physical, which is closely allied to his later interest in idealist efforts to transcend these oppositions.

In addition to demonstrating this continuity in Coleridge's psychological theories, however, this chapter shows how his early descriptions of the dependence of thought on inarticulate feeling developed, firstly, into the distinction between 'true' and 'false' feeling which I discuss more extensively in Chapter 3, and secondly, into the theory that all genuine thought or reflection involves an attempt to verbalize emotions which naturally resist expression.

'True' feeling, for Coleridge, is always something unambiguously internal, and unrelated to the demands of ambition or popular taste. Such feeling, he argues, can never be fully or adequately expressed, yet those who come closest to expressing it, or who devote the greatest effort to doing so, are the truest and profoundest thinkers. Much writing of the period, however, is described by Coleridge as arising from the 'false' or superficial kinds of feeling which he associates with the term 'sensation', and by implication with the automatic generation of ideas from external impressions described by Hartley. Since it derives chiefly from conformity to popular opinion or from repetition of received ideas, such writing can neither express nor bear witness to fundamental truth. Hence there is a close alliance in Coleridge's thought between the internality of feeling and the validity of the ideas derived from it. At the same time, however, the inexpressibleness of feeling becomes for Coleridge a central criterion of its genuineness, and his writing thus continually gestures towards a mysterious essence of emotion underlying and preceding his thought and language.

One aspect of his experience, however, continually emerges as a threat to these analyses of thought and emotion – namely the process of dreaming. The fact that, on waking, he often seemed to discover physical causes for his dreams – whether in the effects of opium, or in specific physical discomforts – though during those dreams he had been unaware of such causes, appeared to support Hartley's theory that our ideas arise from physical processes of which we are unconscious. In an effort to avoid this conclusion, Coleridge suggested that physical discomforts, or the disturbing influence of opium, might merely disrupt our usual state of unconsciousness in sleep, allowing the mind to perceive its own essential state with unusual directness. Because his dreams were so often of a disturbing nature, however, this means of avoiding a Hartleian conclusion was itself profoundly threatening, and rather than persisting in his search for a non-materialist explanation of his nightmares, Coleridge repeatedly seems willing to accept that Hartley's model has at least a limited validity. This counter-argument to his view of both feeling and thought as arising independently of external impressions is thus itself a fascinating illustration of the extent to which Coleridge's thought is determined not merely by personal conviction, but also by a search for practical liberation from the negations of experience.

1. FEELING AND SENSATION

In a lecture of 1819, Coleridge forcefully rejected any materialist explanation of thought. The notion 'that sensation and thought are precisely the same', and 'that this same sensation ... at once becomes philosophical and intellectual as soon as it passes into the marrow of my skull', he said, was 'an outrage to common sense and to morality ... a complete circle of dogmatic, mere unsupported, assertions' (*PLects*, 353). What Coleridge was attacking was the notion of a continuity between impressions and ideas, or more precisely, the construction of a single substance which at one extremity is sensation, and at the other is thought. He attacked this conception partly because it seemed to eliminate the will and the reason, representing morality as an illusion and thought as automatic and irrational, but also because it was contradictory and ungrounded. Starting with the idea of matter, the materialist ended with something heterogeneous from matter, and whose only connection with it was his assertion of their identity.[2] Moreover, this very assertion seemed to contradict itself: in order to be valid, it must itself have arisen automatically; yet the fact of its having done so could scarcely be in favour of its validity. Such explanations of thought were common in the eighteenth century, yet they were rarely so unqualified as Coleridge implies.[3] Hartley's system, for example, is chiefly concerned with fleshing out the bare assertion that matter is identical with sensations and ideas. Yet having elaborated gradations of internality from 'the Organs of the Hand, Eye, Ear, &c.' to 'the spinal Marrow and Nerves', thence to the brain, and thence to 'the sensitive Soul, or the Sensorium' (*OM*, 1: 31), he is nevertheless unwilling to admit 'that Matter can be endued with the Power of Sensation', and admits the impossibility of discovering 'in what Way Vibrations cause, or are connected with ... Ideas' (*OM*, 1: 33–4). As Christensen points out, his religious beliefs seem to have forced Hartley into the hypothesis of an 'infinitesimal elementary Body ... intermediate between the Soul and gross Body' (*OM*, 1: 34).[4] Though the *sine qua non* of his thesis is an identification of thought with the vibrations which also produce sensation, he is finally unable to tolerate this assertion, and obscures the issue with an ambiguous mediation.[5]

Coleridge himself was far from being consistent in his opinions on this matter. Yet even his announcement to Southey that he was 'a compleat Necessitarian', but went further than Hartley in believing 'the corporeality of *thought*', was accompanied by a passage effectively ridiculing Hartley's mode of explanation.[6] As Christensen comments, this peculiar conjunction shows 'that even in the first flush of his enthusiasm for Hartley, Coleridge preserved a distance from his conviction that neither Hartley nor Priestley ever exhibited'.[7] There can be little doubt, moreover, that the mature Coleridge was entirely opposed to believing 'the corporeality of thought', at least in the Hartleian sense of this expression. If one had to assign a date to his conversion, it would be in March 1801, when he claimed to have 'overthrown the doctrine of Association, as taught by Hartley, and with it all the irreligious metaphysics of modern Infidels' (*CL*, 2: 706). Before this date, however, Coleridge had often expressed opinions radically opposed to materialism. One of his most revealing pronouncements on the concept of life, for example, dates from four years earlier, when he wrote to John Thelwall opposing various contemporary explanations of it. Rather than being 'the result of organized matter', or identical with the blood or even the soul, he says, life is beyond explanation, and identical with the thinking consciousness.[8] Similarly, the death of his son Berkeley in 1799 prompted Coleridge to describe life as an ineradicable and continuously progressive force, in no way subject to material extinction.[9]

By February 1801, when he wrote a series of philosophical letters to Josiah Wedgwood, his early enthusiasm for Locke had almost entirely disappeared.[10] Though his principal concern in these letters is to demonstrate the injustice of Locke's celebrity, he also makes several revealing comments on the meaning and etymology of the word 'mind'. Whereas 'a staunch materialist' would affirm that the mind is '*innate in*' the brain, Coleridge can only allow that it may be '*connate* with' the brain.[11] More importantly, his discussion of the etymology of 'mind' both here and in a contemporary notebook entry consistently interprets it as meaning 'vibratory yet progressive motion' (*CN*, 1:378). 'The oldest meaning of the word mahen' – according to Coleridge, the origin not only of 'mind' but also of the German *meinen* and *mahnen* ('to mind') – he writes, is

> ... to move forward & backward, yet still progressively – thence applied to the motion of the Scythe in mowing... To mow is the same as the Latin movere which was pronounced mow-ere— & monere in like manner is only the reduplicative of mow-ere... This word in the time of Ennius was *menere*, & hence *mens*—the

> Swedish word for Mind is Mon—the Islandic [*sic*] Mene. The Greek μναόμαι, i.e. μενά ομαι, from whence μνήμη, the memory, is the same word—and all alike mean a repetition of similar motion, as in a scythe.[12]

This passage shows at least one respect in which Coleridge had by this time 'overthrown' the doctrine of association. The point of his etymology of 'mind' is that there is no 'Thought-Box' of the kind which both Locke and Hartley assumed – that we are wrong to think of our ideas as originating or residing in a pre-existent intellect or mind.[13] We may be unable to dispense with the concept of a subject of our thoughts, and Coleridge does not attempt to do so; yet both here and in his letters to Wedgwood, he challenges the view that we can either conceive or describe their origin.

This view contrasts interestingly with his description, six years earlier, of the respect in which his opinion went 'further than Hartley': 'I…believe the corporeality of *thought*', he wrote, '– namely, that it is motion.' Whereas the equation of mind with motion really equates it with the activity we call 'thinking', and challenges the derivation of thought from physiology or external impressions, the equation of *thought* with motion need not represent such a challenge. Since thought is a process rather than an object capable of stasis, any identification of it with motion is in a sense tautologous, and forces us to ask what sort of motion, or motion *of what*, thought represents, if we are to attach any meaning to it.

The obvious answer, considering Coleridge's explicit declaration of his allegiance to Hartley, is that the motion in question is a corporeal one, consisting of physical vibrations in the 'medullary Substance' of the brain.[14] Christensen, however, points out that Coleridge's assertion of 'the corporeality of *thought*' is immediately preceded in his letter by a poem describing how a lover's passion expresses itself in his heart's throbbing, and suggests that Coleridge's philosophical assertion may therefore be 'an hyperbolic gloss on the association of the heart's throb with the soul's passion'.[15] This is important because, as we shall see, Hartley does not in fact consider the relationship between thought and emotion, but only the supposed effects of external impressions on mental phenomena – of which, moreover, he has a somewhat limited conception.[16] In highlighting the ambiguous relationship between thought and emotion, and the frequent difficulty of distinguishing between them, therefore, Coleridge would have passed beyond the naive Hartleian conception of thought as a consequence of external impressions moving through the body in successive sequences of vibrations. In order to have meaning, he suggests, our ideas must be connected with sensations or impressions; but if we describe the latter as exclusively physical, we not only dissociate thought from feeling, but are also forced to postulate an unconscious connection between body and mind.[17] As Coleridge makes clear, what Hartley failed to recognize was 'The dependence of ideas ... on states of bodily or mental *Feeling*' (*CN*, 2: 2638). So strong is the impulse to distinguish mental and physical, yet at the same time to regard thinking as an effect of the brain, that the real nature of our experience is lost in a morass of contradictions.[18]

Coleridge, however, was consistent in his insight:

> I hold, that association depends in a much greater degree on the recurrence of resembling states of Feeling, than on Trains of Idea/that the recollection of early childhood in latest old age depends on, & is explicable by this—& if this be true, Hartley's System totters ... Believe me, Southey! a metaphysical Solution, that does not instantly *tell* for something in the Heart, is grievously to be suspected as apocry[p]hal. I almost think, that Ideas *never* recall Ideas, as far as they are Ideas—any more than Leaves in a forest create each other's motion—The Breeze it is that runs thro' them/it is the Soul, the State of Feeling—.
>
> (*CL*, 2: 961)

Superficially, Coleridge seems here rather to be defending the view that sensation 'becomes ... intellectual as soon as it passes into the marrow of my skull', than to be opposing it. What he rejects in Hartley, however, is primarily his theory that ideas are formed unconsciously through the repetition of particular sensations and the consequent production of 'miniature vibrations' in the brain. According to Hartley, association occurs among ideas when the sensations which generate them have been repeated simultaneously a sufficient number of times. It is not necessary for sensation B to occur in order for the corresponding idea 'b' to be recalled; rather, it is sufficient that sensation A, which previously occurred in conjuction with sensation B, should occur in isolation, for idea 'b' to be recalled along with idea 'a'.[19] The aspects of Hartley which Coleridge opposes, therefore, are, firstly, his radical distinction between sensations and ideas, whereby the latter are merely 'traces' of the former, and can recombine independently of them, and secondly, the notion of an unconscious transformation of the physical into the intellectual, whereby sensations give rise to ideas. Unconsciousness is indispensable to this relationship in Hartley, since his system cannot account for any consciousness other than that produced by sensation: if we were aware of sensations becoming ideas, this very awareness would need to have been produced by other sensations, which is absurd. The feeling which Coleridge describes as the cause of association, therefore, is precisely what Hartley excludes from this process; and what Coleridge rejects is the notion of an automatic process giving rise to knowledge, from which not only willing or reasoning, but all self-consciousness is excluded. In themselves, he implies, ideas can have no contexture or combinative principle. They cannot recall each other, because they are mere counters or images – not even the 'matter' of intellection, but fragments artificially siphoned off from the diverse combinations and processes in which they always occur. In order to have meaning – in order to be more than such fictional counters – ideas must be part of a larger movement of the mind, which in this instance he identifies not just with 'the state of feeling', but also with 'the Soul'.[20] Whereas Hartley's system includes no concept of thinking, and implies that his theory is itself an accidental product of sensations, Coleridge makes feeling the *sine qua non* of thinking, without which even the mind is inconceivable.

Coleridge's early response to Hartley is thus connected with his later Schellingian thought by far more than their common emphasis on an ascent or progression from matter to mind, and from the insensate to the voluntary. The emphasis on the inseparableness of feelings and ideas which characterizes his discussion of Hartley clearly prefigures his later view that mind and matter are two aspects of a single process which cannot be identified with either.[21] Yet at the same time, his early description of mind as inconceivable apart from the activity of feelings and ideas which constitutes thinking has much in common with his later, idealist view that (as *Biographia* puts it) 'intelligence is a self-developement, not a quality supervening to a substance' (*BL*, 1: 286). In describing thought as an attempt to articulate feelings ambiguously poised between the mental and the physical, that is, even the early Coleridge suggests that this activity cannot be located in a pre-existent substance, but is rather a self-generating process which transcends the distinction of matter and spirit.

2. PASSION AND EXCITEMENT

What, then, is the 'feeling' which Coleridge contrasts with Hartley's concept of sensation, and which he argued was the true cause of association? In E. H. Coleridge's edition, the letter to Southey quoted above was mistranscribed as saying that 'a metaphysical solution which does not instantly *tell you* something in the heart is ... to be suspected as apocryphal' – a phrase suggesting a valorization of emotion above intellectual rigour, or the view that truth should be determined by some form of emotional gratification.[22] Coleridge's actual words, however, were 'a metaphysical solution which does not instantly *tell for* something in the Heart'[23] – a phrase which, though suggesting that truth is discovered at least partly through emotion, also involves the idea of a correspondence between emotion and theory, or the fulfilment by philosophy of a condition or conditions existing prior to reflection. What precisely these conditions consist of is not immediately evident; yet they are clearly neither purely physical nor purely intellectual. In order to construct a satisfactory theory, Coleridge implies, we must produce through that theory a feeling which corresponds to one already existing, and from which we set out on the construction of it.[24]

A further clarification of Coleridge's view of the relationship between feelings and ideas occurs in his critique of Wordsworth's Preface to *Lyrical Ballads* in *Biographia*. Having misquoted Wordsworth as celebrating the real language of men '*in a state of excitement*',[25] Coleridge writes that excitement *per se* can be of no value to the quality of speech, because

> ... the nature of a man's words, when he is strongly affected by joy, grief, or anger, must necessarily depend on the number and quality of the general truths, conceptions and images, and of the words expressing them, with which his mind had been previously stored. For the property of passion is not to *create*; but to set in increased activity.
>
> (*BL*, 2: 56–7)

Rather than being created by sensation and associating with each other on the repetition of a given sensation, therefore, ideas are set in motion by an emotion which played no part in their production – a point which Coleridge clarifies in his next sentence. 'At least', he adds,

> ... whatever new connections of thoughts or images, or (which is equally, if not more than equally, the appropriate effect of strong

> excitement) whatever generalizations of truth or experience, the heat of passion may produce; yet the terms of their conveyance must have pre-existed in his former conversations, and are only collected and crowded together by the unusual stimulation.
>
> (*BL*, 2: 57)

The 'increased activity' in question, then, is not just association; indeed it is hard to see how association, as a mere mechanical emergence of pre-existent ideas, could be called 'activity' at all. Rather, it is 'generalizations of truth or experience' that are peculiarly the effect of strong excitement – that is, relations of a much stronger, more complex, and more intellectual kind than any described by Hartley. As noted earlier, Hartley makes little attempt to describe or to account for the process of thinking.[26] Automatic and unconscious association is the only kind of relationship he describes as occurring between ideas. For Coleridge, on the other hand, the principal form of relationship between ideas is categorization. In a state of 'strong excitement', he says, we are inclined to generalize – that is, to establish new connections between ideas and images, or to produce general conclusions and theories which explain them. Passion may be the precipitating cause of this process; yet though it sets thought in increased activity, whatever associations it produces are subject to a criticism and organization which passion alone could not engender.

The view that excitement alone cannot give rise to thought is highlighted by a letter to William Godwin of 1800, where Coleridge describes the effect of alcohol on his habits of conversation:

> An idea starts up in my hand [head?]—away I follow it thro' thick & thin, Wood & Marsh, Brake and Briar—with all the apparent Interest of a man who was defending one of his old and long-established Principles—Exactly of this kind was the Conversation, with which I quitted you/I do not believe it possible for a human Being to have a greater horror of the Feelings that usually accompany such principles as I then supported, or a deeper Conviction of their irrationality than myself—but the whole Thinking of my Life will not bear me up against the accidental Press & Crowd of my mind, when it is elevated beyond it's natural Pitch/.
>
> (*CL*, 1: 580)[27]

In this passage, Coleridge describes how an irrational excitement disrupted his voluntary and rationally held beliefs. Thinking, indeed, is described as the opposite of his mental activity in this instance. Though he was arguing, and intelligibly defending certain 'principles', he was doing so automatically, without the engagement of his moral and critical faculties. Emotion, however, plays no definite part in this process: it is, indeed, conspicuous by its absence. The 'elevation' which Coleridge describes has no affective content and no determinative value. It is 'unnatural' precisely because it excludes or overrides his usual aversion to the views he is expressing; his conversation is random disputation, without any governing objective or moral constraint. 'The Feelings that usually accompany such principles as I then supported' are mentioned as the implication of his talking rather than its origin. Like Hartley's mechanical intellect, Coleridge has become the victim of accidental associations, devoid of that 'feeling' which is fundamental to rationality. Even his pursuit of the ideas which 'start up' in his head is not strictly his own, but the spontaneous effect of his intoxication, resembling a physical reflex.

To say that on this occasion Coleridge was not thinking, however, would be to go too far in adopting his schema. As in the letter to Southey where he rejects Hartley's theory of association, Coleridge is contrasting the rational with the irrational, and the voluntary with the automatic; yet in order to be intelligible – in order to have been 'defending' a particular position – he must have been making certain kinds of judgements, or at least connecting words with each other in a non-arbitrary manner. Paradoxically, a possible explanation of this activity is suggested by a form of association described by Hartley, in which the opening words of a familiar sentence will automatically recall the remainder.[28] It is not far from this process, occurring independently of judgement or reflection, to the repetition of well-known opinions which Coleridge describes – opinions in which he has no personal interest and which he actually finds repugnant. The ground of distinction between thinking and mere argumentativeness, therefore, would be the presence or absence of a commitment to the opinions in question; and rather than saying that Coleridge was not thinking, we should say that his conversation neither arose from, nor expressed any genuine feeling.

It did not, in other words, '*tell* for [anything] in the Heart'. The view that thought must satisfy an emotional condition, and that meaning consists in an expressive purpose rather than mere logical relations, was among Coleridge's most enduring opinions.[29] How, then, is 'feeling' related to the irrational 'excitement' underlying his conversation with Godwin? The frequent difficulty of distinguishing between the two is highlighted by a passage in More's *Enthusiasmus Triumphatus* (a work with which Coleridge was familiar) describing how '*Melancholy*, as well as *Wine*, makes a man *Rhetorical* or *Poetical*; and that *Genius* how fanciful it is, and full of Allusions and Metaphors and fine resemblances, every one knows'.[30] On the one hand, the effects which More associates with melancholy have much in common with those which Coleridge attributes to alcohol: though melancholy sets thought in increased activity, it is also 'a kind of *naturall inebriation*', and the preternatural eloquence it engenders may itself be a cause of delusion, persuading the affected individual 'that it is the very *Spirit of God* that *then moves* supernaturally in him'.[31] This could scarcely be further from Coleridge's model of emotion as the standard against which we measure the sufficiency of intellectual explanations. Rather than determining the individual's arguments and beliefs, emotion merely produces an agitation of thought and language, and it is this agitation, rather than any feeling he or she might wish to communicate, that causes the individual's delusion. Rather than being the means by which we judge, the emotion described by More and the intoxication described by Coleridge are similarly responsible for the disruption of our judgement and the loss of self-control. On the other hand, however, the qualities of thought and language which More associates with melancholic intoxication are precisely those which Coleridge associates with a person 'strongly affected by joy, grief, or anger'. According to Coleridge, 'generalizations of truth or experience' are what the heat of passion especially produces; its effects are neither repetitious nor automatic, but intellectual and original.[32] Similarly in More, '*Melancholy* ... makes a man *Rhetorical* or *Poetical*'; its '*Genius*' (used here in the sense of 'character' or 'tendency')[33] is 'full of Allusions and Metaphors and fine resemblances'. Yet while admiring, no less than Coleridge, the *style* of the language which passion engenders, More nevertheless represents this style as usurping judgement and control. What he describes as negating true judgement, in other words, is not so much passion as the rhetorical brilliance it engenders. The speaker is impressed with his own power; yet this very power is what deludes him.

Coleridge also, however, was not averse to reflecting on the power of rhetoric to deceive its originator. In his discussions of the younger Pitt, this idea is part of a larger distinction between the internal and the external, or between inward feeling and outward expression. Pitt's 'unnatural dexterity in the combination of words', he wrote in the *Morning Post*, '... must of necessity have diverted his attention from present objects, obscured his impressions, and deadened his genuine feelings' (*EOT*, 1: 219). His eloquence

> ... consisted not in the ready application of a general system to particular questions, but in the facility of arguing for or against any question by specious generalities, without reference to any system.
> (*EOT*, 1: 222)

That which rendered Pitt untrustworthy as an orator, it seems, was also what caused him to be deceived: namely, an absorption in words to the exclusion or suppression both of his 'genuine feelings' and of all systematic thinking. Repeatedly in his comments on Pitt, Coleridge contrasts the 'outside' – by which I mean not only language but also the pleasure produced by language in the speaker and his listeners – with the 'inside' which is truth and conviction:

> Not the *thing* on which he was speaking, but the praises to be gained by the speech, were present to his intuition; hence he associated all the operations of his faculties with words, and his pleasures with the surprise excited by them.
> (*EOT*, 1: 219–20)

Insofar as he is absorbed in language and the pleasures of language, insofar as his objective is not self-expression but the achievement of some ulterior end by the facility of his performance, Pitt's interiority – what Coleridge might call his 'soul' – is overridden and suppressed.[34] He *is* an automaton, despite the fact that his words are so 'finely arranged, and so dexterously consequent, that the whole bears the semblance of argument' (*EOT*, 1: 224). Because of this distinction, we can no longer call Pitt the originator of his own rhetoric. He, in the sense of that self-consciousness which would break through the web of verbiage and adulation, which would will the subservience of language to a truth felt internally, no longer exists in Coleridge's analysis.

The value of generalization as a mark of internality, of a soul acting and originating rather than being overridden by excitement, is therefore considerably weakened. Though 'the ... application of a general system to particular questions' implies a greater intensity of thought than 'arguing for or against any question by specious generalities', indeed, Coleridge is more concerned to elaborate an opposition between the mechanical and the voluntary than to say how this distinction shows itself in the qualities of thought or language. Some form of *excitement*, it seems, is necessary for 'generalization' to occur; yet from the examples I have given, excitement seems to be much more a quality of the outside, of automatism and repetition, than of the will or any standard of judgement. Passion may incline people 'to generalize; to connect by remotest analogy; to express the most universal positions of reason in the most glowing figures of fancy' (*LS*, 15); yet such thinking cannot be regarded as evidence of truth, and may well be a mark of delusion.

3. THE INSIDE AND THE OUTSIDE

One positive point, however, does emerge from Coleridge's reflections on Pitt: namely that in order to avoid being deceived and taken over by the words we use and the circumstances in which we use them, we must be driven to communicate by a feeling which our words cannot contain or adequately express. It was because Pitt's mind was 'founded and elemented in words and generalities' that his language became the enemy of expression. If he had not possessed such a 'power and facility in combining images', Coleridge implies, if he had experienced the inadequacies of language rather than merely enjoying its effects, he would have been both more truthful and more human, the source of meaning rather than the locus of its destruction.[35] Truth and language are in conflict to the extent that there must always be something left unsaid; and if we do not feel that burden of interiority, we are the prisoners of our own perspicuity.

The idea that truth consists in a tension between feeling and expression, between the inward conviction and the outward husk, was a central and consistent part of Coleridge's philosophy. In the moral sphere, as Archbishop Leighton reveals in a passage annotated by Coleridge, it implied that linguistic facility could be both destructive and sinful, an outward show at the expense of moral purpose and conviction. 'If any one's Head or Tongue should grow apace, and all the rest stand at a Stay', Leighton wrote,

> ... it would certainly make him a Monster; and they are no other, that are knowing and discoursing Christians, and grow daily in that, but not at all in Holiness of Heart and Life, which is the proper Growth of the Children of God.[36]

Coleridge's response is to suggest that he is precisely the 'monster' described by Leighton, and to appeal to God's mercy.[37] His view of the relationship between truth and language, however, not only reflected a Christian distinction between internal and external values, but was also closely connected with the philosophical challenge to materialism. By avowing his own sinfulness in this context, he is also expressing a commitment to that 'life' which cannot be circumscribed or understood, a sublime trust in an origin beyond linguistic articulation.[38]

His commitment to an interior standard of feeling, however, often led Coleridge to mistrust expression *per se*. In the act of recommending a philosophical position, he suggests, we may automatically become involved in a certain hostility to the truth itself. 'Do not degrade the Truth in thee by disputing,' the *'voice of Conscience'* urged him: 'I cannot, I *may* not bear the reproach of profaning the Truth, which is *my Life*, in moments when all passions heterogeneous to it are eclipsing ... its dimmest ray' (*CN*, 2: 2196). Yet it was not only the *'passion* of proselytism' (ibid.) that he feared might eclipse his interior conviction. In a letter of 1822 to his friend and benefactor Thomas Allsop, he suggests not only that expression is in danger of overwhelming true feeling – that communication may destroy the meaning we wish to communicate – but even that the two are mutually exclusive. Remarking on 'the very rare Occurrence of strong and deep Feeling in conjunction with free power and vivacity in the expression of it', he continues:

> The most eminent Tragedians, Garrick for instance, are known to have had their emotions as much at command and almost as much on the surface, as the muscles of their Countenances—and the French, who are all actors, are proverbially heartless. Is it that it is a false and feverous state for the Center to live in the Circumference? The vital warmth seldom rises to the surface in the form of sensible Heat without becoming hectic and inimical to the Life within, the only source of real sensibility.
>
> (*CL*, 5: 239)[39]

In this passage, Coleridge's philosophy of interiority – of a feeling which is at once the truth and our only evidence of the truth – has clearly rendered his distinction between feeling and expression more absolute than usual. That which is outside, the *natura naturata* or *forma formata*, is of course deceptive, partial, and fragmentary.[40]

Just as no material object can express the power of its originator, so our words and gestures are insufficient to express our own creative potential. Hence it becomes, for Coleridge, a religious duty to deny that language and expression can be other than deceptive. Nevertheless, this view is usually balanced in his writing by the admission that only through trying to state the truth do we realize the impossibility of doing so: the effort of intellection becomes the monument of a feeling it cannot encapsulate. In the letter to Allsop quoted above, however, Coleridge fixes the opposition between feeling and expression in such a way as to deny the possibility of any contact between them. To seem to articulate emotion effectively, he suggests, is to have no real emotion to articulate. Deep feeling is not merely too great to be expressed, but destroyed by expression. The superficial coherence of these statements, however, belies the fact that Coleridge has given no adequate explanation of the supposed mutually exclusive relationship between feeling and expression. As we have seen, the process of arguing may be feverous or intoxicating, and subject to impulses other than the pursuit of truth; yet this does not explain why expression is destructive of feeling, nor why effective communication must be deceptive. The opposition between inside and outside, the source and the product, has become so absolute that it no longer concerns the role of feeling in determining thought – in fact denies, a priori, that such a relation is conceivable.

As we have seen, however, at other times Coleridge did not deny the possibility of this relationship, but rather revealed its centrality to his own thought and language. As we have seen, generalization – or the construction of analogies – is not in itself evidence of profound feeling, but may rather be the effect of an 'excitement' which overleaps the will and the reason, manufacturing opinions to suit the occasion. In an important notebook entry, however, Coleridge describes his own tendency to construct analogies not as something automatic or out of his control, but rather as the essence of that interiority which combats or opposes a preoccupation with externals. Though this tendency may reduce the clarity of his writing by its multiplication of illustrations for every thesis he attempts to communicate, he suggests, his tracing of such resemblances may itself reveal a truth more important than any of the arguments which it disrupts – namely the inward unity of those phenomena which our habitual interpretation of the world separates and opposes to each other – a unity which is not independent of ourselves, but rather arises from our unconscious role in producing the world which we perceive. 'My illustrations swallow up my thesis', he writes:

> ...I feel too intensely the omnipresence of all in each, platonically speaking—or psychologically my brain-fibres, or the spiritual Light which abides in th~~at~~e brain marrow as visible Light appears to do in sundry rotten mackerel & other *smashy* matters, is of too general an affinity with all things/and tho' it perceives the *difference* of things, yet is eternally pursuing the likeness~~ness~~es ...'
>
> (*CN*, 2: 2372)

The most distinctive feature of this passage is its apparent surmounting of the oppositions between matter and mind, and between thought and feeling. His 'spiritual Light', Coleridge says, 'abides in ... [the] brain marrow'; the expressions 'brain-fibres' and 'spiritual Light' are used paratactically, as if both referred to the same thing, though neither could fully express its true nature. The combination of these elements is used to explain his feeling or conviction of 'the omnipresence of all in each' – a feeling which, he claims, gives rise to his habitual discovery of analogies. To say that he senses this unity, according to Coleridge, is to say that an element of himself which is neither purely mental nor purely physical, but both in one, shares in the unity of all that he perceives. By what means it does so is not made explicit; yet because it is at once a spiritual and a physical element, it is clear that the universe as Coleridge conceives it is one in which the physical and the mental are not independent or opposed, but rather two aspects of a single process. Such an identification of thought with the functioning of the brain is almost unique in Coleridge's writing; yet despite his verbal identification of them, 'spiritual Light' remains something which 'brain-fibres' as such have not explained any more than they did in Hartley. In other words, Coleridge's mystical intuition of oneness, his *feeling* of 'the omnipresence of all in each', has overridden the demand for a rational explanation of it. This feeling itself, however, is implied by the structure of his sentence to be not merely a consequence of, but the same thing as the functioning of his spiritual Light or brain-fibres. Not only is the mental physical, but feeling is also identical with that union of the mental and physical which, through its affinity with the universe in general, constitutes his insight.[41]

This unification of opposites has important implications for questions raised earlier in this chapter concerning the relationship between insight and expression. Whereas, in my earlier examples, Coleridge contrasted the outside with the inside, claiming that facility of expression is actually inimical to philosophic insight and to profound thinking in general, in this passage not only his conviction of unity, but even the inward constitution of the universe is described as expressing itself in his habitual creation of verbal analogies. Whereas an absorption in the pleasures of language was described as undermining profound conviction, and rendering thought the mechanical appendage of accidental sensations, here it is precisely Coleridge's spontaneous production of analogies that is described as revealing the mental/physical complex which constitutes both his insight and the nature of all things. Clearly, his sense of 'the omnipresence of all in each' is implied to be a different variety of feeling from the pleasure which Pitt derived from his own eloquence, and which Coleridge described as 'deadening' his 'genuine feelings'. Coleridge's claim that the analogies which 'swallow up' his arguments arise from more than such linguistic self-indulgence, however, is so obviously favourable to his own moral status, as well as his metaphysical opinions, as to require more substantial justification. His most persuasive argument for distinguishing between Pitt's and his own use of language, indeed, does not concern any difference between the varieties of feeling they express, but rather the effects of their expression, which on the one hand (that of Pitt and the French) are to produce pleasure in their listeners – a pleasure which the speakers then become preoccupied with producing – and on the other hand (that of Coleridge) are to prevent his pronouncements from being easily understood or enjoyed. Whereas Pitt was criticized for his orientation towards popularity, that is, the relative difficulty of Coleridge's own writing is described as paradoxically meritorious. Just as, in *The Friend*, he criticizes his own style only to assert the 'intrinsic excellence' of those on which it is modelled, so having admitted that his illustrations 'swallow up' his main arguments, Coleridge explains how that very submergence is an expression of the profoundest knowledge.[42] Obscurity and unpopularity, he implies, are closely connected with truthfulness; and though this connection – like the notion of an identity underlying his analogies – is clearly favourable to himself, the process of interpreting this passage suggests an additional explanation for it. By challenging the interpretative skills of the reader, that is, Coleridge's text stimulates precisely that contemplation of sublime ideas which he elsewhere describes as the ultimate aim of philosophy.[43] Hence whatever feelings may have engendered his writing, it has the potential to stimulate that restless search for understanding which is the basis of the Romantic sublime, and which the very perspicuity of Pitt's oratory implicitly prevented.

4. BODY INTO MIND: DREAMS AND WAKING CONSCIOUSNESS

In the first part of this chapter I argued that Coleridge – at least after 1801 – was committed to the view that the activities traditionally classified as mental are neither effects of the body nor of a mind which pre-exists them, yet that a 'feeling' entirely distinct from the 'sensation' which Hartley described is nevertheless an indispensable part of all intellectual and associative processes. Certain experiences, however, forced Coleridge to question the independence of such processes from physical determinants. The vividly recollected nightmares he suffered often seemed to be directly related to physical disturbances or discomforts, and in many cases were clearly induced by opium. Such experiences, he wrote to the Swedenborgian C. A. Tulk in 1826,

> ... have almost forced my attention to the obscure subject of dreams—and the extraordinary tendency to a sort of allegoric personification of the processes & incidents of vital Action, that is so characteristic of Sleep when the lower Bowels are deranged.
>
> (*CL*, 6: 607)

This transformation of sensations into images, insistently recorded and analysed in Coleridge's notebooks, had also been noted by Hartley. In dreams, Hartley writes,

> ... the State of the Body suggests such Ideas, amongst those that have been lately impressed, as are most suitable to the various Kinds and Degrees of pleasant and painful Vibrations excited in the Stomach, Brain, or some other Part. Thus a Person who has taken Opium, sees either gay Scenes, or ghastly ones, according as the Opium excites pleasant or painful Vibrations in the Stomach.[44]

Coleridge's avoidance of such associationist language cannot conceal the similarity of the processes described by the two authors. Transcendental idealism might find alternative explanations for the appearance of physical causes, yet in his letter to Tulk Coleridge makes little attempt to challenge or philosophize the evidence of his senses. Physical sensation, it appears, has the power to transform itself into ideas, despite the impossibility of explaining how material processes could give rise to consciousness.[45]

In itself, however, this physical influence on dreams was not a threat to Coleridge's view of thinking as a freely determined continuum of feelings and ideas. In a notebook entry of 1805 he suggests that our dream images rise up automatically, and are only shown to be connected with particular *sensations* by the brief continuance of their connection in the moments of waking.[46] Yet this does not imply that thinking, which at least appears to involve free will and conscious reflection, is in fact produced by unconscious sensations or other physical causes. By referring, in general terms, to 'The dependence of ideas on states of bodily or *mental Feeling*' (*CN*, 2: 2638), Coleridge allows the possibility that the ideas of waking consciousness may arise or be deduced from feelings which are as much mental as physical – a view he made more explicit in a letter to John Thelwall of 1796.[47] Even Hartley, indeed, affirms the difference between the ideational processes of sleep and waking consciousness. The 'Wildness and Inconsistency in our Dreams', he suggests, is due to the intervention of immediate sensations, rather than to the repetition and conjunction of external impressions (*OM*, 1: 385). Indeed, Hartley seems to be forced into this distinction by the universally evident nature of such connections as Coleridge describes: since, according to Hartley, our conscious thoughts are also products of sensation, their origin must be distinguished from that which we can feel and understand.

The fact that our dreams can seem to be determined by the body, however, clearly raises important philosophical problems. If, as Coleridge suggested in a note on Jeremy Taylor, the mind can be unconsciously acted on by 'the presence of irritating matters in the lower abdomen',[48] how can we explain the independence of the soul from the body, and its continuance after the dissolution of the body? Coleridge's chief solution to this problem concerns, firstly, the inactivity of the will and of our rational faculties when we are dreaming, and secondly, the different relationship which obtains between feelings and images when we are awake.

In dreams, he wrote to the newspaper editor Daniel Stuart in 1816:

> … Images and Thoughts possess a power in and of themselves, independent of that act of the Judgement or Understanding by which we affirm or deny the existence of a reality correspondent to them … The Forms and Thoughts act merely by their own inherent power: and the strong feelings at times apparently connected with them are in point of fact bodily sensations, which are the causes or occasions of the Images, not (as when we are awake) the effects of them.
>
> (*CL*, 4: 641–2)

In dreams, then, we are taken over by our sensations. These engender the images which appear to be the causes of our feelings.[49] To say that we *believe* in such a causative relation, however, is to Coleridge inaccurate in two respects. Firstly, because when dreaming we are unable to judge of the reality of anything: 'with the will the comparing power is suspended', he writes, 'and without the comparing power any act of Judgement, whether affirmation or denial, is impossible'.[50] Secondly, however, because in dreams there is no separation between feelings and thoughts or images. Whereas in waking consciousness we judge of the reality of our circumstances and feel certain emotions as a result of our judgement, the emotions of our dreams are in fact the same as physical sensations, and produce the images and thoughts we experience.

In a notebook entry of 1811, however, Coleridge went even further in distinguishing the feelings and images of waking consciousness from those which occur in dreams. Reason, he says, 'can exert no influence' over the terrors of a nightmare, not because reason is *a priori* suspended in sleep, but because the feeling in question

> … is not true Terror: i.e. apprehension of Danger, but a sensation as much as the Tooth-ache, a Cramp—I.e. the Terror does not *arise* out of … a painful Sensation, but is itself a specific sensation, = terror corporeus sive materialis.[51]

In this passage, even the notion of a reversal, in dreams, of the usual relationship between feelings and images, has disappeared. It has done so because the terror we feel in nightmares is not what Coleridge means by 'feeling', but something much closer to what Hartley calls 'sensation'. Whereas true terror is not only a consequence of judgement, but actually indistinguishable from the apprehension of danger, the terror we feel in a nightmare is indistinguishable from a physical sensation, and shares the pattern of Hartley's theory, in which impressions are transformed into ideas through a continuous physical reaction. Whether or not the emotions of waking consciousness are also 'bodily sensations', they are intellectual and depend upon the will – in this case, the will to survive or to avoid destruction. The real difference between dreams and waking consciousness, Coleridge suggests, is not a matter of causative direction, but of the presence or absence of intellection and of the feeling which is its consequence.[52]

Thus, he suggests, we may be determined in Hartleian mode when we are asleep, but this does not mean either that we are so determined when awake, or that consciousness in general can be explained by physical causes. Yet though in the above passage he suggests an almost hyperbolic role for reason in waking consciousness, he neither absolutely denies that it is subject to a material influence, nor explains how reason and judgement could connect or interact with such an influence. Moreover, since he often denied the existence of a material universe other than that which we unconsciously produce in the act of perception, the notion of a material influence determining our dreams through physical or associative processes of which we are unconscious was no less problematic. It was perhaps for this reason that he questioned the popular assumption of such an influence. Concerning 'the seeming appropriation of … Dream Images & Incidents to affections of particular organs, & viscera', he asked:

> Do the material causes act *positively*, so that with the removal of the Body by Death the total cause is removed & of course the Effects? Or only *negatively* and *indirectly* by lessening & suspending that continuous texture of organic sensation, which by drawing outward the attention of the [soul], *sheaths* her from her own state & its correspondent activities?[53]

The alternative, then, to a bodily determination of dream images is that they are present in the mind prior to our becoming conscious of them, and that bodily disturbances merely interrupt that unselfconsciousness which normally prevails in sleep. This, of course, does not solve the problem of material influence *per se*, since the 'attention' of the soul is said to be normally drawn 'outward' by 'the continuous texture of organic sensation'. This 'drawing outward', however, does not involve consciousness, but is rather precisely what prevents the soul from becoming conscious of its own activities. Hence what we see or think in sleep is not occasioned by anything external to the mind. Nothing – not even the body – 'impresses' itself on the soul; what we see is not a consequence of anything except our spiritual condition.[54]

This very substantial elimination of the bodily influence, however, was itself a cause of great anxiety to Coleridge. The question, whether dream images originate within or outside the soul, was, he said in the same passage,

> A fearful Question, which I too often agitate, and which agitates me, even in my Dreams, when most commonly I am in one of Swedenborg's Hells, doubtful whether I am once more to be *awaked*, & thinking our Dreams to be the true state of the soul disembodied when not united with Christ. On awaking from such dreams, I never fail to find some local *pain*, circa- or infra-umbilical, Kidney affection, & at the base of the Bladder with vast water-scenery.[55]

Coleridge's debate as to whether his dreams have a spiritual or a physical origin is paralleled by several of his discussions of Swedenborg, and especially of whether Swedenborg's apparent power of converting his 'thoughts into things' – that is, into images seeming to have an independent existence – was the result of disease, or of an obscure spiritual influence resembling divine revelation.[56] Additionally, Coleridge's comparison of internal and external consciousness parallels Swedenborg's description of the conjunction of inward sinfulness with outward virtue in a passage discussing the state of man immediately after death, which Coleridge quoted in a notebook entry of 1821.[57] Coleridge's interest in these topics, however, is clearly an intensely personal one. That explanation of dream images which would save him from admitting that the body can unconsciously determine our ideas is itself terrifying, and something he would much rather not believe. The situation is rendered more complex, however, by the fact that he experiences this fear within the dreams which are in question. He dreams he is being punished with an anxiety about whether this very 'agitation' is the true state of the soul in hell, or merely an effect of the body. To be in hell, he implies, is not to know whether or not one is in hell. He is not agitated *about* anything, except whether his agitation will continue.

His description of this fear is an ironic, if deeply felt, commentary on the quotation from St Ambrose to which it is appended, namely that 'death is a haven of rest'. The real haven, it appears, is rather a belief in the physical causation of his dreams – a point he makes more explicit in the concluding chapter of *Biographia*, when discussing the consolation to be derived from understanding the chains of cause and effect which determine our experience. 'It is,' he writes,

> ... within the experience of many medical practitioners, that a patient, with strange and unusual symptoms of disease, has been more distressed in mind ... from the fact of being unintelligible to himself and others, than from the pain or danger of the disease: nay, that he has received more solid comfort, and resumed a genial and enduring chearfulness, from some new symptom or product, that had at once determined the name and nature of his complaint, and rendered it an intelligible effect of an intelligible cause: even though the discovery did at the same time preclude all hope of restoration. Hence the mystic theologians ... have joined in representing the state of the reprobate spirits as a dreadful dream in which there is no sense of reality, not even of the pangs they are enduring—an eternity without time, and as it were below it.
>
> (*BL*, 2: 234–5)[58]

The comfort to be derived from understanding the *causes* of our sufferings is thus connected by Coleridge with a very similar experience to that described in his note on Taylor. When compared with this note, indeed, the discussion in *Biographia* suggests that even though the establishment of a physical cause for his nightmare may threaten his belief in the immateriality of the soul, it nevertheless provides great consolation, by releasing him from the sense of being disconnected from reality, and – as he puts it here – unintelligible to himself. Indeed, the emphasis in this passage on confusion or lack of certainty, and on anxiety itself (rather than any specific fear) as the greatest cause of mental suffering, suggests that these two passages derive from the same dream experience, which seems from his notebooks to have been a repeated and memorable one. His attempt to argue away the physical influence, and to produce an idealist theory of dreams, thus seems to have been decisively thwarted, or put into reverse, by the emotional necessity of comprehending and explaining his nightmares, and re-establishing his grasp on the 'matter' of waking consciousness and physical existence.

Coleridge's analyses of dreams thus arise from an attempt to accommodate the appearance of their physical causation within an anti-materialist psychology. Paradoxically, however, several factors lead him to emphasize the physical origin of dreams. Firstly, his wish to accentuate the distinctive freedom and rationality of thought requires that dreams be distinguished from it. If our dream images were held to arise in the same way as thoughts, that is, the experience of active choice in thinking would no longer be a ground for distinguishing it from the process of dreaming, whatever claims we might make as to the mental, rather than physical, origin of either. Secondly, however, Coleridge wishes to escape from the unpleasant consequences of believing that nightmares originate in the eternal soul or spirit rather than the accidents of sensation, and this need to re-establish a firm grasp on perceptual reality is a powerful influence on the interpretation of dreams in his later notes and marginalia. His intellectual judgement that matter and spirit can never be divided is thus effectively overturned both by his emphasis on the unique experience of thinking, and by his search for a sense of certainty and security. That such consolation could be derived from believing in the physical origin of dreams, as well as from asserting the priority of consciousness to its objects, indeed, is a particularly vivid illustration of the fact that far from being a purely intellectual matter, his persistent quest for freedom or transcendence was centrally concerned with overcoming the emotions of fear and helplessness by which he was so often afflicted.

3

The Feeling of Knowledge: Insight and Delusion in Coleridge

Coleridge's repeated claim that thought depends on intuition or feeling, and that philosophical insight can only be derived from personal conviction, raises obvious questions as to how one should distinguish a 'true' or revelatory conviction from a false one.[1] His continual quest for a feeling of the sublime is rationalized as a pursuit of fundamental truths which are beyond human understanding; yet the very impossibility of demonstrating these truths reveals their dependence on Coleridge's will to believe in them, or on his search for a sublime feeling which is essentially a substitute for any form of argument. Similarly, his preoccupation with Neoplatonic theories of the upward movement of nature and intellect towards union with the deity seems to have been motivated by a desire not only to establish grounds for an optimism which his practical circumstances tended to undermine, but also to celebrate the intellectual efforts which he evidently found so rewarding.[2] To say that his philosophical writing proposes 'the communication and *acquirement* of truth' as its 'immediate object' would therefore seem to involve too uncritical an acceptance of his metaphysical conclusions.[3] Coleridge himself renders these problematic, not only by his consistent pursuit of insights principally represented by sensations, but also by his candid descriptions of the pleasures of thinking and of the vital roles of intuition and emotion in metaphysical discovery.[4] Hence his thought is continually on a cusp between claims to absolute knowledge, and self-descriptions which seem to undermine them.

The apparent contradictions may be partly resolved by Coleridge's concept of the will, and especially his view of faith as a form of 'active knowledge'.[5] His argument that by choosing to believe in certain supersensible objects we move towards fulfilling our spiritual destiny may be a circular one, but it has at least the sanction of a long tradition. Coleridge himself, however, seems to have been dissatisfied by the intrinsic ambiguity of such theories, and repeatedly sought additional means of justifying his metaphysics and distinguishing them from self-indulgence or delusion. His principal means of doing so was to focus on the types of feeling usually accompanying metaphysical insight, and to contrast these with the feelings of those who in various ways are distracted from the truth. The apparent mundanity of this analysis may be surprising in an author usually so dedicated to ideas of the sublime and ineffable. Yet his discussions of the role of sensation and emotion in determining our ideas not only show the importance of feeling to Coleridge's own reflective processes, but also suggest a persistent anxiety about the reliableness of a philosophy so extensively guided by irrational or subjective forces.

1. MYSTICS AND VISIONARIES

As noted in Chapter 2, Coleridge's distinction between 'feeling' and 'sensation' not only contrasts those emotions whose origin is internal with those which derive from outside influences, but also implies that genuine thought and insight can only arise from an accurate expression or analysis of the former. His conceptions of 'true' and 'false' feeling thus also involve the ideas of the true and false opinions they give rise to, yet precisely how we should distinguish a valid intuition from an externally derived delusion is by no means always apparent. From the extent and variety of Coleridge's own thoughts on this issue, however, the distinction of insightful from delusive states of feeling seems to have been a matter of personal, and not merely rhetorical, interest to him, underlying the very possibility of trusting his convictions. Of greatest importance to the justification of his metaphysics are his reflections on those thinkers who lay claim to a knowledge revealing itself through sensation or emotion. Coleridge himself belongs to this class: hence his interest in mystics such as Jacob Boehme, and in specifying the mental states which led them either into error, or into the profoundest knowledge.

This specification is often arranged by Coleridge under two sets of opposed headings: his distinctions between 'enthusiasm' and 'fanaticism', and between 'certainty' and 'positiveness', are primarily between the types of mystical excitement which lead to knowledge and to delusion. When he discusses mystical delusions in isolation from these schemata, however, his comments involve no less clear a dichotomy; only here the opposite of error is not an abstract condition of insight, but consists rather in his own supposed ability to recognize and understand the diseases in question. An individual with such insight into waywardness, we are supposed to believe, could not possibly share the same delusions. In this way, Coleridge's general critique of mysticism acts as a rhetorical support to his metaphysical assertions.

These unformalized discussions of mystical delusion chiefly concern the dangers afflicting the 'uneducated man of genius' – a type of which Boehme is for Coleridge the chief representative. His manner of describing these dangers, however, clearly has its roots in pre-Enlightenment notions of melancholy, with which he was familiar from his reading of seventeenth-century authors. The Platonist Henry More, for example, describes in his *Enthusiasmus Triumphatus* how those intoxicated with melancholy may be so impressed by their own imaginative brilliance as to believe they are possessed by the spirit of God.[6] Similarly, Richard Baxter, in his *Preservatives Against Melancholy*, describes a condition in which people

> ... seem to feel something besides themselves, as it were *speaking in them*, and saying this or that to them, and bidding them do this or that ... and they will hardly believe how much of it is the Disease of their Imagination.
>
> In this case they are exceeding prone to think they have *Revelations*, and whatever comes into their Minds, they think some *Revelation* brought it thither ...[7]

Though Coleridge never adopted the idea of melancholic intoxication – that mysterious transformation of the physical into the mental described by More and Baxter – the type of delusion they attributed to this process was one which particularly interested him, and for which he found a variety of explanations. At one extreme, Coleridge can be surprisingly modern in his psychological analysis, though also suggesting physical causes which seem to endanger any rigorous distinction of mind from body. His notebook discussion of St Teresa of Avila is notable in both these respects. It was, Coleridge says,

> ... almost impossible ... that a young Spanish Maiden so innocent, & so susceptible, of an imagination so lively by nature & so

> fever-kindled by disease & its occasions...should not mistake, & often, the less painful and in such a frame the sometimes pleasurable approaches to bodily Deliquium, and her imperfect Fainting-fits for divine Transports, & momentary Union with God—especially if with a thoughtful yet pure psychology you join the force of suppressed Instincts stirring in the heart & bodily frame, of a mind unconscious of their nature/and these in the keenly-sensitive body, in the innocent and loving Soul of a Teresa ...
>
> (*CN*, 3: 3911)

The chief advance on More in this passage is a diversification of the monolithic 'melancholy' into a complex interrelation of psychological and physical elements. Rather than a chemical sublimation, Coleridge describes one which is almost Freudian; disease was one of the things which predisposed Teresa to delusion, but what produced it was repressed desire and an instinctual valorization of pleasure.[8] What I wish to emphasize, however, is that Coleridge's more modern and superficially more sympathetic interpretation of religious enthusiasm shares the same structure as More's: firstly in that the personal is mistaken for the universal, or the phenomenal for the transcendent; and secondly in that the causes of this mistake are either physical, or psychological only insofar as they are also part of an inherited and predetermined psycho-physical complex. Most unusually for Coleridge, the movement of transcendence is immediately interpreted as a form of delusion. The truth, he implies, lies in 'suppressed Instincts', just as for More the truth of enthusiasm lies in vapours from the lowest region of the body. Coleridge, in other words, seems to adopt that attitude towards St Teresa which advocates of psychoanalysis might adopt towards his own case.[9]

As we shall see, however, Coleridge's usual interpretation of enthusiastic delirium is more traditional than this, and makes no explicit reference to physical or instinctual causes. His image of 'the fanatic who abandons himself to the wild workings of the magic cauldron of his own brain mistaking every form of delirium for reality' (*PLects*, 186) serves more effectively to offset his own clear-headedness. It is an old-fashioned image, making no concessions to modern science or psychology, and sharing the antiquated and mysterious flavour of its seventeenth-century antecedents. The 'magic cauldron' is neither physical nor mental, but rather an image whose very obscurity is implicitly attributed to the thoughts of the deluded individual. The antiquated style of Coleridge's description becomes a means of distancing himself from the phenomena he is describing, of locating them firmly in a pre-scientific scenario.

His discussion of Boehme is intermediate between these two extremes; for while he is not so Freudian as in the case of St Teresa, nor is he so mysterious about the causes of Boehme's delusion as to invoke a seventeenth-century interpretation. In chapter nine of *Biographia*, for example, he seeks as much to justify Boehme's ideas (and those of 'mystics' in general) as to explain their origins. His evocation of Boehme's experience expresses a degree of sympathy which prevents Coleridge from merely dismissing his thinking, leading him instead to distinguish its merits from its evils. The chapter, indeed, is entitled 'Obligations to the Mystics, and its tone is so much one of sympathetic reappraisal as paradoxically to implicate Coleridge in the very condition he is describing[10] – a fact which is particularly evident in the following passage:

> O! it requires deeper feeling, and a stronger imagination, than belong to most of those, to whom reasoning and fluent expression have been as a trade learnt in boyhood, to conceive with what *might*, with what inward *strivings* and *commotion*, the perception of a new and vital TRUTH takes possession of an uneducated man of genius. His meditations are almost inevitably employed on the eternal, or the everlasting; for '*the world is not his friend, nor the world's law*'. Need we then be surprised, that under an excitement at once so strong and so unusual, the man's body should sympathize with the struggles of his mind; or that he should at times be so far deluded, as to mistake the tumultuous sensations of his nerves, and the co-existing spectres of his fancy, as parts or symbols of the truths which were opening on him?
>
> (*BL*, 1: 150–1)

According to this passage, Coleridge is one of the few highly educated people who *can* conceive 'with what *might* ... the perception of a new and vital TRUTH takes possession of an uneducated man of genius'. Not only can he feel gratitude towards those mystics who 'contributed to keep alive the *heart* in the *head*' by transgressing the boundaries of a shallow and dead philosophy, he can also understand the feeling which occasionally led them into error.[11] The central theme of this chapter is that the mystics in question perceived and expressed truth in ways which the philosophical and religious conventions of their time prohibited among the learned. Only because they were not bridled by these conventions could their instinctual desire for a deeper understanding be fulfilled. Yet in giving way to this desire they became so excited that they could not always distinguish the objects of their insight from the sensations and images accompanying them. The duality of insightful and delusive feeling is expressed in the above passage by the words 'strivings' and 'commotion': the former gave rise to the latter, but in its absence there would only have been the 'rattling twigs and sprays' of a dogmatic system.[12]

It is in terms of this duality that, in a marginal note on Boehme, Coleridge distinguishes between two senses of the word 'visionary'. Boehme, he says,

> ... was ... a Visionary in two very different senses of that word. Frequently does he mistake the dreams of his own over-excited Nerves, the phantoms and witcheries from the cauldron of his own seething Fancy, for parts or symbols of a universal Process; but frequently likewise does he give incontestible proofs, that he possessed in very truth
>
> 'The Vision and Faculty divine!' (*CM*, 1: 558)[13]

Though Coleridge here constructs a clearer distinction between the admirable and regrettable aspects of Boehme's mysticism, this very clarity draws attention to the obscure basis of his distinction. To say that excitement can lead to delusion is not to explain how true conceptions can be distinguished from false ones.[14] Some explanation of the mechanism underlying mystical confusion was given in *Biographia*: mental excitement, Coleridge suggested, may also produce physical agitation, resulting in a tendency to mistake the sensations of the body and the images of fancy for revelations. Yet though, in *Biographia*, he clearly implies that the source of this error lies in the body's 'sympathizing' with the mind, in his marginal note this is not so clearly implied, Coleridge's emphasis being rather on the peculiar images and excitements which Boehme misinterpreted, than on what caused him to misinterpret them. The only clear distinction, indeed, is between Boehme's insight ('The Vision and Faculty divine') and his confusion: neither their relationship, nor Coleridge's own method of distinguishing the one from the other, is explained.

His distinction, in *On the Constitution of the Church and State*, between two senses of the word 'mystic' brings us no closer to discovering how deceptive feeling can be distinguished from that which is necessary to metaphysical insight. As we saw in *Biographia*, the same excitement can act in both directions, and the mystic who suppresses his craving for knowledge will be void of enlightenment as well as delusion. In *Church and State*, however, the delusive effects of such excitement are said to affect mystics only in a secondary sense of the term 'mystic'. 'Where a person mistakes the anomalous misgrowths of his own individuality for ideas, or truths of universal reason', Coleridge writes in a glossary of terms

> ... he may, without impropriety, be called a *Mystic*, in the abusive sense of the term, though pseudo-mystic, or phantast, would be the more proper designation. Heraclitus, Plato, Bacon, Leibnitz, were Mystics, in the primary sense of the term: Iamblichus, and his successors, Phantasts.
>
> (*C&S*, 165)

What, then, is the 'primary sense' of 'mystic', and how does it differ from the abusive? *Church and State* does not explain this, and all we can conclude either from the above passage or from chapter nine of *Biographia* is that a 'true' mystic would be one who did not make the mistakes I have described.

A notebook entry of 1819, however, is more specific in indicating the ideas and experiences associated with 'true' mysticism, or the kind which Coleridge wishes to recommend. The term 'Mystic', he suggests, is commonly used to denote one who bases his beliefs 'on *blind feelings* or incommunicable Experiences', though empiricists use the term to 'confound and discredit' those (including Coleridge himself) who 'receive and worship God in spirit and in truth'. According to Coleridge, however, those most guilty of the weakness commonly referred to as 'mysticism' are empiricists themselves, in regarding mere sensation as the basis of reality, and rejecting the insights of idealist thinkers. Genuine 'Pietists', on the other hand, though sometimes mistaking their sensations and images for revelations, only do this in 'exceptions and *fits*' (*CN*, 4: 4605). Hence, though his definition of 'Mystics' is largely a negative one, Coleridge claims that those usually called by this name in fact have genuine insights, albeit occasionally falling into error. 'Mystics' thus remains a highly ambiguous term, partly denoting 'self-misapprehending' visionaries, and partly expressing the polemical intentions of its user, yet also – in a use which is specific to Coleridge – referring to those who are unjustly accused of suffering from delusions.

His conclusion on 'Mystics and Mysticism' in *Aids to Reflection*, however, clearly defines a mystic as one who makes precisely the mistakes which, in *Church and State*, he attributes only to a 'pseudo-mystic' or a phantast:

> When a Man refers to *inward feelings* and *experiences*, of which Mankind at large are not conscious, as evidences of the truth of any opinion—such a Man I call a MYSTIC: and the grounding of any theory or belief on accidents and anomalies of individual sensations or fancies, and the use of peculiar terms invented or perverted from their ordinary significations, for the purpose of expressing these *idiosyncrasies*, and pretended facts of interior consciousness, I name MYSTICISM.
>
> (*AR*, 389)

According to *Aids to Reflection*, therefore, the central facts about mysticism are that it is at once a pretence to knowledge and a consequence of anomalous sensations. Idiosyncrasy, diversion or perversion from the tenets of true religion or philosophy, seems to be the object of Coleridge's criticism here. Whereas in *Biographia* he praised mystics for the insight which resulted from their greater feeling and lesser constraint, here he writes only of 'anomalous sensations' and 'pretended facts of interior consciousness'. The idea of pretence, however, is obviously in conflict with that of being taken over by feeling, or of merely mistaking 'the anomalous misgrowths of [one's] own individuality' for universal truths. Whereas in *Church and State* Coleridge implies that those properly to be called mystics have misunderstood their feelings and images, here he accuses them of consciously foisting off their false imaginings as revelation, and seeking to mislead their readers.

The additional accusation that they use 'peculiar terms… perverted from their ordinary significations, for the purpose of *expressing* these idiosyncrasies',[15] is in retrospect an unwise one to have made. For Coleridge himself, in a less fanatically orthodox moment, did precisely this with the term 'mystic'. As several critics have shown, desynonymy was Coleridge's principal means of legitimating private distinctions. By drawing up lists of the terms in other languages whose diverse meanings had been confused in English, he sought to demonstrate that reality was more complex than our habitual use of language implied.[16] In the case of 'mystic', however, such desynonymy does not seem to have been practicable. All he can do is invoke an etymology:

> MYSTES, from the Greek μύω—one who *muses* with closed lips, as meditating on *Ideas* which may indeed be suggested and awakened, but cannot, like the images of sense and the conceptions of the understanding, be adequately *expressed* by words
>
> (*C&S*, 165)

To meditate on ideas which cannot be adequately expressed by words is necessarily to make one's feelings the ground of one's belief, or as Coleridge puts it in *Aids to Reflection*, to refer 'to *inward feelings* and *experiences*, of which Mankind at large are not conscious', as evidences of the truth of an opinion. This, however, was how Coleridge defined mysticism in the 'abusive' sense. The etymology which he intended to distinguish the 'primary' sense of mystic from the abusive thus turns out to describe only one subjective condition, containing no internal ground of distinction. Only insofar as the ideas entertained by a 'pseudo-mystic' are 'anomalous misgrowths', while those of a true mystic are not, can they be contrasted with each other.

Further statements, indeed, more directly implicate Coleridge in the mysticism he is alternately denigrating and praising. 'In the Bible', he wrote,

> ...there is more, *that finds me* than...I have experienced in all other books put together...and...whatever finds me brings with it an irresistible evidence of its having proceeded from the Holy Spirit.
>
> (*SWF*, 2: 1123)[17]

This is precisely the kind of delusion which More and Baxter described: the taking of inward feelings as evidences of divine inspiration. Perhaps there can be no other ground for belief in such inspiration; yet beyond the criterion of conforming to established opinion (a quality which, as noted earlier, Coleridge deprecates in his philosophical opponents), there is equally no means of distinguishing it from the error of a 'self-misapprehending' visionary.

2. ENTHUSIASM AND FANATICISM

When More described those who mistake their own feelings of power for divine inspiration, however, he was writing not about mysticism but about 'enthusiasm'. Insofar as More and Coleridge are discussing the same phenomenon, the different names they give to it may be of little importance. Yet Coleridge also used the word 'enthusiasm', not as a synonym of mysticism, but rather as one element in a dualism which is largely independent from his definitions of mysticism. As far as Coleridge is concerned, 'enthusiasm' seems to denote a more specific set of characteristics than mysticism, and one which he habitually contrasted with fanaticism. In *Aids to Reflection*, indeed, he describes enthusiasm and fanaticism as two types of mysticism. Having first given the deprecatory definition of mysticism quoted above, he continues:

> Where the error consists simply in the Mystic's attaching to these anomalies of his individual temperament the character of Reality, and in receiving them as Permanent Truths, having a subsistence in the Divine Mind, though revealed to himself alone; but entertains this persuasion without demanding or expecting the same faith in his neighbours—I should regard it as a species of ENTHUSIASM ... But when the Mystic by ambition or still meaner passions, or ... by an uneasy and self-doubting state of mind that seeks confirmation in outward sympathy, is led to impose his faith, as a duty, on mankind generally ... such a Mystic is a FANATIC ...
>
> (*AR*, 389)

Despite appearances, this distinction does not remove the contradictions involved in the deprecatory definition of mysticism which precedes it. Insofar as mysticism involved mistaking the personal for the universal, it seemed unreasonable to accuse its sufferer of seeking to mislead other people. The accusation that mystics express 'pretended facts of interior consciousness' was obviously problematic; for though on the one hand the revelations they believe themselves to experience may not be genuine, their expression of these apparent revelations does not involve them in any deception. In the passage I have just quoted, however, Coleridge seems to distinguish between those who intend to deceive, whom he calls fanatics, and those who subjectively attach the character of reality 'to [the] anomalies of [their] individual temperament[s]', whom he calls enthusiasts. There is still considerable ambiguity as to the intention of the fanatic, for though he 'seeks confirmation [for his opinions] in outward sympathy', one must doubt whether deception can be his aim even before persuasion of others has secured his certainty. It seems clear, at least, that whereas enthusiasm is something personal and private, not involving any imposition on others, fanaticism always involves such imposition. Yet unless enthusiasts are wholly uncommunicative, in which case none would have come to Coleridge's attention, it is hard to see how they could avoid the danger of misleading others. Hence we can find no secure ground of distinction either in the fanatic's intention to deceive or in the enthusiast's avoidance of deception. Coleridge clearly prefers enthusiasm to fanaticism, for whereas the former, though 'always ... to be deprecated', is 'capable of co-existing with many excellent qualities both of Head and Heart', the fanatic is 'in certain states of the public mind a dangerous Member of Society' (*AR*, 389). Yet this is not a true opposition, and merely indicates the same desire to praise one aspect of mysticism and criticize another as emerged from his distinction between those 'inward strivings' which are necessary to truth, and that 'commotion which leads to delusion.

Coleridge's most detailed distinction between enthusiasm and fanaticism, however, occurs in a marginal note on Birch's *Sermon on the Prevalence of Infidelity and Enthusiasm* (1818). 'Enthusiasm', Coleridge notes,

> ... is the absorption of the individual in the object contemplated from the vividness or intensity of his conceptions and convictions: fanaticism is heat, or accumulation and direction, of feeling acquired by contagion, and relying on the sympathy of sect or confederacy; intense sensation with confused or dim conceptions. Hence the fanatic can exist only in a crowd, from inward weakness anxious for outer confirmation; and therefore, an eager proselyter and intolerant. The enthusiast, on the contrary, is a solitary, who lives in a world of his own peopling, and for that cause is disinclined to outward action.
>
> (*CM*, 1: 496)[18]

Here we have at least one clear distinction between the processes involved in enthusiasm and fanaticism. Whereas the former involves intense conceptions and convictions, the latter only involves intense sensations, and it is its very lack of conviction that needs to be filled up by confederacy and proselytism. Whereas the enthusiast is 'absorbed' in the objects of his contemplation, the fanatic – it seems – wants to be so absorbed, but can only find certainty in the concurrence of others. Since, however, fanaticism also arises 'by contagion', and itself depends on 'the sympathy of sect or confederacy', it cannot be described as a disposition, but only as a form of communal excitement. It may be that certain individuals are disposed, by 'inward weakness', to *become* fanatics, but they will not *be* such until they are gathered together.[19]

Thus we can develop a distinction, parallel but not identical with Coleridge's, between enthusiasm, which is a process of having strong feelings and images and at least potentially being 'taken over' by them, and fanaticism, which is rather an image of heat or excitement voluntarily created by the interaction of weak or unfruitful minds. Whereas the enthusiast is fulfilled in the contemplation of what arises automatically from or within his mind, the fanatic is effectively empty, and can only find or have meaning in conjunction with others of his kind. In *Biographia*, Coleridge is more specific about the technical aspects of fanaticism, yet also emphasizes the idea that fanatics are not real individuals or separate minds, but rather something analogous to 'damp hay':

> A debility and dimness of the imaginative power, and a consequent necessity of reliance on the impressions of the senses, do, we well know, render the mind liable to superstition and fanaticism. Having a deficient portion of internal and proper warmth, minds of this class seek in the crowd *circum fana* for a warmth in common, which they do not possess singly. Cold and phlegmatic in their own nature, like damp hay, they heat and inflame by co-acervation; or like bees they become restless and irritable through the increased temperature of collected multitudes. Hence the German word for fanaticism (such at least was its original import) is derived from the swarming of bees, namely, Schwärmen, Schwärmerey.
>
> (*BL*, 1: 30)

These images, repeated separately in other places, serve to exonerate Coleridge by contrasting his own creativity and independent conviction with the debilitated and almost physical interdependence of fanatics.[20] What they lack is warmth and imagination; hence they live only in the realm of the external senses. *As* fanatics, they only exist insofar as they inflame each other. They do not think, but act in a way quite different from rational beings. Enthusiasm, Coleridge implies, is perhaps excusable when the powers which cause it are also necessary to transcending such a debilitated condition. That he is exonerating himself in this distinction is made still more evident by his statement that the enthusiast 'is a solitary, who lives in a world of his own peopling, and for that cause is disinclined to outward action'. Because the fanatic is characterized by the impossibility of his independent existence, solitary creativity and the private world of thought become intrinsic values, which in his commentary on Birch's *Sermon* Coleridge does little to moderate.[21] Similarly, in praise of Boehme Coleridge writes:

> A meek and shy quietist, his intellectual powers were never stimulated into fev'rous energy by crowds of proselytes or by the ambition of proselyting [*sic*]. He was an enthusiast in the strictest sense, as not merely distinguished but as contra-distinguished from a fanatic.
>
> (*PLects*, 327)

Far from being stigmatized, then, enthusiasm is gradually depleted of its disadvantages by comparison with the intrinsically negative and dangerous phenomenon of fanaticism. In *Aids to Reflection* Coleridge writes that even a mysticism exempt from fanatical proselytizing is 'always to be deprecated'. But this was not always his opinion. 'Nothing great was ever atchieved without enthusiasm', he wrote in 1816. 'For what is enthusiasm but the oblivion and swallowing-up of self in an object dearer than self, or in an idea more vivid?'[22] Insofar as it is opposed to fanaticism, such 'absorption of the individual in the object contemplated' seems to be an unambiguous good.[23] It is only when enthusiasm and fanaticism are considered as two categories of mysticism that the importance of creative excitement is eclipsed by the critique of delusion. Quite explicitly, what Coleridge values in enthusiasm is the same as its definition: independent and original meditation. What the enthusiast challenges is the complacent and unthinking consensus of fanaticism.

3. CERTAINTY AND POSITIVENESS

Coleridge's distinction between 'certainty' and 'positiveness', on the other hand, is concerned less with individuality or creative energy *per se* than with the importance of a certain kind of feeling. We cannot say unambiguously that Coleridge wishes to determine what kind of feeling is conducive to the discovery of truth, since – as in his distinction between enthusiasm and fanaticism – he is primarily seeking to establish his own integrity by criticizing particular excesses. Insofar as he expresses a largely consistent valorization of one kind of feeling over another, however, he also implies the possibility of an ideal or correct relationship between feeling and thought. My aim in this section will be to discover how the ideal implied by this dualism relates to the values of his wider philosophy.

One rather unusual context of this distinction relates it to the different kinds of feeling which Coleridge suggests are involved in the practice of geometry. In a *Courier* article of 1809 he deprecated those who can reason on subjects of great moral importance 'in as cold-blooded a tone, as if [they] were demonstrating a problem in geometry' (*EOT*, 2: 78). A notebook entry of 1807, however, states that as 'Love' is to 'Likings', so 'the sense of *certainty*' in geometry is to 'the sensation of positiveness' (*CN*, 2: 3095).[24] The obvious implication is that geometrical reasoning, though perhaps 'cold-blooded', involves varying intensities of conviction, and that 'certainty' is a more powerful conviction than 'positiveness'.

Coleridge's most frequent explanation of the difference between certainty and positiveness, however, concerns the relative calmness of the former, and turbulence of the latter. 'I shall hereafter endeavour to prove', he wrote in the periodical *Friend*,

> ... how distinct and different the sensation of positiveness is from the sense of certainty, the turbulent heat of temporary fermentation from the mild warmth of essential life.
>
> (*Friend*, 2: 7)

The expression 'mild warmth' clearly suggests a lesser intensity of feeling than 'turbulent heat', and in this respect *The Friend* seems to contradict Coleridge's distinction in his notebook. If love is a 'mild warmth', 'likings' cannot denote 'turbulent heat', so that in terms of their intensity the relation between certainty and positiveness seems to have been inverted. The two statements are consistent, however, in suggesting that certainty is something more profound and enduring than positiveness. This view is repeated in a marginal note on Taylor's *Discourse of Confirmation*, where Coleridge remarks how 'professional Divines ... identify themselves with the theological scheme, to which they have been *articled*', and bemoans

> ... the nature and the power, the effect and the consequences of a wilful Faith, where the sensation of Positiveness is substituted for the sense of Certainty, and the stubborn Clutch for quiet Insight ...[25]

This passage again characterizes certainty at least partly by its relative calmness. Positiveness, however, is here not merely a briefer or more violent feeling than certainty, but also the principal cause of dogmatic adherence to received opinion. How this feeling might more specifically be described is not made clear. Yet if we take this case as the paradigm for Coleridge's distinction between certainty and positiveness, we can say that the calmness he recommends corresponds to insight, while the turbulence he deprecates corresponds to dogmatism.

This interpretation, however, does not seem adequate to account for the imagery he uses in *The Friend*. Can dogmatism, mere stubborn orthodoxy or obscurantism, really be identified with 'the turbulent heat of temporary fermentation'? Certainly 'the mild warmth of essential life' is quite appropriate to the nature of insight as Coleridge elsewhere conceives it.[26] The turbulent priest, moreover, may also be the stubbornly orthodox one; yet in *The Friend* it is not dogmatism, but rather the reckless enthusiasm of youth that Coleridge criticizes under the heading of 'positiveness'. In our youth, he says,

> The pleasurable heat which the Blood or the Breathing generates, the sense of external reality which comes with the strong Grasp of the hand or the vigorous Tread of the foot, may indifferently become associated with the rich eloquence of a Shaftesbury, imposing on us man's possible perfections for his existing nature; or with the cheerless and hardier impieties of a Hobbes, while cutting the gordian knot he denies the reality of either vice or virtue ...
>
> (*Friend*, 2: 7)

To this youthful 'turbulence', as to the dogmatism of orthodoxy, Coleridge equally opposes the 'quiet insight' of certainty. What these two kinds of positiveness have in common is 'acquiescence without insight'.[27] Indeed, Coleridge emphasizes the difference between certainty and positiveness by calling the former a 'sense' and the latter a 'sensation'. Precisely what sensation can be said to belong to religious dogmatists is not explained, but it appears to be something analogous to the fanatical 'inflammation' discussed earlier in this chapter.[28] Lacking the certainty of insight, the dogmatist finds conviction through imposing his opinions on others. His strength is dependent on community. And just as conformity seems, according to Coleridge's definition, to be a necessary feature of fanaticism, so it is the orthodoxy of the wilful priest that makes him 'positive'.

What Coleridge recommends in these passages, therefore, is the grounding of one's beliefs on thought rather than on tradition or feeling. In the *Omniana* paragraph entitled 'Voluntary Belief', indeed, he seems to contrast belief with feeling. According to Jeremy Taylor, he writes,

> 'It is possible ... for a man to bring himself to believe any thing he hath a mind to.' But what is this belief?—Analyse it into its constituents;—is it more than certain passions or feelings converging into the sensation of positiveness as their focus, and then associated with certain sounds or images?[29]

The same process is given a more detailed description in the 'Conciones ad Populum' of 1795, albeit that here he places it under the heading of 'fanaticism'. 'The mind', Coleridge says,

> ... is predisposed by its situations: and when the prejudices of a man are strong, the most over-powering Evidence becomes weak ... Some unmeaning Term generally becomes the Watchword, and acquires almost a mechanical power over his frame. The indistinctness of the Ideas associated with it increases its effect, as 'objects look gigantic thro' a mist.'
>
> (*Lects 1795*, 52)

Passion, then, can overwhelm a person's intellect, endowing words or images with an unreasonable significance. We should not assume from this, however, that Coleridge recommends detachment or emotional indifference, whether in philosophy or any other form of inquiry. Even in the case of geometry, an intensity of feeling analogous to that of 'love' was valorized over the relatively superficial feeling corresponding to 'likings'. In *The Friend*, moreover, Coleridge emphasizes the necessity of his appealing to 'the feelings, the imagination, and ... the fancy' if he is to arouse in his reader a conviction of noumenal realities.[30] The very intensity of human passions, he suggests, is evidence of their belonging 'as by a natural right to those obscure ideas that are necessary to the moral perfection of the human being'; the tendency of deep feelings to associate with obscure ideas is not regrettable so long as these feelings are directed towards the ideas of 'Being, Form, Life, the Reason, the Law of Conscience, Freedom, Immortality, God'.[31]

A notebook entry of 1800, however, presents an ideal of moderation which contrasts dramatically with *The Friend*'s enthusiastic enlistment of the reader's passion, suggesting that the capacity for perceiving truth depends on a condition intermediate between heat and coldness, passion and indifference:

> Hotheaded men confuse, your cool-headed Gentry jumble, the man of warm feelings only produces order & true connections ...
> (*CN*, 1: 868)

To be lacking in passion, Coleridge implied in *The Courier*, was no less dangerous than to be overcome by the accidental association of passion with meaningless watch-words.[32] To reason geometrically, as Hume did, with regard to noumenal objects, is even in a sense to be 'positive' rather than 'certain'; for it involves the application of an inappropriate faculty, and a stubborn clinging to the realm of the intelligible.[33] Yet if Coleridge retained this ideal of moderation, *The Friend* does not obviously espouse it; and though Coleridge's individualism seems to exempt him from the charge of fanaticism, he offers us no obvious ground for distinguishing his later philosophy from that 'positiveness' which is excited by the obscure.

4

Thought into Feeling

Coleridge's diverse misfortunes – emotional, physical, and economic – and their interaction with the often negative effects of narcotics have been explored by numerous critics and biographers.[1] That the experiences of elevation and tranquillity arising from his philosophical explorations were an increasingly vital source of solace from these evils is suggested not only by his descriptions of the liberating pleasures of thought, but also by the passionate enthusiasm with which he repeatedly seeks to evoke the transcendent origin of consciousness or the ascent of being towards union with the divine.[2] Merely to regard his philosophy as escapism, however, would be to adopt precisely the objectifying and deterministic view of the individual which Coleridge himself associated with the 'philosophy of death' propounded by empiricists, and which seems itself to have played a major role in producing his experiences of negation and near-despair.[3] Similarly, to relocate the meaning of his texts in the unconscious is to express a degree of satisfaction with the self as reified 'other' which – as Derrida, among others, has demonstrated – can only result from failing to consider the implications of that reduction for the interpretative process within which it occurs.[4] That Coleridge's criticism of such attempts to 'arrest' or stabilize being was associated with contrasting experiences of elevation or sublimity, moreover, indicates at least one respect in which he was not limited or defined by the mental pain which is repeatedly so prominent in his writing.[5] Similarly in Fichte's and Schelling's thought, the deliberate interpretation of the material world, and every objectification of the self, as issuing from a mind or process which necessarily transcends its products, illustrates the extent to which Romantic thought eludes and pre-empts the psychological reductionism which, in different forms, achieved such dominance in both the eighteenth and the twentieth century.[6]

That his thinking not only had a certain affective value for Coleridge, but was also shaped by a repeated quest for, and effort to express, the feelings it engendered, however, will be a central thesis of this chapter. By celebrating a continual process of self-criticism in which the highest truths are repeatedly found to be inconceivable or inexpressible, Coleridge valorizes an essentially open-ended form of discourse which provides extensive opportunities for pursuing the sublime. This quest for intellectual pleasure or emotional liberation, however, cannot be separated from his attempts to articulate fundamental truth. Without the search for understanding, that is, no gratifying sense of the incomprehensible grandeur of one's own ideas would (as Kant observes) be able to emerge.[7] Hence Coleridge's conception of the nature of ultimate truth seems to derive not only from the emotional necessity of transcending limitation, but also from a process of intellectual inquiry which continually seeks (and fails) to give logical form to that conviction. As I will show, Coleridge himself denies that the aim of philosophy is to produce pleasure, though admitting that pleasure may result from the effort to communicate truth. In contrasting the aims of philosophy with those of poetry, however, he tends to conceal the vital role which emotion and the pursuit of pleasure play in his own philosophizing; and his numerous attempts to distinguish the terms denoting any form of pleasure from those he uses to describe the feelings accompanying philosophical reflection highlight the considerable moral importance he attached to this distinction.

1. ESCAPISM OR TRANSCENDENCE?

Coleridge has often been accused of escapism in his philosophy, and encouraged this accusation in his autobiography, poems, and letters. In 'Dejection' and chapter 1 of *Biographia*, he described a pattern of experience in which feeling was suppressed or stifled by metaphysics. Not only his thwarted love for Sara Hutchinson, but also 'bodily pain', he suggested, could be escaped in 'abstruse researches, which exercised the strength and subtlety of the understanding without awakening the feelings of the heart' (*BL*, 1: 17).[8] His description of philosophy as a 'refuge' or 'asylum' from intolerable emotions has been repeated, largely unchanged, in the opinions of several critics.[9] Yet as we have seen, feeling was also described by Coleridge as an indispensable part of the reflective process, both animating or connecting our ideas, and enabling us to distinguish true from false philosophy. Feeling thus has two general roles in Coleridge's explanation of his thinking: firstly as the suffering which he flees, and secondly as the intuition which he rationalizes.[10] The relationship between the two has been explored both from psychoanalytic and from existentialist viewpoints. Fields's Freudian study is problematic (if characteristic of its genre) in the extent of its failure to engage with Coleridge's own theories, or to grasp their relationships with conscious (rather than merely unconscious) feeling, as well as with the intellectual milieu which he inhabited.[11] Lockridge and Mileur, however, find little reason to resort to abnormal psychology in order to explain the causes and effects of Coleridge's dejection. Both argue that a widely-shared experience of 'alienation' was the dominant cause of his suffering, and an important influence on his theories. Lockridge, indeed, even claims that Coleridge 'is the first thinker in England to formulate what could loosely be called an existential viewpoint: one must act beyond one's essence, become more than what one is'.[12] Though indicating a central impulse in Coleridge's thought, this statement conceals an important difference between Coleridge's theory of the self and the Sartrian principle with which Lockridge implicitly compares it. Whereas Sartre locates transcendence solely in the conscious negation of externally-defined identity or 'facticity', that is, Coleridge argues that our transcendence of phenomenal being is permanent and absolute, albeit only recognized through a liberating process of reflection analogous to that described by Sartre.[13] 'Considered merely intellectually', he wrote in *The Friend*,

> ... individuality ... is only conceivable as with and in the Universal and Infinite ... The finite form can neither be laid hold of, nor is it any thing of itself real, but merely an apprehension, a frame-work which the human imagination forms by its own limits ... and the sole truth of which we must again refer to the divine imagination, in virtue of its omniformity.
>
> (*Friend*, 1: 520)

Knowledge and reasoning are thus contrasted by Coleridge with the condition in which 'we think of ourselves as separated beings, and place nature in antithesis to the mind, as object to subject, thing to thought, death to life' (ibid.). The central paradox of individuality is that our idea of it only arises as one form of the divine imagination. Hence, in the light of reason, individuality is not individuality, but only one more manifestation of a unity which goes beyond selfhood, and beyond the distinction of subject and object.

The value which this theory held for Coleridge, however, seems to have resembled that which Sartre attaches to the act of transcending or 'negating' one's phenomenal self. As Lockridge suggests, it is hard to avoid concluding that Coleridge's interpretation of individual identity as just one aspect of the deceptive world of understanding arose from his need to escape from the negative judgements of others and to transcend the often miserable self-consciousness revealed in his notebooks and letters. 'The society of loveless observers sits in judgment on each of us', Lockridge writes, 'but ironically it is made up of all of us: we cooperate in framing the cruel arena in which human action is to be played out and judged.'[14] As Mileur suggests, however, any interpreter of Coleridge's theory is faced with a choice between accepting that the phenomenal self is merely a product of the mechanical understanding, and explaining this theory as an attempt to escape from the more absolute realities of his own psyche.[15] Certain of Coleridge's insights seem undeniable: the phenomenal self is always something distinct from the mind which thinks that self, or which conceives the individual as an object. Moreover, when we distinguish ourselves from our phenomenal existences there are clearly no qualities left to distinguish one 'self' from another: insofar as we conceived such qualities, we would be thinking of an object which could never be identified with our immediate thought-processes.[16] In addition, however, Coleridge often claims that the indistinguishableness of selves beyond the phenomenal realm implies their identity as parts of an infinite unity originating in God. Our '*true* Self', he writes, is to be found 'in theat *distinctness*, where no division can be—in the eternal I AM, the <ever-living WORD>' (*SWF*, 2: 1155).[17] In one sense, this merely extends the principle that what is active or creative in nature is ultimately one with the deity: the mind which conceives, he suggests, is part of the *natura naturans* or *forma formans*, and characterized by an inexplicable priority to phenomena.[18] At the same time, however, this theory cannot be separated from the bodily and emotional vulnerability which many critics have regarded as the most important influences on his philosophy. As Mileur shows, his act of faith was itself an act of freedom or transcendence: rather than accept his helplessness, he interpreted it as delusion.[19]

This very delusion, however, was seen by Coleridge to be a potential tool in the recommendation of his thesis. As if describing his own reaction to fear and bereavement, he thus consoled Thomas Poole on the death of his mother:

> As all things pass away, & those Habits are broken up which constituted our own & particular Self, our nature by a moral instinct cherishes the desire of an unchangeable Something, & thereby awakens or stirs up anew the passion to promote *permanent* Good, & facilitates that grand business of our Existence—still further, & further still, to generalize our affections, till *Existence* itself is swallowed up in *Being*, & we are in Christ even as he is in the Father.
>
> (*CL*, 2: 758)

The death of an individual – than which there could be no clearer mark of our weakness, separateness, and subjection to a material existence – is thus described as enabling us to recognize that selfhood is itself a delusion. Though it is in reaction to bereavement that we cherish the idea 'of an unchangeable Something', this idea – Coleridge suggests – is itself a revelation of our destiny. Being weak and helpless, destined to extinction in the world of the senses, we discover that this world is 'but a Shadow', and seek to intensify the consciousness of our permanent and undifferentiated being, thus moving closer to our final union with God.[20] This richly ambiguous conception is one which only the role of spiritual adviser enabled Coleridge to elaborate. His own reaction to bereavement is too personal and immediate to be simultaneously compensation and revelation. In his letters to Poole and to his wife on the death of their infant son Berkeley, Coleridge does not stand back from his sorrow and his philosophical compensation for it – does not pontificate on the 'advantages' of bereavement for our personal growth and the good of mankind in general – but rather enacts the response which is theorized in terms of these advantages.[21] In the letter to Poole, indeed, he does not deny that he is compensating: the 'advantage' is wholly temporal; yet he is nevertheless passionate in his conviction.

> I find it wise and human to believe, even on slight evidence, opinions, the contrary of which cannot be proved, & which promote our happiness without hampering our Intellect. —My Baby has not lived in vain—this life has been to him what it is to all of us, education & developement! Fling yourself forward into your

immortality only a few thousand years, & how small will not the difference between one year old & sixty years appear!

(*CL*, 1: 479)

In similar vein he wrote to his wife, asserting not only the value of his son's short life but also the necessity of its continuance beyond the grave:

Can cold and darkness come from the Sun? where the Sun is not—there is cold and darkness!—But the living God is every where, & works every where—and where is there room for Death?—To look back on the life of my Baby, how short it seems!—but consider it referently to non-existence, and what a manifold and majestic Thing does it not become?

(*CL*, 1: 481–2)[22]

Despite revealing the importance of Coleridge's faith as a compensation for bereavement and a liberation from the fear of futility, such declarations cannot be reduced to any simple model of the relation between feeling and intellection. We cannot say what feeling they are informed by, unless it is a desire for the feeling they engender. Or rather, *hope* is at once the cause and the effect of Coleridge's statements here: it is what they express, and it is the nature of the 'happiness' which can be derived from believing them.

Coleridge himself described this dual role of hope in an essay on the war with France. 'In order to brave thoughts', he wrote,

…we must have pleasurable feelings, that is, hopes: for what is hope but a pleasurable feeling, which, connecting itself with definite images of future things, becomes at once both impulse and motive?

(*EOT*, 1: 424)

Hope, in other words, is both what we seek from our contemplation of an excellent future, and the only possible source of that contemplation.[23] Moreover, hope is also one of the words which Coleridge uses to describe the feeling of the sublime. Just as mountainous landscapes give us 'a continual Inducement to look forward to the distance', he wrote in 1803, so the 'intellectual movement connected with looking forward' involves 'a feeling of Hope, a stirring

& inquietude of Fancy' (*CN*, 1: 1675). Though (as Modiano points out) this passage is largely translated from Christian Garve's essay 'Über einige Schönheiten der Gebirgsgegenden' ('On Some Beauties of Mountainous Regions'),[24] it reveals the importance of hope not only to Coleridge's faith but also to the nature of his faith. It is his ability thus to 'look forward' which enables him to will his own sublimity, and to contrast the eternal power and purpose of God with the 'shadows' of 'necessity and general law'.[25] What he values is *out* of this world, beyond the husks of perception and disappointment. It is not merely gratifying, but also depends for its conceivableness on his ability to will such a sublime unity. It is as if Coleridge's philosophy were pre-formed in the feeling of his reaction against sorrow. Hence, in stating this philosophy, he simultaneously valorizes the feeling which produces it, which it is designed to produce, and which largely determines its form:

> Hope [is] the Master Element of a Commanding Genius, meeting with an active & combining Intellect, and an Imagination of just that degree of vividness which disquiets & impels the Soul to try to realize its Images—greatly increase this creative Power, & the Images become a satisfying world of themselves—i.e. we have the Poet, or original Philosopher.
>
> (*Lects 1808–19*, 1: 137)

Coleridge's discussions of hope thus not only reveal the dependence of his philosophy on an optimism which reproduces and intensifies itself in the act of thinking, but also celebrate that philosophy as a liberation from the tawdry and disappointing world of sense.[26] His famous descriptions of philosophy as suppressing emotions too painful to express in verse, indeed, seem inadequate to account for the great optimism and vivacity of much of his theoretical writing.[27] Even if, as Emmet claims, 'the creative power of the mind depends…on a deep underlying state which Coleridge calls Joy', this 'Joy' seems often to have been generated by the process of philosophizing, rather than being the spontaneous, prereflective phenomenon described in 'Dejection'.[28] That he did not in fact 'abandon' poetry in 1802 (as claimed in a letter of that year),[29] but rather continued to produce significant quantities of verse until 1833, moreover, suggests that poetic composition also retained considerable importance for Coleridge, even if the spontaneous optimism of the Conversation Poems is largely replaced in his later verse by attempts to alleviate suffering through the imaginative evocation of it. Perhaps the most important difference between his early and later work, indeed, is that the philosophical optimism of his early poetry has its closest parallel in his later theoretical writings, while his later poems (as well as 'Dejection' itself) focus more directly on the emotional context of his thought, and especially on the relationship between despair and hope.[30] Not only 'Dejection', but also 'Work Without Hope' suggests that any productive effort was threatened by the extremes of negative emotion also evoked in poems such as 'Limbo' and 'Ne Plus Ultra'.[31] Yet their repeated evocations of negation and the inadequacy of imagination in language of great musical and imaginative power suggests that such poems also serve a consolatory function, paradoxically liberating their author by giving external form to his profoundest experiences of loss and despair.[32]

A possible explanation of this transition, in Coleridge's poetry, from speculative philosophical optimism to often pessimistic explorations of personal emotion emerges from a passage in his marginalia on Swedenborg's *De Coelo et Inferno* which also highlights the importance, in Coleridge's later religious thought, of a search for both immediate and lasting relief from the guilt and suffering associated with his addiction to opium.[33] 'For a man enthralled in any *habit* condemned by himself, and bitterly bitterly [*sic*] incessantly groaned over—exempli gratia, the ruinous use of anadynes [*sic*] and opiates', he writes, Swedenborg's assertion 'that no one can be received into heaven by an act of immediate mercy', and that recalcitrant sinners must therefore become inhabitants of hell, 'is of unspeakable Horror'. Yet, he adds, 'There are ... other Passages in Sw[edenborg]'s works, thro' which a Ray of Promise breaks'—namely that if he is diseased only in his 'organs' rather than their 'vital principle', a sufficient degree of penitence and 'earnest unselfish Love & Thankfulness toward the believed Redeemer, the Lord God of Forgiveness' will facilitate the redemption of the suffering individual.[34] Only this need to believe in the possibility of a final liberation from suffering and redemption from his perceived guilt – a need growing with his advancing years – I would argue, enables us to understand the increasing extent to which Coleridge's later prose writings replace the metaphysical speculations of his earlier poetry with a devotional repetition of symbols for the inexpressible truths of religion, and above all those of the *logos* and the Trinity.[35] His fear of a hell more permanent than that of his opium-dreams, that is, seems to have played a central part in determining the course of his later thinking, and especially his increasing desire to separate all references to the divine from the vivid evocations of natural and human creativity which make the metaphysical speculations of his early poems so vivid and memorable.[36]

Without compromising Coleridge's own statements on this matter, therefore, we can discover consistent patterns in his thinking which explain the liberating effect that he ascribes to it. His widespread plagiarism might lead us to question the intuitive origin of many of his ideas; yet both his descriptions of the experience of thinking, and the quest for religious consolation underlying much of his thought, suggest that its value was closely linked to the nature of his concepts, and specifically that it was in search of hope, and liberation from the negations of experience, that he reflected so consistently on humankind's progress towards unity with the divine.[37] Though debates as to the causes of his 'dejection' must remain at least partly speculative, therefore, Coleridge's transcendence is so transparently linked to the nature of his ideas and to the process of constructing his texts that we can discover a set of motivations for his work which was both immediate and enduring – a network of affective consequences which also determined both its contents and its form.

2. WARMTH AND CALMNESS: THE CONSEQUENCES OF PHILOSOPHY

In a *Courier* article of 1809, Coleridge criticized those 'who make a point of rejecting or disregarding all arguments that are enforced with warmth of feeling and illustrated by the lights of imagination'. 'Woe to that man', he wrote,

> ... who on circumstances which vitally affect the weal and woe of the whole human race in time and for eternity, can reason in as cold-blooded a tone, as if he were demonstrating a problem in geometry. The warmth, which the development and disclosure of such truths occasions, is altogether different from the heat of passion; and by the frivolous and unfeeling alone will the earnestness of a deep conviction be confounded with the irritability of self-mistrusting positiveness.
>
> (*EOT*, 2: 77–8)

This passage highlights a major ambiguity in Coleridge's view of the relationship between thought and emotion. Enthusiasm, he suggests, is only of value insofar as it informs our reflection on the most important issues. To say that we should feel strongly on such matters, however, is to assume that their importance is self-evident, and requires no cooler reasoning in order to be established. Hence our knowledge about which issues should affect us strongly is itself implied to depend on a conviction with no rational basis. This is not the only role which this passage attributes to feeling, however, for warmth is also 'occasioned' by the disclosure of central truths. There is a peculiar slippage in Coleridge's argument, whereby the 'circumstances' on which one reasons suddenly become the 'truths' one has discovered, and feeling is transformed from what enables us to discover the fundamental questions into what results from their solution. Warmth, it seems, gives rise to warmth; and only when it is present *a priori* will we experience the insight which leads to its reduplication.

Coleridge consistently maintained the necessity of warm feelings to philosophic insight.[38] This theory was useful to him in two respects: firstly because, if true, it would justify his own enjoyment of such feelings, and secondly because it implied that the enthusiastic tenor of his writings was at least in favour of their truthfulness, albeit providing no conclusive evidence. The ambiguity as to whether warm feelings are the causes or the effects of his insight provides a further weapon with which to challenge accusations of hedonism. These feelings, he suggests, spontaneously surge up and require him to affirm a transcendent reality. Yet they must also arise necessarily from his contemplation of that reality: otherwise his conviction would be merely a creature of emotion.

This complex and paradoxical pattern of ideas is expressed most clearly in a passage of *The Friend* where Coleridge defends himself against the accusation of 'bewildering' himself and others with metaphysics. 'What are my metaphysics?' he asks:

> ... To what purposes do I, or am I about to employ them? To perplex our clearest notions and living moral instincts? To deaden the feelings of will and free power, to extinguish the light of love and of conscience, to make myself and others worthless, soulless, God-less? No! to expose the folly and the legerdemain of those who have thus abused the blessed machine of language; to support all old and venerable truths; and by them to support, to

> kindle, to project the spirit; to make the reason spread light over our feelings, to make our feelings, with their vital warmth, actualize our reason:—these are my objects, these are my subjects, and are these the metaphysics which the bad spirits in hell delight in?
>
> (*Friend*, 1: 108)[39]

The circular and mutual influence of feeling and intellection is rarely so explicit as in this passage. By supporting 'old and venerable truths', Coleridge suggests, he will 'kindle' the spirit – not only his reader's, but also his own – and in so doing produce a warmth of feeling which will itself enliven their reflection. 'Spirit', however, is obviously an ambiguous term – on the one hand suggesting emotion, or the direction in which his emotions persuade him to argue, and on the other hand referring to the soul, or that element of each individual which is destined to eternal life, and (in Coleridge's theory) to a continuous upward progression towards the divinity. His use of the term here combines its two senses: through being 'kindled', each individual achieves that knowledge which is the means of our advance; the soul is literally projected forwards by the proselytism which moves its conviction. His use of the word 'spirit' in the singular, moreover, accentuates its dual significance; for insofar as they subscribe to one philosophy, Coleridge and his readers will be 'one spirit', the transcendent element of humanity in which all individuality is lost.

In different circumstances, however, Coleridge was more explicit in describing the dominant purpose of his philosophy as consisting in its emotional effects. 'All is vanity', he wrote of his studies,

> ... that does not lead to Quietness & Unity of Heart, and to the silent aweful idealess Watching of that living Spirit, & of that Life within us, which is the motion of that Spirit—that Life, which passeth all understanding.
>
> (*CL*, 2: 1008)

Thus Coleridge first acknowledges that what he seeks from philosophy is some relief or abatement of internal conflict, and then seeks to justify this personal aim with the concepts of self-intuition and spiritual enlightenment. The situation is interestingly reversed in a notebook entry of 1801, where he first describes this perfect 'idealess Watching' of the spirit, and then the feeling which it produces:

> I think of the Wall—it is before me, a distinct Image—here. I necessarily think of the *Idea* & the Thinking I as two distinct & opposite Things. Now <let me> think of *myself*—of the thinking Being—the Idea becomes dim whatever it be—so dim that I know not what it is—but the Feeling is deep & steady—and this I call *I*...identifying the Percipient & the Perceived—.
>
> (*CN*, 1: 921)[40]

The 'silent ... idealess Watching', then, is in fact nothing but the absence of any idea, accompanied by a certain 'deep and steady' feeling. This experience, or at least the 'Quietness & Unity of Heart' which it involves, seems to be what Coleridge seeks from his philosophy: a certain retreat from thwarted love and a diversity of guilts, conceptualized in a purity of intuition which is beyond psychology and the variety of individual experience.

This ideal of intellectual tranquillity – of a meditation in which the mind empties itself of phenomena and becomes 'a naked Spirit', perceiving nothing but itself – appears to conflict with Coleridge's valorization of warmth and excitement in philosophy.[41] When he writes of 'the honest warmth, which results from the strength of the particular conviction' and 'the emotions, which accompany all vivid perceptions' (*Friend*, 1: 278), he is clearly not celebrating the evacuation of mind to its primary and minimal essence, but rather the multiplication of feelings by ideas and vice versa. As we shall see, both of these conditions can be classified as forms of pleasure, or at least of a certain 'intellectual happiness'; yet it is hard to see how they can be connected. Coleridge gives a clue to their relationship in a notebook entry of 1809, where he asks

> ... whether the ~~pleasures~~ Gladness of intellectual Activity, of Tranquillity from intellectual Certainty, &c are really 'PLEASURE', i.e. likewise *modes* of the same Substance as the sensations of the Palate &c—
>
> (*CN*, 3: 3558)[42]

The purpose of Coleridge's distinction between happiness and pleasure will be discussed later in this chapter. What I wish to emphasize here is his distinction between 'Activity' and 'Certainty', and his connection of the former with 'Gladness' and the latter with 'Tranquillity'. Certainty would thus seem to involve a 'spiritual complacency' resembling that which, in *Aids to Reflection*, he describes as resulting from a sense of one's own virtue.[43] The creative activity of the mind, on the other hand, would involve a feeling of elevation such as he evoked in a letter to Thomas Wedgwood describing the effect of mountain-climbing on his spiritual condition.[44] This 'wild activity, of thoughts, imaginations, feelings, and impulses of motion' is clearly something very different from 'the silent...idealess Watching of [the] living Spirit'. The latter, I would argue, is rather the consequence or after-effect of elevated thinking than its accompaniment or immediate result. In two successive notebook entries of 1803, Coleridge proposes to distinguish 'The feeling of positiveness from the sense of Certainty' and 'The heat of fermentation from the warmth of Life/ the bustling Dotage of Composition & the calm long-subsequent admiration' (*CN*, 1: 1409–10). 'Positiveness', then – though he often sought to distance it from his thinking, and to stigmatize it by contrast with certainty – would seem to denote the wilful affirmation of what one's feeling demands or implies, the spontaneous conversion of emotion into a somewhat dubious 'knowledge'. Coleridge contrasts this 'fermentation' on the one hand with 'the warmth of Life', and on the other with 'the calm long-subsequent admiration' of his achievements during the period of energetic creativity. This clearly suggests that his 'silent ... idealess Watching' or 'Quietness & Unity of Heart' was the result or end-product of energetic thinking. A certain exhaustion and self-satisfaction, he implies, generally follows the activity of giving way to the whims of sensation, and letting one's words be determined by the search for ever greater excitement.[45]

This rest from intellectual labour seems to correspond to the condition which, in *Aids to Reflection*, he describes as resulting from the possession of a good conscience. Virtue, he says, may add to the pleasures of bodily health and vigour

> ... a good of another kind, a higher good, perhaps, than the worldly mind is capable of understanding, a spiritual complacency, of which in your present sensualized state you can form no idea. It may add, I say, but it cannot detract from it. Thus the reflected rays of the sun that give light, distinction, and endless multiformity to the mind, give at the same time the pleasurable sensation of warmth to the body.
>
> (*AR*, 49)

The word 'complacency' did not always have its present pejorative meaning, and in this case is clearly used in its earlier sense of 'The fact or state of being pleased with a thing or person', or in other words 'tranquil satisfaction'.[46] Paradoxically, however, Coleridge's use of the term here expresses precisely the self-satisfaction which it has since come to denote: by contrasting the feelings of the virtuous individual with those of his readers, who from their 'present sensualized state' cannot even form any idea of his complacency, that is, he implicitly identifies himself with the former. Yet while the complacency of which he writes is a 'good' beyond the understanding of ordinary mortals, it is also a form of pleasure which, though not purely physical, cannot be unambiguously separated from physical sensation. In the final sentence of my quotation, indeed, even the distinction between physical pleasure and 'complacency' is confused by his invocation of the Platonic analogy between virtue and the sun.[47] That good which is beyond the understandings of the sensual, it seems, is at least partly a physical sensation indistinguishable from pleasure.

3. THE END AND THE MEANS: COLERIDGE AND THE VALUE OF PHILOSOPHY

It is an explicit conclusion of *The Friend* that the highest ideas – those about which we should feel most strongly – are necessarily obscure. Though we should reason clearly concerning all things 'that are the possible objects of clear conception', Coleridge writes, we should reserve our deep feelings

> ... for objects, which their very sublimity renders indefinite, no less than their indefiniteness renders them sublime: namely, to the Ideas of Being, Form, Life, the Reason, the Law of Conscience, Freedom, Immortality, God! To connect with the objects of our senses the obscure notions and consequent vivid feelings, which are due only to immaterial and permanent things, is profanation relatively to the heart, and superstition in the understanding.
>
> (*Friend*, 1: 106)

Rather than describing his philosophy as merely a pursuit of pleasure, therefore, Coleridge suggests that the pursuit of truth, though ultimately unproductive, may have a high moral value insofar as it leads us to revere the deity and our own infinite potential. Yet a philosopher who neither pursues, nor believes he can achieve, any discovery is a highly paradoxical one, and in fact incompatible with Coleridge's aesthetic of sublimity. 'There is no way of arriving at any sciential End', he wrote to his son Hartley,

> ... but by finding it at every step. The End is in the Means: or the adequacy of each Mean is already it's end. Southey once said to me: You are nosing every nettle along the Hedge, while the Greyhound (meaning himself, I presume) wants only to get sight of the Hare, & FLASH!—strait as a line!—he has it in his mouth!—Even so, I replied, might a Cannibal say to an Anatomist, whom he had watched dissecting a body. But the fact is—I do not care twopence for the *Hare*; but I value most highly the excellencies of scent, patience, discrimination, free Activity; and find a Hare in every Nettle, I make myself acquainted with. (*CL*, 5: 98)[48]

The paradox is inescapable: without an object, without an end in view, Coleridge cannot have any 'scent' to follow; yet – he says – he 'does not care twopence' for the result of his philosophy, and is only interested in the pleasure which this prospect produces. Intellectual inquiry gives him an opportunity to exercise his talents, and were it not that this exercise depends on an idea or feeling of purpose, he would gladly dispense with the objective of knowledge. It is this preference for intellectual activity that expresses itself in Coleridge's persistent valorization of thinking over thoughts, and power over its products:[49] by comparing this activity to the divine creative energy, he attributes to it a mysteriousness and sublimity which would render the question of its pleasurableness all but irrelevant.

It is not just any form of inquiry, however, that can provide the fulfilling experiences of 'scent, patience, discrimination, [and] free Activity'. Rather, what gives Coleridge these experiences, I will suggest, is chiefly the attempt to justify their value philosophically. Much of his writing, that is, argues that by meditating on the unknowable we both imitate and move closer to God, who has ordained this project for mankind. In constructing such arguments, however, Coleridge is at once seeking to justify the intellectual pleasures which – in a less formal context – he described as his principal objectives, and pursuing precisely these experiences of sublime elevation.

These very activities, however, are also described by Coleridge as involving a disinterested virtue resembling that which Kant described in the *Groundwork of the Metaphysic of Morals*:

> To possess the end in the means, as it is essential to morality in the moral world, and the contradistinction of goodness from mere prudence, so is it, in the intellectual world, the *moral* constituent of genius, and that by which true genius is contradistinguished from mere *talent*. (*Friend*, 1: 415)[50]

Thus, just as 'goodness' consists in obeying a moral law rather than calculating the consequences of one's actions, so – according to Coleridge – the moral value of genius depends on finding one's fulfilment in the activity of thinking rather than in any truth one might discover. This analogy can only make sense, however, insofar as we artificially separate philosophy from the sphere of choices which Coleridge designates as 'the moral world'. As we have seen, the 'end' which he possesses in the means to its attainment is not the fulfilment of a moral law, but solely concerns his personal satisfaction. Though the law which he obeys in his philosophizing may resemble the categorical imperative in prohibiting the calculations of prudence, therefore, it differs from the categorical imperative in recommending the pursuit of pleasure – an aim which, paradoxically, resembles the merely selfish and prudential considerations which Kant rejected.[51] As the above passage shows, moreover, it is not an end which Coleridge can recommend everyone to pursue; rather, it is only appropriate to those, such as himself, whom he admits to the title of 'genius', and his argument therefore seeks to justify his obvious failure to obey the categorical imperative.

Yet although Coleridge could not, on this evidence, truly have believed that his philosophy was an example of virtue on the Kantian model, we must allow the possibility that it resulted in a sense of virtue which he was unable to explain philosophically. As we have seen, the moral law which Coleridge obeys in his thinking recommends the pursuit of pleasure rather than of truth. Insofar as this pleasure itself depends on a conviction of virtue (and this was his theory in a passage from *Aids to Reflection* discussed earlier), however, we will have to admit that something more than mere hedonism was at the basis of his philosophy. This question is addressed indirectly by a passage in the *TableTalk* where he considers in general terms the 'pleasure' produced by a sense of virtue:

> So you object, with old Hobbes, that I do good actions *for* the pleasure of a good conscience; and so, after all, I am only a refined sensualist! ... Don't you see that if conscience, which is in its nature a consequence, were thus anticipated and made an antecedent—a party instead of a judge—it would dishonour your draft upon it—it would not pay on demand?
>
> (*TT*, 2: 144)

Whether or not we accept its validity, this theory draws attention to a possibility which can easily be submerged by Coleridge's pretentious claims to disinterested virtue: namely that in addition to justifying his work to others, these arguments were central to Coleridge's own conception of its value. Moreover, *The Statesman's Manual* suggests a means by which an activity which was an end in itself might also be designed for the improvement of humankind more generally. Insofar as this improvement involves encouraging a popular pursuit of the same pleasures and convictions as Coleridge found in thinking, that is, and insofar as his own quest for these feelings was the best means of persuading others to pursue them, an end external to his own philosophizing might be achieved by suspending his intention to achieve it.[52]

Such complexities, however, belie the fact that Coleridge's communicative intention was as much a quest for persuasive power over his readers – hence also, for the pleasures associated with such power – as for the encouragement of virtue. The subjective value of such power is considered in a marginal note on Fichte's *System der Sittenlehre*. To Fichte's argument that human beings cannot be driven only by selfishness, since if this were the case they would have no reason to communicate the fact, Coleridge answers:

> ... I fear that these arguments would have little weight with the Hobbists & Mandevillians. They would answer, there is a pleasure attached by Nature to the Communication of such Ideas, & to the knowledge ... or belief that our Ideas influence those of others. It is *power*—and with all acts of Power we associate pleasure, because the greater number of our keenest pleasures are procure[d] & retained by acts of power—
>
> (*CM*, 2: 636)

The fact that this response would be that of 'Hobbists & Mandevillians' does not seem to diminish Coleridge's subscription to it.[53] The pleasure of power is inseparable from his own communicative effort, as also is the decidedly 'external' objective of persuasion. It may be that, as he says of *The Friend*, he is 'making an experiment whether throughout the Kingdom a sufficient number of readers can be found for a periodical Work, which does not appeal to Curiosity, or Personality' (*CL*, 3: 237) – that, in other words, he wishes to involve his readers in the same 'pure' or altruistic thinking as his own. Yet this cannot alter the desire for power and persuasion involved in this very experiment.

His reflections on the nature of the insight – or other virtuous activity – which might be communicated by his efforts are no less ambiguous. According to the letter to his son Hartley discussed above, Coleridge did 'not care twopence for the Hare', but valued 'most highly the excellencies of scent, patience, discrimination, [and] free Activity'. He is not alone in this attitude. Locke, for example, is almost as emphatic as Coleridge in preferring the 'chase' to the 'quarry'. Of the 'understanding' he writes that

> *... as it is the most elevated Faculty of the Soul, so it is employed with a greater, and more constant Delight than any of the other. Its searches after Truth, are a sort of Hawking and Hunting, wherein the very pursuit makes a great part of the Pleasure ...*
>
> *... Thus he who ... sets his own Thought on work, to find and follow Truth, will (whatever he lights on) not miss the Hunter's Satisfaction; every moment of his Pursuit, will reward his Pains with some Delight; and he will have Reason to think his time not ill spent, even when he cannot much boast of any great Acquisition.*[54]

But though in 1820 Coleridge went even further than Locke, claiming such an indifference to intellectual 'acquisitions' as would appear to make his philosophy futile and unworthy of the name, only four years earlier he observed that in the 'inspired Writings' of Christianity, knowledge

> ... is not only extolled as the Crown and Honor of a Man, but to seek after it is again and again commanded us as one of our most sacred duties. Yea, the very perfection and final bliss of the glorified spirit is represented by the Apostle as a plain aspect,

> or intuitive beholding of truth in its eternal and immutable source.
>
> (*LS*, 48)[55]

Coleridge, in other words, has two ways of looking at knowledge. On the one hand it is an objective unworthy of genius, and to seek it is the very opposite of finding 'the end in the means'. 'The adequacy of each Mean is already its end', he wrote to his son Hartley; and the pleasure of thinking is his only explanation of this adequacy. On the other hand, knowledge is truth, or the sublime conviction of God's infinite power and our own participation in his productive energy. In this sense, to contemplate truths 'for their TRUTH'S SAKE' is not to seek pleasure, but rather to approach as close as we can in this life to our ultimate union with God. In the above passage from *The Statesman's Manual*, Coleridge compares knowledge with the 'perfection and final bliss of the glorified spirit' described by St Paul. As Suther observes, it is often unclear whether he expects such bliss in this life or the next. Even in his attitude to Sara Hutchinson, he 'is longing ... for something like the beatific vision, a complete presence and union in full knowledge, which according to mystical theology takes place only in the afterlife'.[56]

Knowledge itself, however, was often contrasted by Coleridge with the activity of thinking. It was not just a matter of distinguishing between different kinds of knowledge – the religious and the phenomenal, or that which the individual mind produces as against that with which it is filled from external sources. Rather, it is knowledge as such, or the objective products of thinking, that Coleridge habitually contrasts with creative activity, and devalues in the comparison. A notebook entry of 1805 suggests that the Platonic 'saws against Book-knowledge' derive

> ... from Times when Books conveyed only abstract Science or abstract Morality & Religion/whereas in the present day what is there of real Life, in all its goings on...that is not *in books*.
>
> (*CN*, 2: 2526)[57]

Expressions of this sentiment, however, are greatly outnumbered in Coleridge's work by rejections of whatever can be written down or encapsulated in formulae.[58] These statements often suggest an equation of truth with the process of thinking, and of particular truths or propositions with fragments siphoned-off from their appropriate contexts, as a consequence of which they have become intellectual 'idols' of the kind described by Bacon.[59] Truth, Coleridge noted (quoting Milton's *Areopagitica*),

> ... is compared in scripture to a streaming fountain; if her waters flow not in perpetual progression, they stagnate into a muddy pool of conformity & tradition.
>
> (*CN*, 1: 119)[60]

Truth, then, is the process of thinking – not what has been thought, nor any imaginable discovery, but rather the development from one belief or interpretation to another. The view expressed in Milton's statement, indeed, is immediately recognizable as that which Hegel, above all others of Coleridge's period, made the foundation and central topic of his philosophy. Philosophy, Hegel writes in the preface to his *Phenomenology*,

> ... is the process which begets and traverses its own moments, and this whole movement constitutes what is positive [in it] and its truth. This truth therefore includes the negative also, what would be called the false, if it could be regarded as something from which one might abstract. The evanescent itself must, on the contrary, be regarded as essential, not as something fixed, cut off from the True, and left lying who knows where outside it, any more than the True is to be regarded as something on the other side, positive and dead. Appearance is the arising and passing away that does not itself arise and pass away, but is 'in itself' [i.e. subsists intrinsically], and constitutes the actuality and the movement of the life of truth.[61]

Coleridge is rarely so explicit as Hegel in defining truth as the process of philosophy, or the whole succession of contradictory insights by means of which we progress; as we have seen, his religious convictions also held out the possibility of a knowledge that was intuitive and non-verbal, a direct communion with the deity. Celebration of intellectual movement, however, is central to Coleridge's aesthetic, especially in the early and middle periods of his writing; and his valorization of this movement involves the double conception of the significance of individual propositions which Hegel also expresses. 'We imagine ourselves discoverers', he writes, '& that we have struck a Light, when in reality at most we have only snuffed a Candle' (*CN*, 1: 1315). Or in other words, we move in the direction of truth by realizing that each thing we say is false, but necessary to that progression. Truth as process is the totalizing concept implied in this paradox or double vision, though it is not objectified as in Hegel.

As Kessler points out, the metaphor of the 'forward-moving stream' is of particular importance in Coleridge's descriptions of what philosophy should involve.[62] The attractiveness of this image seems to have been due partly to its ability to represent thought not as something isolated and independent of the natural world, but as itself a part of the progressive and indomitable life of nature. Philosophical investigation, Coleridge implies in *The Friend*, is ultimately one with its object: in pursuing an explanation of phenomena, we are actually pursuing the ground of our own subjective consciousness – namely that 'life-ebullient stream which breaks through every momentary embankment, again, indeed, and evermore to embank itself, but within no banks to stagnate or be imprisoned' (*Friend*, 1: 519).

Like other instances of the 'stream' image in Coleridge, however, this passage involves the paradox that while thought is progressing it is also limited – that it is in a state of continuous tension with the fixed forms of knowledge. This paradox is of central importance to Coleridge's definition of scientific method, originally developed for the *Encyclopaedia Metropolitana*, but most fully expressed in the 1818 *Friend*, where it takes two distinct forms.[63] On the one hand, because it involves a challenge to the prejudices of understanding, an attempt to transcend received opinion and never to rest in one's own conclusions, method depends as much on our 'passive impressions' as on 'the mind's own re-action' to them.[64] On the other hand, however, methodical or progressive thought cannot occur without some intuition of its forthcoming trajectory. 'Method', Coleridge writes,

> ... implies a *progressive transition*, and it is the meaning of the word in the original language. The Greek Μεθοδος, is literally *a way*, or *path of transit* ... But as, without continuous transition, there can be no Method, so without a pre-conception there can be no transition with continuity.
>
> (*Friend*, 1: 457)[65]

Superficially, this contradicts Coleridge's vision of method as a transcendence of all information 'that can be *conveyed into* [the intellect] from without' (*Friend*, 1: 473). Genius, he writes earlier in *The Friend*, is 'the faculty which *adds* to the existing stock of power, and knowledge by new views, new combinations, &c.', and can therefore be defined 'as originality in intellectual construction' (*Friend*, 1: 419).[66] Yet as we have seen, he also envisaged an ultimate destination for his thinking, namely an 'intuitive beholding' of the infinite and divine. This objective, moreover, is not in conflict with the ideal of progress discussed above. For what Coleridge describes as 'the ground of all comprehension' is itself that ceaseless flow which he thought should be exemplified in philosophical thinking.[67] To transcend opinion and the forms of understanding, he argues, is also to contemplate the infinite. We must be looking *towards* God, in order that our thinking may imitate the illimitable freedom of his nature.[68]

Coleridge's attitude towards knowledge is thus highly complex. On the one hand he states that he is only interested in the activity of philosophizing: knowledge, he implies, is of value only as an objective, never as an achievement. His explanations of this attitude are on the one hand sensational, and on the other theoretical. According to the letter to his son Hartley, it is only the *pleasures* of philosophic activity that interest him, though as we have seen, he also implied that the ability to experience these pleasures involves a certain disinterested virtue; other passages, however, imply that his valorization of intellectual process was based partly on a Hegelian conception of truth as 'the whole' – as the entire history of philosophic exploration rather than any static or definable position. In still other contexts Coleridge describes a form of knowledge involving a 'direct beholding' of the divinity, and communicated to human beings by means of that 'reason' which is both human and divine.

Apart from the last, or Pauline, conception of knowledge, however, these theories all centre on the opposition between activity and stasis, thought and its products, and represent different ways of justifying a consistent valorization of the first term in each of these distinctions.[69] This system of values is also the basis of Coleridge's preoccupation with progress and with the importance of philosophy to the moral improvement of mankind. And it is in terms of these preoccupations that the value of intellectual movement can be reconciled with that of the religious intuition which he evokes in the words of St Paul. In this life, he argues, we cannot progress beyond a certain degree of knowledge and perfection; yet it is our duty to strive to do so, and both we and the universe take our appointed course through this effort. Since our pursuit of knowledge is central to this value-system, however, it is impossible for Coleridge to place a definite limit on what we can achieve as mortals. Hence he not only looks towards, but sometimes implies the earthly possibility of a knowledge quite different from any we can practically achieve. In terms of this theory, knowledge is not merely an objective for philosophy, not just the motive to an intellectual activity valued for its own sake; it is also the destination – the final union with the deity – to which our intellectual striving will ultimately lead us.

These two attitudes towards truth – on the one hand as destructive stasis, and on the other as the ultimate aim of intellectual effort – can clearly be correlated with the two kinds of feeling which Coleridge describes himself as deriving from philosophy, and which I discussed in section 2 of this chapter. On the one hand the pursuit of truth, which continually postpones the discovery of its object, involves warmth and excitement. These feelings, however, are not valued only for themselves, but also for the calmness and 'complacency' which follows the exercise of creative energy, and which can itself be correlated with the 'bliss' of truth or 'union in full knowledge'. This latter conception would be problematic were it not that Coleridge's pursuit of truth always promises more than it finds, and involves an expectation of knowledge which, for the sake of sublimity and excitement, can never be fulfilled. The bliss of truth is an ideal; the sublime *discovery* is impossible. Yet if we did not wish for such epiphanies we would be unable to enjoy the warmth of contemplation and the conviction of a transcendent reality.

4. POETRY VERSUS PHILOSOPHY

The two objectives which Coleridge associates with philosophy – on the one hand pleasure or satisfaction, and on the other the knowledge whose pursuit produces and justifies it – are interestingly paralleled by those he uses to distinguish between poetry and philosophy. Whereas the immediate purpose of poetry is to communicate pleasure, he writes – 'though truth, either moral or intellectual, ought to be the *ultimate* end' – the immediate purpose of works of philosophy or 'science' is to communicate truth – though 'Pleasure, and that of the highest and most permanent kind, may *result* from the *attainment* of the end' (*BL*, 2: 12).[70] In terms of the literal structure of these statements, Coleridge's emphasis on 'communication' in philosophy makes logical sense: his topic is 'philosophic disquisition' rather than the pursuit of truth. In thus designing his discussion of philosophy so as to make it comparable with poetry, however, Coleridge places so much emphasis on its textual or verbal aspect as apparently to alter the topic of his discussion. Unless communication were seen as an indispensable aspect of philosophy, indeed, Coleridge's comparison would be solely between varieties of texts, rather than of intellectual or creative processes, and the aims of philosophy itself might be quite different from those he attaches to 'philosophic disquisition'.[71]

The discussion of 'genius' quoted from *The Friend* in chapter four of *Biographia*, however, suggests that Coleridge's emphasis on the textual aspect of philosophy, and apparent omission of its intellectual aims or qualities, is not merely designed to facilitate an effective comparison between poetic and philosophical writing. The context of this passage is a discussion of the distinctive merits of Wordsworth's poetry, yet its significance is far broader. 'In poems, equally as in philosophic disquisitions', he writes, 'genius produces the strongest impressions of novelty, while it rescues the most admitted truths from the impotence caused by the very circumstance of their universal admission.' Coleridge's terminology is the same as in chapter 14: 'philosophic disquisition' is what he compares with poetry. Yet if rescuing or re-animating ancient knowledge is the principal function of genius in philosophic texts, it is hard to see how it could be differently manifested in the act of philosophizing itself. It might be argued that philosophy discovers those truths to which the philosophic text, like the poem, seeks to attach a feeling or appearance of novelty. This view, however, seems to be decisively countered by a slightly earlier passage of Coleridge's quotation:

> To find no contradiction in the union of old and new; to contemplate the ANCIENT of days and all his works with feelings as fresh, as if all had then sprang forth at the first creative fiat; characterizes the mind that feels the riddle of the world, and may help to unravel it.
>
> (*BL*, 1: 80)[72]

The act of unifying old and new, or combining – as chapter 14 puts it – 'the sense of novelty and freshness, with old and familiar objects', is thus described by Coleridge as characterizing not only philosophic texts, but also 'genius' itself. That act of communication which revives our knowledge of fundamental truths by revealing new instances of them is, he implies, characteristic not only of 'philosophic disquisition', but also of philosophy as such, and the pursuit of truth is ultimately inseparable from an effort to communicate it – that is, from the process of putting our intuitions into words and reflecting on their linguistic form.

Coleridge's definition of genius, however, in fact goes further than this obvious truth. Philosophy like poetry, he suggests, is primarily an attempt to find new terms for, and instances of, old and familiar truths. Such an interpretation of Coleridge's philosophy might seem to be justified by his repeated insistence on biblical truths, and pursuit of diverse analogies for them in both contemporary and ancient thought. Yet to admit that his philosophy was primarily a search for conceptual or verbal analogies to a single set of principles would clearly have weakened its claims to be primarily concerned with the pursuit of truth. His emphasis elsewhere on the pleasures of the 'chase' as the central motivation of his thought, indeed, suggests that even believing it was primarily an experiment with the effects of language would have undermined the project of discovery which underpinned his philosophical enjoyments. As far as philosophy was concerned, therefore, Coleridge was forced to attach only a secondary importance to the pleasures of novelty and analogy, maintaining in his analysis the rhetoric which his philosophy itself involved. In discussing poetry, on the other hand, he uses the conventions of poetic excellence to offset the traditional aims of philosophy. A poem, he writes,

> ... is that species of composition, which is opposed to works of science, by proposing for its *immediate* object pleasure, not truth; and from all other species (having *this* object in common with it) it is discriminated by proposing to itself such delight from the *whole*, as is compatible with a distinct gratification from each component *part*.
>
> (*BL*, 2: 13)[73]

The attribution of these objectives to poetry is not in itself controversial; its obvious validity, indeed, is used to conceal the tendentiousness of Coleridge's more important claim in this passage – namely that philosophy does not share these objectives. As his unveiling of the poetic power continues, however, it becomes increasingly clear that what he says about poetry could also be said about philosophy, and that the powers of the poet as Coleridge ideally describes them are very similar to those he elsewhere attributes to philosophic genius. The poet, he writes,

> ... diffuses a tone, and spirit of unity, that blends, and (as it were) *fuses*, each [faculty] into each, by that synthetic and magical power, to which we have exclusively appropriated the name of imagination. This power ... reveals itself in the balance or reconciliation of opposite or discordant qualities: of sameness, with difference; of the general, with the concrete; the idea, with the image; the individual, with the representative; the sense of novelty and freshness, with old and familiar objects; a more than usual state of emotion, with more than usual order; judgement ever awake and steady self-possession, with enthusiasm and feeling profound or vehement; and while it blends and harmonizes the natural and the artificial, still subordinates art to nature; the manner to the matter; and our admiration of the poet to our sympathy with the poetry.
>
> (*BL*, 2: 16–17)

As we have seen, Coleridge elsewhere describes the invention of analogies as the principal characteristic of his own genius; and it is all he is really describing here under the heading of poetic imagination.[74] Most of the 'opposite or discordant qualities' which, he claims, are reconciled by poetic imagination, are in fact nothing more than the qualities which objects acquire through the fact of being made analogous. 'Sameness' and 'difference' only pertain of those things which are compared: their simultaneity or 'reconciliation' is merely the fact of analogy, or identity discovered in diversity. Again, it is only through being used as part of an analogy that an object can become at once 'individual' and 'representative'. The same holds of reconciling 'the sense of novelty and freshness, with old and familiar objects'. Clearly, that 'sense of novelty' which is to be combined with familiar objects cannot pre-exist the novel comparison, analogy, or mode of expression which produces it. The general and the concrete, and the idea and the image, on the other hand, can in fact be compared or 'reconciled' in the way that

Coleridge suggests: it is precisely such opposites which, through being compared, acquire the qualities of 'sameness' and 'difference', and it is precisely their comparison that enables a single term to be both individual and representative.

The combination of 'a more than usual state of emotion' with 'more than usual order', however, raises questions in the context of philosophy which it does not raise in the context of poetry. For while poetry indubitably combines these two, and does so at least partly for the sake of pleasure, the pursuit of truth implies a detachment from emotion and a superiority to the pursuit of pleasure, both of which seem to be at issue in relation to Coleridge's philosophy. Similarly, the ideal of blending 'judgement ever awake and steady self-possession, with enthusiasm and feeling profound or vehement' is ostensibly confined to poetry; yet these elements are precisely those whose relationship is the focus of the most important questions about Coleridge's philosophy. This very ideal, however, obviously tends to suppress any questions about the motivation of Coleridge's writing and the dominant forces in its production. Rather than asking whether 'steady self-possession' is in fact compatible with profound or vehement enthusiasm, and whether logical structure is not sought for the sake of the pleasure it produces, Coleridge celebrates their 'balance or reconciliation' by means of the poetic power. Only because he is discussing poetry can he ignore these questions; yet the fact that his discussion treats precisely those 'opposite or discordant qualities' which are so problematically present in his philosophy, yet specifically suppresses the issues which they generate, must raise the suspicion that in this description of poetry he is also envisaging a philosophy in which, or in relation to which, no such conflict or ambiguity could arise. The idea of poetic imagination, that is, becomes for Coleridge a means of escaping from the moral and philosophical questions which his intellectual practice persistently raises.

When, on the other hand, he is comparing poetry and philosophy, he can no longer merely idealize the reconciliation of feeling and thought, but must rather discuss their different relationships in each genre. His model of the different primary and secondary objectives of poetry and philosophy is almost, but not entirely, symmetrical. Whereas, in philosophy, pleasure may result from 'the *attainment*' of its primary objective, which is the communication of truth, Coleridge cannot explain how 'truth' (or its expression) is to result from poetry's attainment of its primary objective, which is to produce pleasure. His attempt to distance philosophy from the pursuit of pleasure thus produces a definition of poetry which is literally contradictory. Truth, Coleridge says, 'ought to be the *ultimate* end' of poetry; but how can the pursuit of pleasure, or of 'the communication of pleasure', have truth as its ultimate objective? Interestingly, Coleridge does not say that the pursuit of truth and of pleasure (or of the communication of either) can be identical, since this would destroy his chief distinction between poetry and philosophy, as well as any claim for the greater intellectual or moral importance of the latter.

Yet it is not only in terms of their objectives that Coleridge distinguishes between poetry and philosophy: a further difference – at the level of form – is inescapable. Coleridge attempts to incorporate the opposition between prose and metre within his distinction of objectives, suggesting that metre results from that subjection of passion to voluntary control which takes place 'consciously and for the foreseen purpose of pleasure' (*BL*, 2: 64). In a further attempt to strengthen his distinction between poetry and philosophy, he emphasizes the importance of spontaneity in the former. That 'pleasurable emotion, that peculiar state or degree of Excitement, which arises in the Poet himself, in the act of composition', he says, depends upon

> ... the full play of those Powers of Mind, which are spontaneous rather than voluntary, in which the Effort required bears no proportion to the activity enjoyed—
>
> (*Lects 1808–19*, 1: 217)

If passion is to be combined with poetic form, in other words, that form cannot be arbitrary, but must rather be determined by the passion which it organizes.[75] Metrical composition is undertaken for the purpose of pleasure; but it can only achieve that purpose if it is a framework within which passion can act productively.

The opposition between 'a more than usual state of emotion' and 'more than usual order' is thus replaced by an opposition between the 'powers' responsible for these two conditions. In poetry the spontaneous must be the determinant. Yet clearly we cannot have poetry (at least according to Coleridge's definition) without the voluntary introduction of formal constraints; and in terms of its effect this voluntary element is identical with the effort to communicate truth in philosophy. On the one hand we impose poetic form, and the consequence is pleasure; on the other we attempt to communicate or to discover truth, and the consequence is pleasure. It cannot be true that 'the immediate object of poetry is the communication of pleasure' (*Lects 1808–19*, 1: 219), because its immediate object is the combination of passion with external form. And though 'The immediate object of science was the communication & acquirement of truth',

> ... Yet it would be acknowledged by all that when they read Newton's Principia or Locke's works the immediate object was ... to obtain truth which might hereafter enlighten and the pursuit of pleasure [*sic*], or of something nobler, for which we have not a name, but ... which was expressed in the sacred writings as a peace that passeth all understanding, the delight of which could never be known but by experience...
>
> (*Lects 1808–19*, 1: 219)

Once pleasure is admitted to be the object of philosophy – albeit not the 'immediate' object – Coleridge has no other course but to mysticize the pleasures of intellection, thus introducing a distinction on a different level. The pleasure of thinking, he implies, is not only a consequence of discovering or communicating truth, but in some way identical with it: it is a confrontation with the infinite, a religious experience.

This very experience, however, was not always a means of distinguishing philosophy, but was also used by Coleridge to describe the ultimate aim of poetry.[76] The notes taken by John Payne Collier at a lecture given by Coleridge in 1811 report him as saying that 'The grandest effects' of poetry were

> ... where the imagination was called forth, not to produce a distinct form, but a strong working of the mind still producing what it still repels & again calling forth what it again negatives and the result is what the Poet wishes to impress, to substitute a grand feeling of the unimaginable for a mere image—
>
> (*Lects 1808–19*, 1: 311)

If the aim of poetry is to produce pleasure, then the sublimity which is pursued in 'the grandest effects' of poetry must also be a form of pleasure. According to this passage, however, the formal element in poetry does not act so much to produce pleasure as to stimulate intellectual activity. Form is not combined with feeling, but is rather felt to be inadequate for its expression; the aim is not aesthetic pleasure, but the conviction of a noumenal reality.[77] This is the same as the function which Coleridge elsewhere attributed to mystical philosophy. His early reading of the mystics Fox, Boehme, and Law, he wrote in *Biographia*,

> ... contributed to keep alive the *heart* in the *head*; gave me an indistinct, yet stirring and working presentment, that all the products of the mere *reflective* faculty partook of DEATH, and were as the rattling twigs and sprays in winter, into which a sap was yet to be propelled, from some root to which I had not penetrated, if they were to afford my soul either food or shelter.
>
> (*BL*, 1: 152)

The same objectives of the communication of truth and the production of pleasure seem thus to be involved in Coleridge's conceptions of both poetry and philosophy.[78] To say that something is pleasing in its effects is not to say that its purpose is to produce pleasure; yet it is clearly impossible for Coleridge to prove that the object of his philosophy is not to produce pleasure, though we must also admit that the effort to communicate truth, and the discovery of the impossibility of stating the truth, is necessary to its enjoyment. His emphasis on the spontaneous in poetry does not stand up under analysis, since the 'strong working of the mind' which the reading of poetry produces, and which its composition involves, is not spontaneous passion but the very intellectual effort which, in philosophy as in poetry, gives rise to a feeling of the sublime. In his analyses of poetry, Coleridge alternately strives to explain in what respects it differs from philosophy, and describes his own objectives and the value he discovers in poetry. In so doing, he puts in question every distinction between poetry and philosophy except that of their different forms, and at the same time reveals an effort to suppress, through his comparisons of poetry and philosophy, not only the elements they have in common, but also the perilousness of his philosophy's claim to an overriding interest in the truth.

5. HAPPINESS VERSUS PLEASURE

As we have seen, Coleridge was not always unwilling to admit that a certain enjoyment might be derived from intellectual pursuits.

The possibility of such enjoyment, indeed, was fundamental to the project he announced for *The Friend*. 'Having myself experienced', he wrote,

> ...that no delight either in kind or degree, was equal to that which accompanies the distinct perception of a fundamental truth, relative to our moral being... there arose a soothing hope in my mind that a lesser Public might be found, composed of persons susceptible of the same delight, and desirous of attaining it by the same process.
>
> (*Friend*, 1: 15)

The paradox in this statement is one which persistently afflicts Coleridge's efforts to isolate philosophical pleasures from every other kind. The delight of philosophizing must have something in common with those to which it is superior. Yet, he asserts, no delight 'either in kind or degree' is equal to the philosophical. While celebrating philosophy by comparison with other sources of pleasure, he also attempts to set it on a plane where it is not susceptible of such comparisons. Clearly, intellectual pleasures differ from physical ones – we might even argue that they are more noble or more admirable; but if we claim that they are more intense we must also admit that they are forms of pleasure.

This, however, was precisely what Coleridge was unwilling to do. Rather than being pleasure, he argued, the delight of philosophizing was a certain 'happiness'. He explained this distinction in terms of the different activities from which our various pleasures (or 'delights') are derived, and by an intellectualist ethic which celebrates philosophy's pursuit of truth as its primary objective. To say that the pleasures of philosophy are intellectual, while those of eating are sensual, is in a sense to state the obvious; but for Coleridge this difference was both experiential and moral. Rather than being the result of self-indulgence, he claimed, 'intellectual Happiness' is indicative of virtue. In this argument, Coleridge makes use of the three most famous principles of Aristotle's ethics. According to Aristotle, happiness (or *eudaimonia*) is an enduring condition quite different from pleasure. In order to be in a state of happiness, a person must be not merely happy or joyful at a given moment, but generally secure from threats to his or her intellectual, moral, and physical well-being.[79] Of equal importance to Coleridge, however, is Aristotle's principle that happiness is the end of human action, and hence the end of virtue.[80] This theory is attractive to Coleridge primarily because of another by which it is accompanied: namely that the greatest happiness (and hence the greatest virtue) is available only to the philosopher.[81]

It is in terms of this Aristotelian ethic, combined with a puritanism deriving from quite different sources, that we should understand Coleridge's deprecation of 'pleasure' in *The Friend*:

> Pleasure, most often delusive, may be born of delusion. Pleasure, herself a sorceress, may pitch her tents on enchanted ground. But Happiness (or, to use a far more accurate as well as more comprehensive term, solid WELL-BEING) can be built on Virtue alone, and must of necessity have Truth for its foundation.
>
> (*Friend*, 1: 39)

For Coleridge as for Aristotle, the pursuit of truth is the primary source of happiness, and the chief constituent of virtue. What is not so clear, however, is that they coincide in their interpretation of 'happiness'. Certainly in the above passage Coleridge seems to be writing of *eudaimonia*, or an enduring condition of a much broader and more theoretical type than pleasure. Yet he also compared the satisfactions to be derived from eating and philosophizing in such a way as to imply that philosophy, though it *may* be the source of long-term fulfilment and security, is also a source of immediate pleasure.[82] So insistent, indeed, does he sometimes become on this comparison, that the 'happiness' of philosophy is reduced to a series of such momentary satisfactions. Clearly, his aim is to contrast physical pleasures with philosophical fulfilments, and by placing them in close proximity to educe a recognition of their differentness. Yet in so doing he in fact undermines the most important distinction which he adopted from Aristotle.

Coleridge's fullest discussion of the varieties of happiness occurs in his lectures on philosophy of 1818–19. There are, he claims, 'four perfectly distinct states' which we habitually refer to under this heading. The first is that of

> ... a bodily [appetite], in other words a perfect correspondence of the external stimulants to the frame to be stimulated, producing an aggregate of bodily pleasurable sensations; the second, a certain joyousness...as where Pythagoras discovered the proposition that made him cry out 'Eureka', and this every man who has

> intellectual light will refuse to consider—I do not consider—analogous to the pleasure of eating venison or enjoying anything else bodily. He calls it 'intellectual pleasure' forgetting he must find something in common... The third is a speculative point which arises from the consideration of our extreme dependence upon external things. That a man has reason to congratulate himself on having been born in such an hour and climate under such and such circumstances and under such auspicious circumstances, this the ancients called [Εὐτυχία, Εὐδαιμονία] ... the fourth I cannot otherwise express than in the words of the liturgy as 'the peace of God' which every man who has had an approving conscience must know.
>
> (*PLects*, 141)[83]

In this passage, the concept of *eudaimonia* is no longer used to distinguish intellectual pleasures from bodily ones. Coleridge's emphasis, rather, is on the immediate satisfactions to be derived from philosophy, and the experiential qualities which distinguish them. Pythagoras's 'joyousness', he implies, cannot be called 'intellectual pleasure', because it has nothing 'in common' with the pleasure of eating. By identifying pleasure with the physical, Coleridge creates the need for a term to distinguish intellectual pleasure from every other kind; yet at the same time he admits that *eudaimonia* cannot be such a term, denoting as it does the concept of lasting well-being, rather than the sensations (for want of a better term) which we derive from philosophizing. He does, however, describe two distinct kinds of philosophical pleasure, which approximately correspond to the two discussed in the first section of this chapter. On the one hand is Pythagoras' 'joyousness' – a certain excitement and sense of fulfilment which, however, also involves the self-admiration involved in a reflective appraisal of one's achievements. On the other is 'the peace of God', which is more exclusively identified with a conviction of one's own virtue.

In a notebook entry of 1809, however, Coleridge collapsed this distinction, defining 'intellectual Happiness' as 'Joy, Gaudium, the Peace of God which passeth all understanding' (also identified with the Greek *makariotēs*), and contrasting it on the one hand with 'Gladness' (*Laetitia, euphrosunē*), and on the other with 'Pleasure' (*Voluptas, eudaimonia*) (*CN*, 3: 3558).[84] Self-satisfaction is thus unified with joy and reflective tranquillity, in a combination which Coleridge implies is uniquely the product of intellectual activity.

His description of these elements, however, does not explain why they cannot arise in other contexts than intellectual activity, nor why they are not also forms of pleasure. The terms denoting the varieties of happiness and pleasure are the most important locus of desynonymy in Coleridge,[85] and the notebook entry discussed above contains a passage which reveals more clearly than any other how *ad hoc* an instrument desynonymy could be. In the course of a comparison between eating and philosophizing, Coleridge deletes the word 'pleasures' from the context of intellectual activity, and substitutes for it the word 'Gladness', asking

> ... whether the ~~pleasures~~ Gladness of intellectual Activity, of Tranquillity from intellectual Certainty, &c are really 'PLEASURE', i.e. likewise *modes* of the same Substance as the sensations of the Palate &c—
>
> (*CN*, 3: 3558)

Coleridge's lack of foresight in this (originally private) context is a microcosm of the function of desynonymy. As Hamilton demonstrates, according to Coleridge desynonymy is 'a process of showing that words which we think have identical meanings in fact only have similar meanings'.[86] Coleridge describes two distinct kinds of desynonymy, however: on the one hand is the process of showing that 'homoeonymes' ('those words, falsely thought or carelessly used as Synonymes') in fact have different meanings; on the other is the process of giving newly distinct meanings to previously synonymous terms.[87] Both of these processes, however, depend on the assumption that certain phenomena are more different than was previously recognized, and that their differences can be revealed by comparing English words with analogous terms in other (and usually older) languages which more precisely distinguish gradations of meaning.[88] Hence desynonymy is a rhetorical method by which Coleridge seeks to support such statements as that the pleasure derived from philosophizing is so different from any other kind that it cannot be called by the same name. His readers are supposed to be convinced that by failing to use particular terms to express the different meanings which Coleridge is distinguishing, they were in fact identifying those meanings, rather than using several words indifferently to refer to all of them. In the above passage, therefore, the distinction which Coleridge tries to establish is not just between bodily pleasure and intellectual happiness, but also between the popular identification of them and his own discovery of their diversity: the illusion of a new truth is the means by which he seeks to distance intellectual pleasures from bodily ones. Since, however, he initially employs the word 'pleasure' to denote intellectual happiness, this illusion is completely undermined, and the passage becomes merely an illustration of his rhetorical method.

The same notebook entry, however, also contains Coleridge's most substantial analysis of the difference between intellectual and physical enjoyments. 'The strict question', he says,

> ... is simply this—whether in intellectual Happiness ... there is not such an involution of spontaneity, ergo, such a synthesis of itself as an effect or result with its causal *Activity*, as both distinguishes it in kind from the passio—or action of *stimulus*—and thence to ... unite with the first by means of the spontaneity, which it is produced by, but so as to participate—
>
> (*CN*, 3: 3558)

Two important facts are suggested in this passage. Firstly, the difference between the passive experience of a pleasure resulting from outward stimuli, and the energetic activity without which intellectual pleasure is inconceivable. Even the pleasure of passively recalling and admiring one's achievements, we should note, could not occur without a prior activity and production. Secondly, there is the fact that intellectual pleasure, in the strictest sense of that which occurs *during* the process of intellection, is actually indistinguishable from the feeling of activity, of energetic production and fulfilment. These are not grounds for any moral distinction between pleasures; but they are the best possible reasons for admitting a difference in kind between bodily satisfactions and intellectual ones.

One other means employed by Coleridge to encourage our assent to his distinction of pleasures deserves mention: the distinction between 'a taste of' and 'a taste for'. 'I have seen', he writes,

> ... a very elaborate work on taste ... in which the taste of venison and a taste for Milton and a taste for religious sentiment have been all treated of as a species of the same genus, all originating in the palate; and the whole system of criticism both in poetry, painting, statuary, and so forth, is derived from this grammatical mistake of 'a taster of' and 'taste for'.
>
> (*PLects*, 207)

This confusion, he goes on to say, is morally dangerous in that it prevents people from discovering the superiority of certain tastes over others. Since he cannot demonstrate that he enjoys 'more pleasurable feelings in endeavouring to develop my intellectual faculties' than his interlocutor does 'with his pot of porter' (*ibid.*), this 'grammatical' confusion leaves him no option but to admit that *de gustibus non est disputandum*.[89]

That this grammatical mistake also involves a confusion of tastes is not, however, as clear as Coleridge seems to assume. It is true that we cannot refer to 'the taste' of Milton in the same way as we refer to the taste of mutton; but we can certainly speak of having 'a taste for' Milton in exactly the same way as we speak of having a taste for mutton.[90] By indicating the non-existence of such a thing as the taste of Milton, Coleridge seeks to establish that the pleasure produced by intellectual pursuits is more radically different from the pleasure of eating than most people would acknowledge. Rather than achieving this objective, however, he demonstrates nothing more than was previously self-evident. Moreover, his only explanation of the disadvantages of comparing such diverse tastes is that it may lead us to forget the superiority of intellectual pleasures.[91] He would then need to prove this superiority, yet this is precisely what he is unable to do.

5

Power and Progress: Coleridge's Metaphors of Thought

The circular relationship between thought and emotion in Coleridge's work is nowhere more prominent than in the numerous ascending sequences of classes or stages of being which populate his writing from the 1790s to the 1830s. These patterns – variously linked to the philosophical optimism of Hartley, Priestley, and Godwin, to Schelling's transcendental idealism, and to the *Naturphilosophie* of Steffens and Oken – consistently associate intellectual progress with moral improvement and liberation from the merely passive state of plants or animals.[1] In so doing, I will argue, they not only reveal a unity underlying the obvious diversity and inconsistency of Coleridge's theories, but also demonstrate a distinctive circularity whereby these theories both articulate and stimulate the emotions which are their unifying principle. What connects Coleridge's empiricist thought with his idealism and philosophy of nature, in other words, is the expression of an optimism which itself arises from contemplating humankind's unlimited progression towards freedom, happiness, and virtue. Rather than allowing us to differentiate the source from the expression of such emotions, indeed, these theories articulate a state of consciousness which is essentially aspirational, or whose theoretical content cannot be separated from the sublime expectancy which it simultaneously sustains and reveals. What the title of this chapter refers to, therefore, is the way in which Coleridge's theories of progress repeatedly evoke the experiential process from which they emerge – a process in which intellectual effort both informs and is informed by the feelings it produces. That this evocation or metaphorizing of the experience of intellectual or imaginative creation is, for Coleridge's readers, primarily an effect or implication of his writing need scarcely be said; yet since even the purely logical aspects of his theories are similarly dependent on a concept of intention, there is little reason to give less credence – or to attach less importance – to those partly conceptual, partly emotional complexes which unify his otherwise incompatible and contradictory theories, and whose very hybridity is so closely related to the nature of his central concepts.

1. THE SYSTEM OF OPTIMISM

Coleridge's writings of the 1790s often refer to the 'optimistic' philosophies of Hartley, Priestley, and Godwin, yet do not include any detailed discussion of their relative merits or the differences between their theories. His occasional references to the 'system of optimism' seem to invoke a unified theory existing independently of his own – often fragmentary – judgements and speculations.[2] Yet he is so far from consistent in his support for the views of any of these thinkers that the 'system' over which he enthuses cannot easily be located in any of their works.[3] Coleridge's early response to the empirically-based psychological, religious, and political thought of mid- to late-eighteenth-century British philosophers, therefore, seems to be a prime example of the syncretic method which several critics have discovered in his work.[4] Its governing principle, however, is a consistent pursuit of grounds for optimism, and specifically for belief in the necessary and unlimited progression of human beings towards freedom, happiness, and virtue. Broadly speaking, Hartley provides the materialist basis for this 'necessitarianism', claiming to discover physical and scientific grounds for a Neoplatonic conception of humankind's ascent towards the deity. Priestley, however, largely separates Hartley's theology from his psychology, finding different – and in some respects more credible – arguments for philosophical optimism, while also placing greater emphasis on the certainty or inevitability of the moral and spiritual progressions which Hartley envisages. Godwin, on the other hand, combines an interest in humankind's ascent above a merely physical existence with an emphasis on the practical forms of liberation to be derived from our increasing rationality. Coleridge's enthusiasm for the optimistic theories of all these thinkers thus gives a certain unity to doctrines and arguments which cannot easily be combined into a single philosophical system. Underlying his interest in them is a quest for unlimited hope or sublime expectation which is also central to his later enthusiasm for idealist theories of humankind's transcendence of the physical, and for evolutionary systems in which humanity represents a potential link from earthly to celestial existences. Similarly in the political sphere, the incompatibility of the doctrines to which he successively allied himself belies the consistency of his fascination with 'freedom', whether from the oppressions of aristocracy or from what he later regarded as the tyranny of popular opinion.[5] Not to be constrained by force or fashion, but freely to aspire and progress towards an indefinable summit of being, is consistently the principle of Coleridge's conflicting – and often borrowed – ideologies.

His often-quoted description of himself, in 1794, as a 'compleat Necessitarian', explicitly connects this phrase with Hartley's philosophy and the view of thought as motion which I discussed in Chapter 2.[6] Neither the term 'necessitarian' nor its cognate 'necessarian', however, plays an important role in Hartley's *Observations*, though the latter occurs frequently in Priestley's works, as does the conception of 'philosophical necessity', to which Coleridge implicitly expresses his allegiance in this phrase. As I will show, Coleridge's works of the 1790s repeatedly use 'necessitarian' ideas originating in Priestley, though elsewhere he expresses support for both Hartley's and Priestley's ideas, sometimes seeming to identify their theories.[7] This absence of differentiation between the two thinkers, however, is probably due to the fact that Priestley's doctrine of necessity itself builds on Hartley's discussion of humankind's necessary progression towards a condition of greater happiness and spirituality, though Priestley largely separates this conception from the associationist principles with which Hartley connects it.[8] As we shall see, moreover, Priestley also added to Hartley's theory an idea which later became of great importance in Coleridge's writing – namely that the contemplation of our necessary progress can itself be a means to the fulfilment of this destiny.

Hartley's thesis, however, was always a hybrid or at least a paradoxical one, chiefly in terms of its problematic attempt to explain our ascent above the physical as itself arising from purely physical causes. The essence of his argument was that since our 'sensible Pleasures' are more numerous than our 'sensible Pains',

> ... Association would convert a State, in which Pleasure and Pain were both perceived by Turns, into one in which pure Pleasure alone would be perceived; at least, would cause the Beings who were under its Influence to an indefinite Degree, to approach to this last State nearer than by any definite Difference.
>
> (*OM*, 1: 83)

This optimistic view depended on two somewhat tenuous premisses: firstly that our 'sensible Pleasures' *are* more numerous than our 'sensible Pains', and secondly that association will ultimately eliminate our weaker or less frequent impressions (*OM*, 1: 82–3). Hartley also claimed, however, that 'Some Degree of Spirituality is the necessary Consequence of passing through Life', because

> The sensible Pleasures and Pains must be transferred by Association more and more every Day, upon things that afford neither sensible Pleasure nor sensible Pain in themselves, and so beget the intellectual Pleasures and Pains.
>
> (*OM*, 1: 82)

This statement reveals a paradox which, even after his repudiation of Hartley, remained fundamental to Coleridge's thought: namely, the contradiction between a continuous upward progression from matter to ever greater degrees of spirituality, and the continuous or unchanging identity of the subject of this transformation. Hartley's attempt to explain the increasingly mental or 'intellectual' quality of our enjoyments in terms of material processes in fact repeats the conflict at the centre of his theory of association. Though claiming that 'Man consists of two Parts, Body and Mind' (*OM*, 1: i), he consistently attempts to explain away the spiritual realm by identifying it with the bodily. It may be possible to say without contradiction that consciousness arises from physical causes. Yet however much Hartley attempted to do this, he continued to assert the heterogeneity of mind and matter. 'I do not', he wrote,

> ... by ... ascribing the Performance of Sensation to Vibrations excited in the medullary Substance, in the least presume to assert, or intimate, that Matter can be endued with the Power of Sensation.
>
> (*OM*, 1: 33)

This, however, was not the only contradiction which Hartley's theory entailed, since he also sought to combine 'the Necessity of human Actions, and the ultimate Happiness of all Mankind' with

> ... practical Free-will, or that voluntary Power over our Affections and Actions, by which we deliberate, suspend, and choose, and which makes an essential Part of our Ideas of Virtue and Vice, Reward and Punishment ...
>
> (*OM*, 1: 7–8)

Freedom and necessity, however, are combined in Hartley's thought only in the sense of being identified, just as the distinctness of mind and body is affirmed alongside, but never reconciled with, their identity. What enables Hartley so flagrantly to contradict himself, yet also to maintain a certain coherence in his thesis, is the concept of association, which not only explains the unity-yet-distinctness of body and mind, but also the gradual replacement of our sensible pleasures and pains by intellectual pleasures. Just as, according to Hartley, vibrations in the nerves produce vibrations in the medullary substance of the brain, which in turn give rise to miniature vibrations corresponding to ideas, that is, so man – the subject or locus of this process – is continuously progressing upwards towards happiness, spirituality, and virtue. As we have seen, however, free will and spirituality are also in conflict with the very necessity which, according to Hartley, makes them possible. One of his aims is to show 'in what manner [free will] results from the Frame of our Natures,' or in other words, how 'the Necessity of human Actions' allows for voluntary choice and moral significance (*OM*, 1: vii–viii); the other is to show how an increasingly spiritual existence results from material processes in the brain. The union of physical and mental is itself unsustainable; yet it both grounds and vitiates his theory of human progressiveness.

Though Priestley claimed to owe 'much more than I am able to express' to Hartley's work, and himself edited an abridged edition of the *Observations*, his own writings either ignore these problems, or declare them to be insoluble. In the introduction to his abridgement of Hartley, however, Priestley comes down so firmly on the side of matter and its identity with spirit as apparently to pre-empt any notion of an upward progression on the Hartleian model. 'I am rather inclined to think', he writes,

> ... that, though the subject is beyond our comprehension at present, man does not consist of two principles, so essentially different from one another as *matter* and *spirit*, which are always described as having not one common property, by means of which they can affect or act upon each other .... I rather think that the whole man is of some *uniform composition*, and that the property of *perception*, as well as the other powers that are termed *mental*, is the result ... of such an organical structure as that of the brain. Consequently, that the whole man becomes extinct at death, and that we have no hope of surviving the grave but what is derived from the scheme of revelation.[9]

Thus – as if without realizing it – Priestley seems to reject the entire conceptual structure of Hartley's *Observations*.[10] His concluding sentence, however, reveals a tendency to obscurantism which is of great importance to his theory of progression. As far as our understanding of the world extends, he argues, we can find no ground for distinguishing the spiritual from the material, and indeed create irresolvable philosophical problems whenever we do so. Since, however, the subject is 'beyond our comprehension', the conclusion which we necessarily arrive at is not necessarily the truth, but possibly very distant from it. Instead of attempting to mediate between the irreconcilable, therefore, Priestley first asserts their identity, and then denies it. His chief difference from Hartley is that he admits the mysteriousness of mind-body relationships. The paradox of the simultaneous unity and distinctness of matter and mind is the topic of Priestley's discussion, whereas Hartley continually attempts to conceal this underlying structure of his thought.

The paradox which Priestley makes explicit in this passage is also a prominent feature of his writings on philosophical necessity. No attempt is made to explain that 'unerring direction' which steers our lives and the process of the universe towards a 'glorious and happy' conclusion.[11] Rather, Priestley makes our inability to understand this process a central condition of our progression and development. Ostensibly, *The Doctrine of Philosophical Necessity Illustrated* expresses the simple faith that

> Whatever men may intend, or execute, all their designs, and all their actions, are subject to the secret influence and guidance of one who is necessarily the best judge of what will most promote his own excellent purposes. To him, and in his works, all seeming *discord* is real *harmony*, and all apparent *evil*, ultimate *good*.[12]

This 'optimistic' theory combines two distinct claims: on the one hand that the divine will is shaping everything towards an end which, by definition, is excellent and perfect, and on the other that this divinely originated project necessarily involves our own increasing happiness and virtue. These two theses are illustrated, and in part explained, by the principle of salvation by faith. In our present state, Priestley says, we are only permitted to see 'a very little' of the 'great connected chain' in which our actions and experiences are involved. Insofar, however, as we 'can practically believe that there is but *one will* in the whole universe', and 'that this one will, exclusive of all *chance*, or the interference of any other will, disposes of all things, even to their minutest circumstances, and always for the best of purposes', we will both become perfectly happy, and find that our will is indistinguishable from that of God.[13] In the *Doctrine*, Priestley's explanation of his theory goes little further than this. The union of free will and necessity is supposed to come about merely through our acceptance of his initial claim that we are guided in our choices by the deity. Priestley must, however, allow for a case in which this thesis is not accepted, and to this (very large) extent his theory remains at the level of blind faith. The spreading of his own faith is, similarly, the only explanation Priestley offers for the increasing happiness of mankind. *If* we believe that all apparent evil is excluded in the will of the divinity, he says, 'it is impossible but that we must rejoice in, and be thankful for, all events, without distinction'.[14]

In his earlier *Essay on the First Principles of Government*, however, Priestley argues that the increasing happiness of human beings does not depend primarily on faith, but rather on the nature of their intellectual powers. Our feelings as we pass through life, he says, are increasingly influenced 'both by the remembrance of what is past, and the expectation of what is future'. In many cases, moreover,

> These intellectual pleasures and pains ... wholly over power all temporary sensations; whereby some men, of great and superior minds, enjoy a state of permanent and equable felicity, in a great measure independent of the uncertain accidents of life. In such minds the ideas of things, that are seen to be the cause and effect of one another, perfectly coalesce into one, and present but one common image. Thus all the ideas of evil absolutely vanish, in the idea of the greater good with which it is connected, or of which it is productive.[15]

Rather than becoming happy merely by believing that it is our destiny to do so, and that everything is governed by the most perfect being imaginable, therefore, we become so by our increasing comprehension of the very complexity which, according to the *Doctrine*, makes such faith the only secure means to happiness. Rather than imitating God only to the extent that we trust in His infinite wisdom, we can in fact approximate that wisdom, and in so doing escape the 'uncertain accidents' of mortal existence. Priestley's reference to our 'intellectual pleasures and pains' is not his only debt to Hartley in this passage, since the notion of increasing comprehension serves the same purpose in Priestley's *Essay* as that of association serves in Hartley's theory of our progression towards a happier and more spiritual existence. Whereas Hartley seeks to ground our destiny in physiology, that is, Priestley grounds it in the growth of intellect and experience. The most distinctive feature of Priestley's theory both here and in the *Doctrine*, however, is that it refuses to account for a destiny which, he argues, only God can perfectly comprehend. It is an incoherent theory – inconsistent also in its several statements – but one which illustrates more clearly than Hartley's the 'system of optimism' which attracted Coleridge in the 1790s.

Coleridge's most obvious borrowings from Priestley occur in the *Moral and Political Lecture* of 1795, where he briefly paraphrases the dedication to Priestley's *Doctrine*. Most notably, Coleridge celebrates those who look forward

> ... with gladdened heart to that glorious period when Justice shall have established the universal fraternity of Love. These soul ennobling views bestow the virtues which they anticipate. He whose mind is habitually imprest with them soars above the present state of humanity, and may be justly said to dwell in the presence of the most high. Regarding every event even as he that ordains it, evil vanishes from before him, and he views with naked eye the eternal form of universal beauty.
>
> (*Lects 1795*, 13)[16]

Most of these ideas, as well as several words and expressions, derive directly from Priestley, who also writes of the 'soul-ennobling views' revealed by his system – whose central principle is the progression of humankind through their belief in, or increasing knowledge of, this progression – and of the mind receiving 'such a lasting impression' from these views as will inspire 'a serenity and joy, which *the world can neither give nor take away*'.[17] The coincidence of our will with that of the deity is described by Priestley as involving 'a kind of *union with God*', and evil is said to be eliminated in the concept of God's greater project for the universe.[18] In adopting this theory, moreover, Coleridge does little more than Priestley to resolve its contradictions or fill in its lacunae. The moral responsibility of the individual is retained alongside the theoretical impossibility of evil in God's perfect design. This very paradox, indeed, is itself the basis of the development which both authors envisage: through our dedication to a certain doctrine and aesthetic, we are rising upwards from a world in which evil and suffering are inescapable, to one in which they are inconceivable. Coleridge, however, makes no reference in this lecture to the intellectualist version of Priestley's theory expressed in his *Essay on the First Principles of Government*, emphasizing instead the simultaneously aesthetic and moral value of a repeated meditation on the impossibility of evil and the necessity of ultimate perfection – ideas corresponding closely to those in Priestley's *Doctrine*.[19] With regard to the ultimate effect of cultivating this aesthetic, moreover, the two authors are in close agreement: it is a state of perfection and happiness which, in its very other-worldliness, effectively coalesces with the image which produces it. Coleridge, indeed, makes this coalescence explicit in describing how 'These soul ennobling views bestow the virtues which they anticipate.' Why we are becoming happier, at least, is not mysterious; and the disappearance of evil is also described as resulting from our meditation.

The most important respect in which the early Coleridge resembles Priestley, however, is in his repeated description of the universe as structured by the twin polarities of obscurity and clarity, confusion and order. Even in Priestley's *Doctrine*, where the individual's advance involves no growth of understanding, but only a repetition of the same 'soul-ennobling' prospects, the notion of a great system concealed beneath the apparent absurdity of individual lives and occurrences is fundamental to the progression he envisages. Similarly in the *Essay on the First Principles of Government*, where Priestley places no limit on the increase of human understanding, his theory is structured by the conception of an originally incomprehensible order in the universe. Happiness and virtue, he suggests, increase through the gradual replacement of our immediate perceptions with a recognition of their place in God's evolving system. In Coleridge's version of this theory, however, the major difference between Priestley's two expositions of his thesis is largely obscured. Though, as noted earlier, Coleridge's 'Moral and Political Lecture' does not explicitly envisage our increasing comprehension of a pre-existent design, its imagery of widening prospects evokes an optimism which he describes as unifying our own viewpoint with that of God. Similarly in 'Religious Musings', Coleridge multiplies the images of darkness giving way to light and confusion to unity, in such a way as to suggest a more complete union with God's viewpoint than that which faith alone, or the repeated contemplation of an incomprehensible order, can logically engender. The second section of Coleridge's poem initiates the sequence of enlightenments:

> Lovely was the death
> Of Him whose life was Love! Holy with power
> He on the thought-benighted Sceptic beamed
> Manifest Godhead, melting into day
> What floating mists of dark idolatry
> Broke and misshaped the omnipresent Sire:
> And first by Fear uncharmed the drowséd Soul,
> Till of its nobler nature it 'gan feel
> Dim recollections; and thence soared to Hope,
> Strong to believe whate'er of mystic good
> The Eternal dooms for His immortal sons.
> From Hope and firmer Faith to perfect Love
> Attracted and absorbed: and centred there
> God only to behold, and know, and feel,
> Till by exclusive consciousness of God
> All self-annihilated it shall make
> God its Identity: God all in all!
> We and our Father one!
>
> ('Religious Musings', ll. 28–45, *CPW*, 1: 110–11)

The paradox which begins this section encapsulates the structure of reality and illusion which is fundamental to the system of optimism. Like Priestley in the *Doctrine*, Coleridge represents the death of Christ as the supreme example of an evil which is at the same time the highest good.[20] This example is unique in combining participation in the best possible *process* (the process because of which we must 'rejoice in ... all events, without distinction') with an impact on our spiritual welfare deriving not merely from our own religious faith, but also from the sacrifice Christ made for our salvation. The next sentence, however, introduces a more complex paradox in which faith is represented as dissolving the confusion arising from intellectual inquiry. Our 'omnipresent Sire', Coleridge says, was 'Broke and misshaped' by the idolatry of scepticism; or in other words, the necessity and consequent goodness of all events was concealed by an excessive faith in the power of human understanding. The remainder of this passage similarly expresses an ethic and an aesthetic which are essentially those of the later Priestley. Coleridge's chief advance on the *Doctrine*, indeed, is his greater clarity concerning our intuition of unity in the universe and our eventual union with God. His idea that the soul might feel 'Dim recollections' of 'its nobler nature' gives the experience of faith a significance which is far more than merely moral or aesthetic. What we *will* become, he suggests, was known to us even before we were ignorant of it, in a form of 'collective unconscious' which unifies us with the God who made us and to whom we will return – a theory notably anticipating Wordsworth's more celebrated intimations of immortality.[21]

Hartley, however, is invoked in a note to line 43 ('All self-annihilated it shall make') as justifying the content of the latter part of my quotation.[22] In one of the passages Coleridge refers to, Hartley writes:

> Since God is the Source of all Good, and consequently must at last appear to be so, *i.e.* be associated with all our Pleasures, it seems to follow ... that the Idea of God, and of the Ways by which his Goodness and Happiness are made manifest, must, at last, take place of, and absorb all other Ideas, and He himself become, according to the Language of the Scriptures, *All in All*.
>
> (*OM*, 1: 114)

Fairchild takes this and other passages of Hartley's *Observations* as demonstrating that we are wrong to draw too 'black-and-white [a] contrast between the influence of Hartley and the influence of Neoplatonic and other mystics' on Coleridge. Coleridge's assertion in *Biographia* that the two parts of Hartley's system are inconsistent – the first presenting a materialist explanation of intelligence, the second being concerned with 'the existence and attributes of God' – he suggests, is unjustified: 'When [Coleridge] wrote *Religious Musings* ... it was precisely the *dependence* of Hartley's religion upon Hartley's psychology that appealed to him.'[23] Fairchild's comment is valid to the extent that Hartley's explanation of our eventual union with God resembles that proposed by Priestley in the *Doctrine*: in both cases, contemplation of God's perfect but invisible design involves some form of coincidence between humankind and the deity. But whereas in Hartley this coincidence depends on the process of association whereby one idea replaces another, in Priestley and Coleridge association itself is not directly referred to, but only the effect of faith on our relationship with God – that effect which Hartley sought to make a consequence of physiology.[24]

The following paragraph, however, includes the image of men 'Treading beneath their feet all visible things / As steps, that upward to their Father's throne / Lead gradual' (*CPW*, 1: 111) – an idea which more closely resembles Origen's theory of 'a stairway of worlds, superimposed one on another not in space but in time, and leading up, by their ascending grades of perfection, to the consummation in which "God shall be all in all"'.[25] Coleridge's ideal in 'Religious Musings' is not explicitly that of a constant upward progression of world-orders as distinct from the simultaneous emanation and ascent of being described by Plotinus;[26] yet the imagery of social revolution in the final stanzas of the poem shows that Coleridge also envisaged a permanent improvement of humankind's condition – something analogous to the 'miraculous Millenium' of pantisocracy as he later called it – though this vision seems not to have been fully integrated with his necessitarian theories.[27] Both here and in 'The Destiny of Nations', indeed, Coleridge's writing has an obvious millenarian content which has been attributed to various influences, including not only those of Priestley and Erasmus Darwin, but also those of Godwin and – indirectly – of French writers such as Diderot and de Maupertuis.[28] That the millenarianism which Priestley, in particular, expressed in this period (though in different works from those which expound his 'necessitarian' theories) should have attracted Coleridge's interest is scarcely surprising considering his enthusiasm for the notion of an earthly paradise established by physical or psychological forces rather than the second coming of Christ.[29] Such millenarianism, however, is rarely evident in Coleridge's writing even during the 1790s, when revolutionary enthusiasm made it particularly widespread elsewhere;[30] and though the Godwinian project of establishing a 'pantisocracy' (or society in which all rule equally) was prominent among his interests in 1794–5, these socio-political aspects of his thinking also seem not to have been fully integrated with the theories he derived from Hartley and Priestley. His references, at this period, to the 'corruption' which human beings are liable to suffer as a result of living 'in Great Cities', and to the excellent 'Moral Effects' of 'The pleasures, which we receive from rural beauties', seem clearly to connect the ruralist aspect of pantisocracy with Hartley's concept of environmental conditioning.[31]

Yet Godwin's emphasis on the abolition both of government and of private property as means of increasing the happiness and virtue of human beings has little in common either with the physically-based religious optimism of Hartley, or with the more purely psychological theories of Priestley.[32] The chief similarity between Godwin's work and that of 'necessitarian' thinkers, indeed, lies neither in political nor in millenarian optimism, but rather in the visions of a liberating ascent of being from matter to mind, and from the insensate to the voluntary, which characterize not only Hartley's and Priestley's, but also Godwin's ideal of humankind's increasing freedom and rationality.

Like Hartley, indeed, Godwin seeks to reconcile the freedom and ultimate perfectibility of human beings with the derivation of our ideas and actions from impressions *ab extra*. 'The perfection of the human character', he writes,

> ... consists in approaching as nearly as possible to the perfectly voluntary state ... We should remove ourselves to the furthest distance from the state of mere inanimate machines, acted upon by causes of which they have no understanding.[33]

This value and objective, however, are ostensibly incompatible with his equally important tenet that 'the actions and dispositions of mankind are the offspring of circumstances and events, and not of any original determination that they bring into the world'.[34] Godwin's chief problem, therefore, is to explain how, having no 'original determination' to act or proceed in any particular way, and being in all respects the products of accidental circumstance, we can develop our voluntary powers in order to distance ourselves as far as possible from the mechanical origins of thought and action. The means by which he does so has important features in common with Priestley's earlier theory of progression through the growth of experience and understanding. According to this theory, the growth of experience entails a proportionate growth in our understanding of the cosmological process. Priestley does not say that any growth in intellectual power is involved in this development. All that is necessary is that our 'faculties of perception and action' should 'remain in the same vigour', and that our 'recollection and foresight' should be unimpaired.[35] Godwin, on the other hand, both explicitly makes intellectual power a consequence of experience, and attempts to explain how freedom and the power of judgement can arise from experience. His basic premiss is one which Locke most famously affirmed, namely that

> The human mind, so far as we are acquainted with it, is nothing else but a faculty of perception. All our knowledge, all our ideas, everything we possess as intelligent beings, comes from impression. All the minds that exist set out from absolute ignorance. They received first one impression, then a second. As the impressions became more numerous, and were stored by the help of memory, and combined by the faculty of association, so the experience increased, and with the experience the knowledge, the wisdom, everything that distinguishes man from what we understand by a 'clod of the valley'.[36]

Godwin's aim in this and similar passages is gradually to wear away the assumption of a fundamental difference between perception *per se* and the activities of making complex ideas and logical judgements. It is essentially the same procedure as Locke uses in explaining the generation of knowledge:

> Our Observation employ'd either about *external, sensible Objects; or about the internal Operations of our Minds, perceived and reflected on by our selves, is that, which supplies our Understanding with all the materials of thinking.*[37]

Observation, Locke implies, is all that is necessary to organization. Complex ideas arise in precisely the same way as simple ones: the only difference is in the nature of the objects perceived by reflection. Godwin, however, writes not only of the 'faculty of association' as playing a central role in the formation of complex ideas, but also of a certain 'voluntary state' acquired by means of experience. These concepts emphasize his failure to explain how perceptual experience *per se* can either involve or engender the activities of thinking, classifying, and choosing.[38] The lacuna in his theory, however, is also present in Locke's. To say, as Godwin does, that the continuance of perception entails the production of knowledge and wisdom is merely to beg the question what we mean by 'perception'. What Godwin means is impressions *ab extra*, yet he makes no attempt to explain how these can arise. Locke's procedure, on the other hand, is first to explain the activities of classifying and reasoning as merely varieties of observation, and then to say that the activity of choosing is just one of the modes of thinking – that is, something which the agent, and not any faculty (whether innate or generated by experience), must perform.[39] In both cases, the higher activities of mind are supposed to inhere or be implied in the lower, yet the possibility of the lower is not itself accounted for. The twin shibboleths of 'experience' and 'perception' seek to combine yet also to distance the mechanical universe and the progress of intellect.

Like Locke, then, Godwin fails to derive intellect and will from perceptual experience, or, in identifying them, to explain the possibility of either. His emphasis on the moral and practical value of an ascent from mere automatism to perfect freedom, however, encapsulates key aspects of the aesthetic of progress which plays so central a role in the materialist and necessitarian thought to which Coleridge allied himself during the 1790s. Godwin's political ideals share this aesthetic in terms of their optimistic celebration of increasing rationality and freedom;[40] yet though Coleridge's enthusiasm for necessitarian optimism seems not to have disappeared completely until 1801, his interest in Godwin's socio-political theories seems to have evaporated simultaneously with the collapse of his and Southey's project for their practical implementation.[41] The contradictions inherent in Hartley's attempt to derive increasing spirituality and freedom from materialist premises would soon lead Coleridge to explore the alternative explanations of consciousness suggested by idealist thinkers. As we shall see, however, the same fascination with an ascent above the physical entailing the growth of freedom and happiness is fundamental to his interest in theories which, by denying the priority of matter to mind, hold out a clearer prospect of liberation from external determinants. Those critiques of materialism (or of what Fichte and Schelling revealingly call 'dogmatism')[42] which celebrate a repeated process of self-criticism, moreover, seem – in Coleridge's experience – to have been a more effective source of emotional liberation than Priestley's theory of a self-fulfilling contemplation of our progression towards unity with the divine. This progression, however, bears important metaphorical resemblances to the practical liberation which Coleridge himself seems to have derived from contemplating the spiritual destinations which both Hartley and Priestley envisaged; and this striking reflection of the experiential in the theoretical (and vice versa), I would argue, makes Priestley's theories the most important 'metaphors of thought' in Coleridge's early writing.

2. COLERIDGE, TRANSCENDENTAL IDEALISM, AND THE ASCENT OF INTELLIGENCE

Coleridge's borrowings from and adaptations of Schelling provide the most vivid illustrations of the circular interaction of thought and emotion repeatedly evoked by his varied conceptions of the progress or ascent of being. What primarily attracted Coleridge to Schelling was his unification of objective nature with the highest forms of philosophical insight by making them the twin poles of a single progression. Human beings, he argues, start by seeing themselves as subject to external forces and conditions; but as philosophy progresses they perceive that nature's otherness, and their own individuality, are products of a single process, in which a power that transcends the phenomenal self gives rise to a universe made up of these polarities. Having discovered this, the philosopher's problem is how to reconcile his or her own insight – the 'free' or 'conscious' production of this interpretation – with the involuntary and unconscious production of a self and a world set over against it. In order for this interpretation to be true, both forms of production – that performed consciously, and that performed unconsciously – must derive from a single origin preceding the birth of consciousness. According to Schelling, philosophy cannot explain the unity of these two, or in other words, how freedom, which is the essence of philosophy, can be identical with its opposite. This contradiction can only be resolved in the 'intuition of art', which 'ever and again continues to speak to us of what philosophy cannot depict in external form, namely the unconscious element in acting and producing, and its original identity with the conscious'.[43] Hence Schelling's *System* is structured by a gradual unveiling of conclusions which he represents as the necessary process of insight and intellection. As human beings have advanced further in comprehending the universe as he describes it, Schelling claims, so mind has reached an ever higher state of development, gradually abolishing the notion of its distinctness from external nature.[44]

Mind is thus self-subsistent: there is nothing that is not a consequence of our own conscious or unconscious production. But whereas unconscious production issues in a polarized relation of self and other, philosophy seeks to overcome this polarization by a series of dialectical moves which retrace the development of consciousness from an undifferentiated 'Absolute'.[45] Coleridge was attracted by the way in which Schelling made mind at once the unifying concept of evolution, and – in its intellectual transcendence of dualism – the summit of evolutionary development. His habitual valorization of mental labour over sensual pleasure was gratified by this arrangement, in which thought becomes the paradigm of universal progress.[46] Without Schelling's insight, we will remain forever immersed in a misperception of nature as something independent of ourselves; comprehending his work, we can only be the tools of an advancing universe.

Many of the ethical and aesthetic attractions which Schelling held for Coleridge, however, can also be found in other thinkers whose theories he admired or adopted – most obviously those in the Platonic tradition from which Schelling himself derived many of his ideas.[47] Berkeley's *Siris*, for example (a work often referred to by Coleridge),[48] contains many passages which elegantly combine the same values of transcendence, intellect, and freedom. 'Theology and philosophy', Berkeley writes,

> ... gently unbind the ligaments, that chain the soul down to the earth, and assist her flight towards the sovereign Good. There is an instinct or tendency of the mind upwards, which sheweth a natural endeavour to recover and raise ourselves, from our present sensual and low condition, into a state of light, order, and purity.[49]

These values, however, are not the only points which Berkeley and Schelling have in common: for both thinkers, intellectual transcendence of earthly preoccupations also involves the recognition that nature has no independent existence. 'From the outward forms of gross masses which occupy the vulgar', Berkeley writes,

> ... a curious inquirer proceeds to examine the inward structure and minute parts, and from observing the motions in nature, to discover the laws of those motions ... But, if proceeding still in his analysis and inquiry, he ascends from the sensible into the intellectual world, and beholds things in a new light and a new order, he will then change his system and perceive, that what he took for substances and causes are but fleeting shadows; that the mind contains all, and acts all, and is to all created beings the source of unity and identity, harmony and order, existence and stability.[50]

Rudimentary though it is, this formulation of the values of insight and transcendence is an especially clear expression of the aesthetic which informed most of Coleridge's philosophical preoccupations. The movement from ignorance to knowledge is also a movement from fragmentation to unity, from the outward to the inward, and from the helplessness of the individual to the original creativity of consciousness. As in Schelling, the discovery that mind originates both the world which we perceive and the notion of our distinctness from it represents an actual liberation from what previously seemed to determine our existence.

Many analogies with the aesthetic shared by Berkeley and Schelling, however, can also be found in the empiricist thinkers whose ideas most interested the younger Coleridge. In terms of their philosophical premisses, the gulf between Schelling's idealism and the empirical tradition of Enlightenment philosophy is clearly dramatic. Yet in terms of its emotional investment in a teleology of progressive and liberating insight, Schelling's system has obvious elements in common with Godwin's ideal of humankind's increasing freedom and rationality, and our progressive self-liberation from the state of mere 'inanimate machines, acted upon by causes of which they have no understanding'.[51] For Godwin, thought and education are the means by which we liberate ourselves from an original helplessness. By increasing our comprehension of the values of justice and virtue, he argues, we cease to be on a level with the rest of nature, and acquire a superior control over the conditions of our life and society.[52] For Schelling, on the other hand, insight or learning is only a means to our advance insofar as it is also its end. Philosophical knowledge is the nature of a superiority which is not precisely ours, but that of the self-comprehending Absolute expressed in our intellection.[53] For both thinkers, however, there is a movement from human subjection to human insight: knowledge is freedom, whether from the helplessness and brutality of animal existence, or from the misperception of ourselves as set over against an external world.

A comparison of Godwin's views on the progress of intellect with those expressed by Berkeley, however, reveals more detailed similarities. For both thinkers, humankind's advance is a necessary – indeed almost automatic – acquisition of higher forms of mental activity as a consequence of the lower, though both also attach a moral value to this development, and imply that it can be hastened by education. In addition, the insight of mind into its own power is for both thinkers an important part of our progression. According to Godwin, the act of comparison – which as in Locke arises necessarily out of perception –

> ... immediately leads to imperfect abstraction ... Abstraction, which was necessary to the first existence of language, is again assisted in its operations by language. That generalization, which is implied in the very notion of a thinking being, being thus embodied and rendered a matter of sensible impression, makes the mind acquainted with its own powers, and creates a restless desire after further progress.[54]

The theoretical chain of development constructed by Godwin depends on his avoidance (for most purposes) of the concept of independent 'faculties': the necessity of progress resides in the identity of abstraction and perception, or at least the potentiality of the former in the latter. In Berkeley, on the other hand, different faculties provide the materials for each other to work upon, in a series which repeats itself at ever higher powers of thought:

> Sense supplies images to memory. These become subjects for fancy to work upon. Reason considers and judges of the imaginations. And these acts of reason become new objects to the understanding. In this scale, each lower faculty is a step that leads to one above it. And the uppermost naturally leads to the Deity ...[55]

Both Berkeley and Godwin thus describe each new insight as providing the basis for a further progression through the various stages or classes of mental operation. By becoming acquainted 'with its own powers', the mind acquires a higher object for its next abstraction than the sense impressions with which it commenced; the objects of 'understanding' (in Berkeley's terms) are no longer images of an external world but judgements of reason, from which we proceed indefinitely upwards (and, in Berkeley's view, towards an ultimate union with God). Clearly, Godwin does not share Berkeley's religious or idealist premisses. Yet not only the directions, but in many ways also the forms of the intellectual progressions they envisage are all but identical.

Godwin, however, is not the only empirically-orientated thinker of the period who substantially shares the ideals of intellectual and spiritual ascent expressed by both Berkeley and Schelling.

Berkeley's confidence in the self-improving and ultimately religious trajectory of the human mind – a kind of perpetual-motion machine as he describes it – also bears important resemblances to Priestley's conception in *The Doctrine of Philosophical Necessity Illustrated.* For both writers, the ignorance with which we begin is necessary both to our eventual enlightenment and to the fulfilment of God's project for mankind. Only by beginning with a perception of the world as something fragmentary and without purpose can we gradually arrive at a conception of the unity of all things according to a divine intention. The nature of our graduation, and its dependence on a primary ignorance or confusion, is vividly evoked by the following passage from Hartley's *Observations on Man*, quoted at the end of Priestley's *Doctrine.* 'It would', Hartley says,

> ... be a sufficient Answer ... to all our Difficulties and Anxieties from the Folly, Vice, and Misery, which we experience in ourselves, and see in others, to say, that they will all end in unbounded Knowledge, Virtue, and Happiness; and that the Progress of every Individual in his Passage through an eternal Life is from imperfect to perfect, particular to general, less to greater, finite to infinite, and from the Creature to the Creator.[56]

Like Berkeley, therefore, Priestley envisages our enlightenment as consisting in the discovery that what we imagined to be fragmentary and without purpose is in fact perfectly unified, yet that our confusion was necessary to that unity. Both in Priestley's *Doctrine* and in Berkeley's *Siris*, the central concept is such a movement from ignorance to light, the progression – whether through faith or philosophy – from animal confusion to a viewpoint shared with the divinity.

In Schelling's philosophy, the ideas of unity and transcendence are both more formalized and more integrated than in the other thinkers I have been discussing. Whereas Berkeley and Godwin merely adumbrate a repeated cycle of mental operations leading to ever greater insights of the mind into itself, Schelling gives to his analogous progression a rigorous dialectical form based on the initial polarization of consciousness. The principal aim of his system is also evident in Berkeley: namely to transcend the opposition of self and other, free and not-free, by intellectually rediscovering their original unity. Berkeley writes both of an ascending chain of beings and mental states, and of the unity of mind with its objects, yet does not attempt to integrate these two conceptions. Mind's discovery of its identity with the other is certainly a higher state of being than mere perception; yet it is not clear how this discovery fits into the chain connecting us with God. In Schelling, on the other hand, opposition and resolution are states of consciousness which recur throughout the process of philosophy, beginning with the distinction between perception and the objects of perception, and ending with an attempt to reconcile the free production of his philosophy with the necessity of the very polarization it describes and analyses. It is not enough for Schelling merely to write of a theoretically discoverable identity; for by this very conception he reintroduces polarity into his system, contrasting the theoretical consciousness with its object – namely that process whereby the Absolute manifests itself first in the distinction of subject and object, and secondly in the opposed activities of thinking and perceiving. Inward unity and the ascending series are thus connected by more than merely the superiority of the philosophic to the natural viewpoint. The extended and gradual progression which Berkeley refers to but does not illustrate becomes in Schelling identical with the recurrence of opposition and resolution at increasingly higher powers of thought.

Schelling's *System*, therefore, attempts to reach an intellectual position which reflects the original identity of all forms of consciousness in an undifferentiated Absolute.[57] As we have seen, he finally admits the impossibility of doing so, stating that only in the products of imagination can the free and the necessary, or the conscious and the unconscious, be reconciled. In every proposition which seems to reconcile them, subject and object are again opposed to each other. This reawakening of conflict, and the prolonged effort to overcome it, are the driving forces of his philosophy, which represents itself, and its ultimate disappearance into an artistic 'intuition' of oneness, as necessary stages in the progress of self-consciousness.[58]

That certain aspects of Coleridge's theory of imagination closely parallel Schelling's description of the functioning of the imaginative power needs little demonstration here.[59] What I wish to emphasize, rather, is the extent to which Coleridge's adaptations of Schelling preserve those aspects of his theory which emphasize an infinite progression or ascent of being, while rejecting those which seem to render it incompatible with Christianity. According to Schelling, the role of art is to duplicate in its products the unity of opposed activities which philosophy postulates but cannot demonstrate. This artistic resolution, however, is unified with the original identity of all production by the concept of the 'productive power' they have in common. What is unified in terms of 'productive power', in other words, is not just subject and object, conscious and unconscious, freedom and necessity, but also the whole sequence of attitudes or 'intuitions' which leads from the 'primordial intuition' of an external world to that poetic resolution which goes beyond the most that philosophy can achieve. 'This productive power', Schelling writes, 'is the same whereby art also achieves the impossible, namely to resolve an infinite opposition in a finite product.'[60] That his use of the terms 'imagination' and 'poetic gift' to refer to this power deliberately identifies the processes of artistic creativity with those which underlie perception is a fact which, through Coleridge's plagiarism, has become among the best-known aspects of Schelling's philosophy.[61] Schelling, however, does not say that poetic imagination 'dissolves, diffuses, dissipates, in order to recreate' (*BL*, 1: 304): he is not concerned with *how* poetic imagination works, but only with what it achieves. Moreover, the 'primary potentiality' of the poetic gift in Schelling is not a 'repetition' of anything, let alone of 'the eternal act of creation in the infinite I AM' (ibid.): this aspect of 'primary IMAGINATION' in Coleridge was presumably introduced in an attempt to reconcile transcendental idealism with the idea of a deity who creates the world prior to, and independently of the mind's own productiveness.[62] Beyond these differences, however, there is a much more important identity of viewpoint. In Coleridge as in Schelling, there is one power which is called imagination and which in two different forms produces first the world of perception and secondly the work of art, and in both authors this structure entails the idea of a progression from the lowest to the highest form of consciousness.

In a letter of 1818 to his disciple J. H. Green, Coleridge claimed that at the time of writing *Biographia* he was '*taken in*' by Schelling's *System*, 'retrograding from [his] own prior and better Lights' (*CL*, 4: 874). Yet even in those passages which are largely a direct translation of Schelling, Coleridge repeatedly interpolates ideas of his own, and in a manner sufficiently consistent to transform the significance of what is merely borrowed. As noted above, Coleridge's description of primary imagination (Schelling's 'productive intuition' of nature) as merely a 'repetition' of the divine act of creation evokes an obscure network of relationships between our unconscious production of a perceptual world and a deity which Schelling did not refer to, yet whose creativity supports our own. A similar process occurs in chapter 12 of *Biographia*, where Coleridge's translation of Schelling is briefly interrupted by a reference to the divine origin of nature. In the passage which I quote below, the first half of the sentence (up to the semi-colon) is Schelling, while the second half is Coleridge:

> The theory of natural philosophy would then be completed, when all nature was demonstrated to be identical in essence with that, which in its highest known power exists in man as intelligence and self-consciousness; when the heavens and the earth shall declare not only the power of their maker, but the glory and the presence of their God, even as he appeared to the great prophet during the vision of the mount in the skirts of his divinity.
>
> (*BL*, 1: 256)[63]

All Coleridge achieves by this addition is to suggest that, for reasons he has not explained, demonstrating the identity of nature and intelligence involves demonstrating the glory and presence of God. By achieving 'the perfect spiritualization of all the laws of nature into laws of intuition and of intellect', we are supposed to discover God's law as well as the laws of consciousness.[64] Coleridge may only be suggesting that, for a Christian, the miracle of our production of the sensible and intelligible worlds demands to be treated like any other. Though we have created them, still 'The heavens declare the glory of God; and the firmament sheweth his handywork'.[65] This view, however, implicitly challenges any claim of Schelling's philosophy to describe the origin and structure of the universe. However much Coleridge duplicates the conception of a dialectical universe developed in Schelling's *System*, he persistently adds to this a religion which undermines it.

In a marginal note on the Schlegels' *Athenaeum*, Coleridge firmly opposes the apparent atheism of Schelling's *System*. The phrasing of his criticism, however, implies that Schelling shared his own theological views, yet was diverted in this work from expressing these deeper intuitions. Schelling, he says, 'overlooked the I AM in the Absolute' – a statement which implies that Schelling's Absolute is a real rather than a merely theoretical entity, yet that he had only perceived part of its true nature. The continuation of this passage makes Coleridge's 'creative' mode of reading even clearer. For, he says, Schelling 'then confounded the *Absolute* with *Nature* – identified Earth, yea Hell, with Heaven. He terrestrialized the celestial by the abortive attempt to celestialize the Terrestrial' (*CM*, 1: 138). The complaint of pantheism implicit in this passage clearly travesties Schelling's *System*, which not only involves no explicit conception of a deity, but also makes a fundamental distinction between the ground of phenomena and the process of their production. As Bolman notes, there *is* a tendency in Schelling's later work not only to identify ground and process, but also to claim that what is both the origin and the substance of our experience is itself nothing other than God.[66] According to Coleridge, however, the 'Absolute' of Schelling's *System* is also a form of deity, and in his later work he merely identified this implicitly divine Absolute with the productivity underlying phenomena. In this response, the true nature of Schelling's thought is almost wholly excluded. Its effect, however, is to represent him as merely a misguided worker on the path to the true theology.

The reasons for Coleridge's often illogical introduction of theology into the systems of other philosophers are clarified by a passage in *On the Constitution of the Church and State*:

> That in all ages, individuals who have directed their meditations and their studies to the nobler characters of our nature, to the cultivation of those powers and instincts which constitute the man, at least separate him from the animal, and distinguish the nobler from the animal part of his own being, will be led by the *supernatural* in themselves to the contemplation of a power which is likewise super-*human*; that science, and especially moral science, will lead to religion, and remain blended with it—this, I say, will, in all ages, be the course of things.
>
> (*C&S*, 44)

According to this passage, all philosophy that deserves the name participates in a trajectory which begins with our subjection to a world of sense and ends with our acknowledgement of the deity. It seems, indeed, that those who do not reach a theological conclusion are regarded by Coleridge as failing to direct their studies 'to the cultivation of those powers and instincts which constitute the man'. This is so broad a formula, however, that even Hume – according to Coleridge, the arch-enemy of religious and philosophic truth[67] – would have to be included among those thinkers labouring towards an acknowledgement of God. No philosopher can be said not to be cultivating powers which distinguish him or her from lower animals; yet Coleridge can scarcely include a philosophy which aims to undermine theology in the trajectory he attributes to every operation of intellect.

This apparent contradiction, however, seems to arise from the essentially dualistic view of mental operations which (as Wellek notes) Coleridge claimed to discover in Kant, yet which in fact combines Kant's distinction between reason and understanding with earlier conceptions of religious intuition.[68] For Coleridge, 'Reason' is not merely a division of human intellect, but rather a means whereby the 'Supreme Reason', or God, communicates with human beings, providing them with insights which cannot be derived from purely logical inquiry. Hence he does not restrict ideas of reason to the 'regulative' function which Kant attaches to them, describing them rather as the means by which we can arrive at a knowledge that transcends experience, and above all at knowledge of God.[69] The view of philosophy which Coleridge expresses in the passage from *Church and State* quoted above, therefore, reflects his conception of reason as providing insights unavailable to understanding. Those who have dedicated their meditations and studies 'to the cultivation of those powers and instincts which constitute the man', he says, will be led 'by the *supernatural* in themselves to the contemplation of a power which is likewise super-*human*'; or in other words, science will lead to religion. It will do so, however, only because what distinguishes human beings from animals, and the nobler from the animal part of their own nature, is reason – that is, an organ of special insight and divine communication. According to Coleridge, some philosophers never attain the insight of reason. The organ which connects human beings with the deity is never awakened in them, and they remain trapped in the realm of understanding, whose products they idolatrously represent to themselves as the origins of knowledge.[70] This theory, however, is here combined with an Aristotelian conception of the soul as divided into a rational and an irrational element.[71] Understanding thus becomes something 'animal'; we will not be really human, Coleridge suggests, until we begin thinking not just logically, but in accordance with the great trajectory which he attributes to reason.

Coleridge's often illogical Christianizing of Kant and Schelling thus arises from the same key preoccupation as his early enthusiasms for Hartley, Priestley, and Godwin. At the heart of both his pre-Kantian and his post-Kantian theorizing is an image of humanity's ascent, through a combination of faith and intellectual effort, towards a state of unity with God in which every form of conflict and contradiction prevailing in the phenomenal world will be overcome, and understood as a product of the 'mere' understanding. Despite Godwin's celebration of humankind's increasing rationality and freedom, the practical and political emphasis of his vision made his appeal for Coleridge less enduring than that of other thinkers. Yet Hartley's and Priestley's attempts to combine Christianity both with empiricism and with a theory of humankind's necessary moral and intellectual progress clearly anticipate Coleridge's enthusiasm for a version of Schelling which includes God as a Neoplatonic source and consummation of intellectual development. What remains consistent in Coleridge's philosophical interests is principally the teleology of a movement from confusion to comprehension, the material to the intellectual, and the phenomenal to the transcendent; and despite his theological disagreements with Schelling, the dynamic and integrated dialectic of his *System* probably came closer to satisfying Coleridge's demand for such a vision than the ideas of any other thinker.

3. SERIES AND PROGRESSIONS IN NATURE

Coleridge's often-repeated division of all philosophers into Platonists and Aristotelians implicitly deprecates the ideas of the latter;[72] yet as Lovejoy points out, it was Aristotle, rather than Plato, who 'chiefly suggested to naturalists and philosophers of later times the idea of arranging (at least) all animals in a single graded *scala naturae* according to their degree of "perfection"' – an idea which is repeatedly prominent in Coleridge's reflections on the development of nature.[73] Aristotle's argument in *De Animalibus Historia* is neither an evolutionary nor a metaphysical one, but merely arranges natural phenomena according to 'the degree in which they appear to participate in life'. There are, he suggests, no clear boundary lines between plants and animals, or between the animate and the inanimate. Rather, there is a continuous upward transition extending from inanimate materials to the most intelligent forms of life. Nature, he says,

> ... passes so gradually from the inanimate to the animate that their continuity renders the boundary between them

> indistinguishable; and there is a middle kind that belongs to both orders. For plants come immediately after inanimate things; and plants differ from one another in the degree in which they appear to participate in life. For the class taken as a whole seems, in comparison with other bodies, to be clearly animate, but compared with animals to be inanimate. And the transition from plants to animals is continuous; for one might question whether some marine forms are animals or plants, since many of them are attached to the rock and perish if they are separated from it.[74]

In Aristotle, then, the great scale of being neither entails any theory of evolution, nor any notion of the identity of the various phenomena which it connects. They are connected merely in terms of this – so to speak scientific – classification, and the only unifying concept is that of nature, which equally carries no implication of essential unity.[75] Coleridge's most important attempt to classify natural phenomena – the *Theory of Life*, begun in 1816 – follows this Aristotelian model in connecting the varieties of organic life with objects traditionally regarded as inanimate, though as in Plotinus and other Neoplatonic thinkers, this hierarchical conception is combined with a theory of the upward progression of nature towards its divine source.[76] In common with the *Naturphilosophen*, however, Coleridge links this Neoplatonic conception with contemporary scientific theories of the development of higher life forms out of the lower, though his simultaneous commitment to a Christian concept of the soul makes the inclusion of humanity in this process enduringly problematic. His interest in such theories, I will argue, chiefly arises from an attempt to combine Schelling's emphasis on a progression from the lowest to the highest form of consciousness with a system of nature expressing the same values. Though Schelling described outward phenomena in general as belonging to a lower form of consciousness than philosophy or artistic creation, that is, the evidence of hierarchical patterns and evolutionary processes within nature itself seems also to have held a considerable fascination for Coleridge, and to have demanded some reconciliation of scientific with idealist viewpoints.

Hence his repeated suggestion that the inanimate objects which, according to Schelling, arise from a productive process sharing the same origin as his conscious interpretation of them might in some sense be animated in the same way as the more obviously 'living' elements of nature and human consciousness. Coleridge's articulations of this theory borrow from numerous sources, ranging from Aristotle and the Neoplatonists to the *Naturphilosophen* Steffens and Oken, as well as Schelling's own speculations on the origin and significance of natural phenomena. Several features which persistently characterize his evolutionary schemas, however, were prominent in his thinking before he read the *Naturphilosophen*, or indeed Schelling's *System*. In particular, his emphasis on triadic hierarchies of powers or modes of being connects those aspects of his work which clearly derive from contemporary science with others whose sources are far more ancient.[77] His frequent references to 'reproduction', 'irritability', and 'sensibility' as the dominant 'powers' of different forms of life have numerous possible sources, including the biologist Haller in the mid-eighteenth century, as well as his German contemporaries, Steffens, Oken, and Schelling.[78] More importantly, triadic schemas derived from Neoplatonism are prominent in Coleridge's early – and repeated – categorization of life forms in terms of their position on a scale from the merely corporeal to the divinely rational. A notebook entry dating from between 1795 and 1800 is an early example of this conceptuality:

> Brutal Life—in which we pursue mere corporeal pleasures & interests—
> Human Life—in which for the sake of our own Happiness ... & Glory we pursue studies and objects adapted to our intellectual faculties.
> Divine Life—when we die to the creatures & to self and become deiform by following the eternal Laws of order from the pure Love of Order & God.
>
> (*CN*, 1: 256)

As in his later theories of evolution, the distinction between modes of life serves both to emphasize our moral duty and to evoke a continuous upward progression in which we participate by fulfilling that duty. A similar conception is prominent in Plotinus, whose description of the 'three planes on which a man may live' also emphasizes our ability to choose between physical, rational, and god-like forms of existence.[79] The exclusivity which Coleridge sometimes attaches to these categories is problematic, and his later reference to the 'paramount ... highest and especial Power' of each class of organic life-forms implicitly recognizes the importance of reconciling such categorization with the continuous presence of organic forces in human as in animal existence.[80] The highest category in this instance – that of a 'Divine Life' available to human beings through their loving acquiescence in the 'eternal laws' of God's creation – however, not only resembles Plotinus's description of a god-like mode of life which is superior to the merely rational, but also recalls Priestley's theory that faith in the pefection of God's design can bring us 'a kind of *union with God* himself'.[81]

Despite his frequent emphasis on intellectual progress, therefore, Coleridge's conception of the highest form of life attaches the greatest value to a knowledge which is superior to the intellectual, thus resembling his later celebrations of the mysterious power of *logos*, one of whose central characteristics is its capacity to unite the human with the divine.[82] In the above passage, indeed, he seems in somewhat pedagogic fashion to restrict the realm of intellect appropriate to humanity, suggesting that we should pursue studies 'adapted to our intellectual faculties', until by faith and love we merge with the divine. Rationality and a transcendence of the bodily, however, are – he suggests – what separates human beings from a merely 'brutal' existence, though the latter will remain the condition of those who have not lived up to their potential.[83] A similar conception occurs in a *Table Talk* entry from 1830. 'If a man is not tending upwards to be an Angel', Coleridge is reported as saying, 'depend upon it, he is tending downwards to be a Devil'.[84] Not to be participating in the great ascent for which we were created, he implies, entails being worse than the 'beasts' to which we believe ourselves superior.[85] Such passages are unusual in making human life not only the central focus, but also the compass of the evolutionary process they describe, and emphasize the values on which Coleridge's wider evolutionary theory is based. A more orthodox version of this distinction occurs in *On the Constitution of the Church and State*, where he asserts (attributing the remark to St Augustine) that 'there neither are nor can be but three essential differences of Being, viz. the Absolute, the Rational Finite, and the Finite irrational; i.e. God, Man, and Brute!'[86] Despite his repeated suggestion of a continuous progression linking lower with higher forms of life – partly through the moral choices of the individual – therefore, Coleridge in 1829–30 emphatically rejects any blurring of the divisions between the three classes of being which he envisages. That the sharpness of his moral distinction in this passage so closely resembles that in his notebook entry of the 1790s, indeed, is among the clearest indications of continuity in his aesthetic and moral vision.[87]

Between these two extremes of his career, however, Coleridge developed a concept of evolution which combined the projects of intellectual development and moral improvement with a natural history derived from the triadic theories of organic development propounded by the *Naturphilosophen*. The two parts of Coleridge's system are unified by a single set of values, among which the rationality and freedom celebrated both by empiricist and by idealist thinkers are particularly prominent. Human beings, Coleridge argues, are unique in possessing the ability either to will the good or to remain subservient to a merely organic existence, pursuing – as his notebook puts it – 'mere corporeal pleasures & interests'. Superficially, this dualistic conception of humanity resembles Aristotle's distinction between the rational and irrational souls, and recommends a similar ethic of self-governance.[88] By the manner in which they use, or do not use, their intellectual and moral faculties, Coleridge suggests, human beings can choose whether or not to constitute the link from organic to spiritual existences. This moral aspect of his theory, however, does not explain how reason – which brings with it the freedom to determine the course of our lives – can arise out of matter. His suggestion, in a notebook entry of 1805, that varying degrees of memory may explain the more obvious differences between human beings and 'lower' animals, ironically recalls numerous eighteenth-century empiricists' efforts to explain how consciousness arises. 'The different gradations in which the Past or Memory in the power of Imagination modifies the Present Impression', Coleridge writes, 'appear to me a good ground-work for a Theory concerning the Understanding & Souls of Brutes, and their relation to that of man—' (*CN*, 2: 2555). Such theories clearly conflict with the anti-empiricism which predominates in Coleridge's thought after 1800. This passage, indeed, recalls Hartley's theory of the gradual improvement of human beings through their accumulation of associations: the will is absent, and what changes 'brutes' into 'men' seems to be little more than an involuntary increase, through the action of time, in the intellectuality of our ideas. Like Hartley, Coleridge is attempting to explain away the more radical difference he continued to assert, and which any evolutionary theory – like any theory of association – needed to account for, though neither was capable of doing so. Later in the same entry, he reaffirms the importance of 'that chasm, which Reason requires for self-esteem, and sense of distinct difference of kind', and notes 'the bad effects on the moral and intellectual character of the belief of mere difference of degree' (ibid.). [89] These were his predominant sentiments; yet at the same time, his preoccupation with human improvement, arising from the experiential value of philosophy, expressed itself in an evolutionary conception conflicting both with Christianity and with Schellingian idealism.

So great a force, indeed, do these metaphors of intellectual progress and spiritual liberation seem to have held for Coleridge that he persistently seeks – and fails – to reconcile evolution with the 'chasm' between instinct and reason. An important instance of this effort occurs in *Aids to Reflection*, where he describes a progression from protozoa, which 'have neither brain nor nerves' to that 'free will' which combats the forces of automatism. In contrast with Locke, he distinguishes free will from the mere ability to choose, including within the former concept the possession of an internal 'law' to which we may or may not conform.[90] By its very nature, however, such a will is not explicable within the evolutionary sequence which Coleridge is describing. If it could be a consequence of biology, it would belong to the deterministic starting-point of the series, rather than to its liberated conclusion. The two extremes are connected purely by the fact that one follows another, or in Coleridge's terms, by God's design:

> The lowest class of Animals or Protozoa, the Polypi for instance, have neither brain nor nerves. Their motive powers are all from without ... As life ascends, nerves appear; but still only as the conductors of an *external* Influence; next are seen the knots or Ganglions, as so many Foci of *instinctive* agency, that imperfectly imitate the yet wanting *Center*. And now the Promise and Token of a true Individuality are disclosed; both the Reservoir of Sensibility and the imitative power that actuates the Organs of Motion (the Muscles) with the net-work of conductors, are all taken inward and appropriated; the Spontaneous rises into the Voluntary, and finally after various steps and a long Ascent, the Material and Animal Means and Conditions are prepared for the manifestation of a Free Will, having its Law within itself and its motive in the Law—and thus bound to originate its own Acts, not only without but even against alien Stimulants.
>
> (*AR*, 97–8)[91]

The twin triads of organisms and their 'vital powers' which Coleridge found in the *Naturphilosophen* play a prominent role in this passage, forming the first three stages of nature's development. The protozoa, lacking even nerves, merely reproduce, corresponding to the 'glandulo-venous' system in an analogous hierarchy which Coleridge borrowed from Steffens.[92] These are followed by organisms possessing 'conductors of an external influence', or in other words, 'irritability', corresponding to the 'Musculo-arterial' systems in Steffens's hierarchy.[93] The third group of organisms, however – those characterized by sensibility – are here divided into two subclasses – those which only possess 'knots or ganglions, as so many *foci* of instinctive agency', and those in which sensation is centralized in something resembling a brain. Coleridge's text is notably obscure, however, with regard to the intermediate stages between 'knots or ganglions' and the voluntary determination of our actions. Freedom seems to be somehow born out of the appropriation and taking-inward of the 'reservoir of sensibility', the 'imitative power that actuates the organs of motion' and 'the network of conductors', yet how this process occurs is not explained. Suddenly, we have reached the upper limit, and protozoa have been replaced by self-determining beings.

The individuality which Coleridge celebrates in this passage, however, is necessary both to the concept of freedom and to that self-consciousness which plays so central a role in Schelling's idealism. Like self-reflection, willing is impossible except for an individual, and hence the process of 'individuation' becomes an important principle in the ascent towards freedom and rationality. Whereas, in organic terms, individuality is an absolute, and a condition of rationality and freedom, however, Coleridge's concept of individuation chiefly concerns the greater or lesser degrees to which human beings demonstrate individual freedom rather than merely following the dictates of convention and physical existence. Individuality and freedom, that is, are metaphorically asssociated with each other, as two aspects of our gradual emergence from the merely instinctual condition of animals. In our present state, he continues, 'we have only the Dawning of this inward Sun (the perfect Law of Liberty)' (ibid.) – a statement clearly restricting such freedom to the class of beings which begins with man.

In the *Theory of Life*, however, Coleridge makes individuation the sole principle of nature's upward progression. All forms of life and matter, he suggests, are linked and distinguished by the degrees to which they possess individuality.[94] In his introduction to the first edition, Watson argues that Coleridge was the earliest thinker – at least in Britain – to maintain that not only animals and plants, but even 'rocks and mountains, nay, "the great globe itself", share with mankind the gift of Life'.[95] To Watson, this indiscriminate use of the term was problematic. There are, he asserted, 'well known ... uses of the word "Life," to which Mr. Coleridge's speculations, as contained in the accompanying pages, are wholly inapplicable'. His examples are the eternal life of the soul – to which, he says, 'Mr. Coleridge's views of magnetism, electricity, &c., can hardly be thought applicable' – and the 'spiritual sense' of 'life' involved in such expressions as 'I am the resurrection and the *life*'.[96] In saying this, however, Watson neglects the complex structure of Coleridge's concept, which neither excludes eternal life nor attributes it to phenomena in isolation from each other, but rather concerns the unity of all phenomena as progressive transformations of a single shaping force. Though not a Christian concept, Coleridge's 'life' entails both the gradual elevation of being to a supremely spiritual existence, and the eternity of that being, which moves in a circular trajectory, originating in God and returning towards Him.[97]

Plotinus seems to be Coleridge's ultimate source for this conception. As Inge writes, Plotinus's theory that nature arises as a series of 'emanations' from the divine spirit is accompanied by the Aristotelian view that 'Every natural thing ... in its own way longs for the Divine and desires to share in the Divine life as far as it can.'[98] Hence the 'eternal systole and diastole' in which, according to Plotinus, the life of the universe consists:

> The perfect and unchangeable life of the Divine Spirit overflows in an incessant stream of creative activity, which spends itself only when it has reached the lowest confines of being ... And by the side of this outward flow of creative energy there is another current which carries all the creatures back toward the source of their being. It is this centripetal movement that directs the active life of all creatures endowed with Soul. They were created and sent into the world that they might be moulded a little nearer to the Divine image by yearning for the home which they have left.[99]

As Levere points out, the influence of this Neoplatonic theory is also evident in Steffens, from whom Coleridge borrowed extensively in the *Theory of Life*. The notion of a hierarchy of powers – reproduction, irritability, and sensibility – by which Steffens explained the diversity of organisms, moreover, is also prominent in this work, while Coleridge's unification of organic and inorganic nature makes use of Steffens's speculations on the history of geological formations.[100] The *Theory of Life* can thus be described as a Plotinian theory of evolution, borrowing from contemporary scientific theories, but characterizing both inorganic and organic existences as transformations of a single energy and participants in a single trajectory. According to Potter, Coleridge's reworking of this ancient cosmology arose from his inability to reconcile evolution itself with 'the religious doctrines of man's fall and redemption'. Since he could not accept that the highest forms of life actually developed out of the lower, he writes, Coleridge

> ... tried to explain the spirit of the very idea he would not accept, by supposing that an abstract 'Nature' developed and grew in its production of new and increasingly higher forms of life, but that these forms did not grow or develop from each other.[101]

As Potter suggests, Coleridge's theory combines a vision of the increasingly spiritual nature of earthly existences with the view that they originate in the highest, rather than the lowest form of being. He is wrong, however, in suggesting that 'an abstract "Nature"' is what develops and grows in Coleridge's system. Watson notes that Coleridge's frequent personifications of nature in the *Theory* seem to attribute to it an independence which, as 'a pious Christian', he could not have believed in.[102] One is tempted to say that life, rather than nature, is what Coleridge envisages as eternally progressing; yet this would be equally incorrect, since Coleridge's 'life' rather denotes the progression which both is and entails all things, than any subject of these transformations. The mistake of Coleridge's interpreters, therefore, is to have envisaged a Spinozistic 'substance' as grounding the transformations he describes: his system is distinctive in making its teleology the substance of its cosmology.

It is, indeed, the very absence of an independent 'substance' in Coleridge's system which leads to its central paradox. All things are one, he suggests, not because they are different forms of a single essence, but because they are all stages in a single progression. This progression, however, is a process of individuation – that is, a progressive detachment of the individual from the intrinsic unity of phenomena. 'Life' means an upward movement, the progressiveness which links phenomena; yet only by the increasing separation of its individual parts from this progression can any development or growth occur.[103] 'In the lowest forms of the vegetable and animal world', Coleridge writes,

> ... we perceive totality dawning into *individuation*, while in man, as the highest of the class, the individuality is not only perfected in its corporeal sense, but begins a new series beyond the appropriate limits of physiology. The tendency to individuation, more or less obscure, more or less obvious, constitutes the common character of all classes, as far as they maintain for themselves a distinction from the universal life of the planet; while the degrees, both of intensity and extension, to which this tendency is realized, form the species, and their ranks in the great scale of ascent and expansion.
>
> (*SWF*, 1: 516)

Individuation, which both *is* distinction from others and distinguishes the higher from the lower forms of being, thus also constitutes the unity of phenomena, the 'life' which is 'the common character of all classes'. By detaching ourselves from this 'universal life of the planet', we also become part of it, which appears to be a contradiction.[104] This paradox, however, is substantially resolved by Coleridge's definition of life as 'the *tendency* to *individuation*': the varieties of being are unified, not just by active individuation, but also by their potential (which is really the world's, or the universe's potential) for this process.[105] Hence by converting potential into action, beings at once depart from an original unity, and participate in the temporal unity of process. By this ruse, Coleridge manages to combine identity with difference, or in other words to maintain the independence of humanity from lower life forms while affirming our participation in a tendency shared with rocks and plants. We are different in that we are more independent, yet we are the same in that we have the tendency to become more so.[106] This still implies, however, that human beings have arisen from a certain unity with rocks and plants. Coleridge cannot radically distinguish them while he retains the idea of this common tendency; but he cannot describe them as participating in a single process if detachment from that process is its principle. He is caught in a similar paradox to that involved in Hartley's attempt to derive free will from physical processes. Coleridge, that is, wishes to be at once a monist and a dualist, yet in failing to do so, nevertheless produces a system of remarkable subtlety.

One factor above all prevented him from espousing a purely monistic system – namely the Christian tenet that human beings are unique in possessing a soul, which derives directly from God, and hence cannot have precursors or be part of an evolutionary series. It cannot, for example, just be the locus of a greater freedom or individuality than is accorded to animals, or the result of a more prolonged striving for individuality. Rather, its existence manifests a directly contrary movement to that of evolution or the development of life – a downward rather than an upward movement, yet one which does not participate in God's original creation of the upwardly-aspiring universe. The radical distinction between spiritual and earthly existences maintained by Christianity was not the only source of Coleridge's dualism: his faith in human freedom, and resistance to the deterministic theories of empiricism, were similarly powerful ones. In the *Theory of Life*, however, the Christian concept of the soul becomes the dominant focus of Coleridge's resistance to a monistic vision. Radical distinction – the specially inbreathed soul of man – was incompatible with any form of unity between human beings and lower life forms. Hence the only solution to his dilemma was an appeal to ultimate mysteries. 'In what manner this evident interspace is reconciled with the equally evident continuity of the life of Nature', he writes,

> ... is a problem that can be solved by those minds alone, which have intuitively learnt that the whole *actual* life of Nature originates in the existence, and consists in the perpetual reconciliation, and as perpetual resurgency of the primary contradiction, of which universal polarity is the result and the exponent.
>
> (*SWF*, 1: 537)

In *Aids to Reflection*, the dependence of this mystery of 'polarity' on the contradictory nature of Coleridge's intellectual aims is unambiguously evident. Instead of saying that there is a continuous upward progression in nature, yet that we cannot intellectually bridge the gulf between human beings and lower animals, Coleridge presents the ideas of the developmental unity of life and the uniquely human soul in immediate succession, leaving his readers to interpret the contradiction. 'Life is the one universal soul', he writes,

> ... which, by virtue of the enlivening BREATH, and the informing WORD, all organized bodies have in common, each *after its*

> *kind* ... But, in addition to this, God transfused into man a higher gift, and specially imbreathed:—even a living (that is, self-subsisting) soul, a soul having its life in itself.
>
> (*AR*, 15)

The contradiction between a principle of evolution – or the generation of the higher out of the lower forms of life – and the concept of a self-subsisting soul, remained a central problem of Coleridge's thought until the end of his life. Yet it is often difficult to distinguish the effect of Christian belief on his idea of evolution from the effect of idealism *per se*, or an opposition to the view that consciousness and intelligence are explicable as the results of material processes. In both cases, something is held not to be explicable within the structure of evolution, whether it is the mere fact of consciousness or the eternal soul of man. As I have suggested, these two ideas act together to prevent Coleridge from subscribing either to a simple evolutionary schema or to a Neoplatonic circle in which God merely originates the upward progression of being. The soul, effectively, must pre-exist its own emergence in the generative scale of nature, and it can only do so by being akin to God, the source of what it consummates.

As we have seen, it was in Schelling's *System of Transcendental Idealism* that Coleridge found the best model for such a unification of self-subsistence with an evolutionary process. Schellingian evolution, however, does not concern the scale of nature, but only the development of mind.[107] Moreover, there is no room in his *System* for any form of deity, let alone for a Christian concept of the soul. Coleridge's interest in Schelling centres on his explanation of nature as one stage in a developing self-consciousness, rather than on any reconciliation of Christianity with an evolving universe. Mind is at once the origin of a nature contrasted with the self, and – in its recognition of this fact – the consummation of a single process of development. As we have seen, Coleridge rejected Schelling's *System* after he had plagiarized from it, yet the same conception of mind as both the source and the summit of evolution can be found even in Coleridge's latest writings.

In his last major work, *On the Constitution of the Church and State*, he attempted to combine the idea of evolution with that of the soul's priority to any generative process by distinguishing evolution in the conventional sense (that is, a continuous upward progression from one form of being to another) from the idea of potentiality, or the latency of the highest form of being in the lowest. This alternative evolutionary concept enabled him to argue that though each higher form of life 'implies a lower, as the condition of its actual *existence*', yet the lower, or the origins of human reason and intelligence, would themselves be inconceivable in the absence of the highest, which is their destination.[108] The same, he suggests, holds true of the 'powers' which the various classes of natural phenomena are held to possess. The power of 'growth' (to which plants are restricted), for example, could not be lower than that of locomotion (or 'irritability'), unless the destiny of the former were to precede the latter. In the same way, irritability would not be lower than sensibility unless the latter were born out of it, as the next step in the ascending scale of nature. Thus,

> ... in the *idea* of each power the lower derives its *intelligibility* from the higher: and the highest must be presumed to inhere latently or potentially in the lowest, or this latter will be wholly unintelligible, inconceivable—you can have *no conception* of it.
> (*C&S*, 179)[109]

Though an obvious truth about the *idea* of evolutionary stages, this does not explain how the highest can be at once distinct from and continuous with the lowest. Coleridge uses the concepts of generation and conception to construct a circle in which evolution depends on the idea of a completed series. According to this theory, the soul, or that which has the power of comprehending its origin, is both born out of the lower life forms or powers and the condition of their possibility. *As* lower, of course, they do depend on the idea of their destination. Yet Coleridge takes this conceptual dependence as implying the actual dependence of the evolutionary series on a pre-existent intellect or conception. In other words, some design or teleology analogous to his own conception of nature must, according to Coleridge, be presumed to inhere latently or potentially in the precursors of human intelligence. As in the *Theory of Life*, therefore, the teleology of his conception stands in for an explanation of the system he is describing. Nature *is* its progression, and could not be so unless its highest form – that of the philosophic soul which comprehends this process – somehow preceded all of its developments.

This is not to say, however, that Coleridge represents his own insight as actually preceding nature's development. Though the lowest stage of evolution is dependent on the highest, God is still the origin of the series, the source of that teleology which is inherent in nature. Clearly, Coleridge cannot resolve the conflict of unity and diversity unless the human soul is itself the source of evolution, producing both external nature and the explanation of it. Such a theory was often attractive to him; yet in much of his later work it is replaced by a combination of evolution with God's special intervention in creating the human soul. Within human beings, the progress of nature is continued by the progressive 'irradiation' of the understanding by the reason. Thus humanity is both at one with the divine, and at the same time striving upwards, like the rest of nature, to achieve that unity. According to a letter of 1821 from Coleridge to C. A. Tulk,

> ... vital or zoo-organic Power, Instinct, and Understanding fall all three under the same definition *in genere*, and the very additions by which the definition is applied from the first to the second, and from the second to the third, are themselves expressive of degrees only...
>
> (*CL*, 5: 137)

In Reason, on the other hand, 'there is and can be no *degree*. Deus introit aut non introit'. Moreover, 'in Reason there are no *means* nor ends: Reason itself being one with the ultimate end, of which it is the manifestation' (ibid.). Most importantly, however,

> From the Understanding to the Reason there is no continuous *ascent* possible, it is a metabasis εἰς ἄλλο γένος, even as from the air to the Light. The true essential peculiarity of the Human Understanding consists in it's capability of being irradiated by the reason—in it's recipiency—& even this is *given* to it by the presence of a higher power than itself.
>
> (*CL*, 5: 138)

This final twist, in which reason's unbridgeable superiority to understanding is reabsorbed within the divine programme, reaffirms Coleridge's desire to have unity as well as diversity, and never to allow one aspect of his philosophy to exclude the other. Monism and dualism had to coexist; and though they could not do so, this repeated dialectical turning and re-turning makes the closest possible approximation to their simultaneity.

6

The Limits of Expression: Language, Consciousness, and the Sublime

Coleridge's repeated evocation of analogies between human consciousness or creativity and aspects of the divine is among the most distinctive and problematic aspects of his work. As early as 1796, Charles Lamb wrote to him – perhaps in response to 'The Eolian Harp', first published earlier that year – 'You seem to have been straining your comparing faculties to bring together things infinitely distinct and unlike; the feeble narrow-sphered operations of the human intellect and the everywhere diffused mind of Deity, the peerless wisdom of Jehovah.'[1] Such tendencies, however, are by no means chiefly characteristic of Coleridge's earlier work. As several recent studies have shown, attempts to mediate between human and divine are of central importance to the reflections on Reason, *logos*, and the Trinity which become increasingly prevalent in his later notebooks and marginalia.[2] That these ideas have an important devotional function – simultaneously expressing his reverence for the mysterious reconciliation of opposites which they evoke, and seeking to justify the insights he claims to derive from this unity – is evident not only from their obvious dependence on faith or intuition, but also from their occasional adjacency to descriptions of his desperate quest for release and redemption from the suffering and guilt associated with his addiction to opium.[3] As these devotional concerns become more central, however, so the vivid and dynamic analogies between the energy or creativity of consciousness, of nature, and of the divine which characterize many of his earlier writings are increasingly replaced by mediations of a far more abstract and theoretical kind. Whether – as Reid and Perkins suggest – Coleridge's late reflections on the nature and functions of *logos* represent his major contribution to philosophical and religious thought depends primarily on how much historical importance we attach to such symbolic resolutions of philosophically insoluble problems.[4] One of my arguments in this chapter will be that unless one shares his devotional commitment, their interest must lie primarily in the circular process by which – here as in his earlier writings – Coleridge strives to express an intuition which itself arises primarily from that quest for expression. Despite the increasing degree of abstraction noted above, that is, Coleridge's ideas of God and of the processes of human intellect are consistently characterized by an emphasis on their inexpressibleness which can only arise from a continual confrontation with the limits of language.

As we shall see, the question of what intuition precedes the quest for expression underlying both his early, more sensuous and dynamic analogies, and his later, more abstract and theologically acceptable ones, was of considerable interest to Coleridge himself, who continually sought to isolate the pre-linguistic essence of subjective consciousness. This distinctively Romantic quest, however, was repeatedly thwarted by the impossibility of practically unifying the objects of consciousness with the act or process of contemplating them – a problem which Schelling had particularly highlighted.[5] Whenever Coleridge attempted to describe or envisage such an essence, that is, it inevitably became an object distinct from the process of reflection, and from any description that might be given of it. In its priority to all phenomena, however, the theoretical essence of consciousness itself resembled the absolute unity of subject and object which, extending Schelling's non-theological principle, Coleridge located in God, and which he argued had its practical reflection in the assumption of self-consciousness (or of the continuity of consciousness) implied in every process of thinking.[6] As I will show, this latter analogy is of central importance to Coleridge's conception of 'Reason' or 'logos' as uniting human and divine through the act of faith which (he argued) every reflective process must therefore involve.[7] Though the energetic process of thinking gradually becomes a less prominent factor in his reflections on this activity, however, and though his quest for a self-justifying explanation of religious intuition becomes increasingly important after 1818, the dependence of these analogies on the experience of striving to objectify the origin of his ideas and language remains continually apparent.[8]

The first section of this chapter explores the ways in which both Coleridge's earlier analogies between human and divine, and the systems of symbols through which his later thought attempts to represent their relationship, reflect this process of striving to comprehend or express the origin of expression – an intrinsically contradictory exercise which can only be understood in terms of the 'religious utilitarianism' of Coleridge's thought, according to which (as Marcel observes) 'pure speculation ... is only of interest insofar as it sustains us in those hopes which alone can give value or meaning to our lives'.[9] The second section shows how the same experience of seeking to verbalize that which is defined, *a priori*, as beyond linguistic expression underlies Coleridge's theories of value in prose writing. By seeking to 'dramatize' the process of reflection in the energetic obscurities and suspensions of his prose, I argue, Coleridge not only celebrates his own attempts to articulate the inexpressible, but also seeks to involve his readers in an analogous confrontation with the infinite. As I show in the final section, however, the perplexity of contemporary readers was more often focused on the obscurity of Coleridge's writing or the impressiveness of the intellect which it evoked, than on the sublime ideas to which he explicitly sought to redirect their thoughts and emotions. However great Coleridge's own efforts to interpret the experiences of thinking and writing in terms of a higher truth connecting his own intuitions with the essence of the divine, therefore, it is to the power of his own thought, and to the perplexing force of his language, that Coleridge's greatest prose writing persistently directs us.

1. A CREATIVITY BEYOND EXPRESSION: CONSCIOUSNESS AND THE DIVINE

As we saw in Chapter 2, it was among the views of the early Coleridge that mind should not be conceived as having any existence prior to thinking, and that the view of the mind as 'containing' its ideas involved a misconception of the nature of thought and the origin of our representations. The importance he attached to these opinions is highlighted by his repeated distinctions between the act and the product of thinking. In numerous notebook entries dating from between 1801 and 1809, 'thought' is envisaged as what precedes all representations, the noumenal origin always implied but never comprehended. 'Thought', we are told in a typical recourse to etymologies, 'is the participle past of Thing' (*CN*, 3: 3587). In other words, it is not itself a 'thing' or an object of knowledge, but rather the origin of all such objects, including any description of the process of thinking.[10] 'Thought', however, is not the only term which Coleridge uses to refer to the noumenal creativity underlying phenomena. In several passages he not only contrasts 'thought' or 'thinking' with 'thoughts' or 'things', but constructs a series of oppositions which, though ostensibly between the general and the particular, implicitly attach a noumenal status to the former. Thus, in 1801, he writes:

> *A Thought* and Thoughts are quite different words from *Thought*—as a Fancy from Fancy, a Work from Work, a Life from Life, a Force & Forces from Force, a Feeling, a Writing &c ...
>
> (*CN*, 1:1077)[11]

Although, in this passage, 'fancy' is compared with 'thought' as the locus of an opposition between two senses – at once the general versus the particular, and the productive versus the product – Coleridge's principal concern is clearly neither with language nor with faculty psychology. Rather, he is indicating different terms in which the relationship between general and particular can be combined with the opposition between an active and a passive aspect. These oppositions suggest, on the one hand, a variety of contexts for the distinction between noumenon and phenomenon, and on the other, a variety of names for the polarities which Coleridge is concerned with. That 'Writing' should be one such context or name suggests that this comparison originates in the experience of thinking, and especially of the relationship between producing a text and the finished product, whose external and objective nature divorces it from the effort to fashion such an object. This experience of literary production – of the effort always failing to be represented in its outcome and objective – is metaphorized in a series of terms which *qua* general denote activities or potentialities, and *qua* particular denote representations or results. In its general sense, for example, 'Feeling' denotes the capacity for sensation or emotion, while 'Life' denotes something wholly mysterious which contains the possibility of all representations.[12]

The significance of Coleridge's distinctions between 'thought' and 'thoughts', and between 'thought' and 'things', is thus considerably extended. 'Thought', in this context, is always ambiguous, denoting on the one hand an effort or activity whose product does not seem adequately to record it, and on the other, an origin or ground which is implicit in all our thinking, yet by its very nature cannot be presented to us. Though the experience of thinking can be described in a general sense, Coleridge suggests, it is also the origin of every description, and hence can never itself be fully represented.[13] Moreover, to 'describe' thinking is impossible except in terms so general that they seem to have little to do with the specificity of subjective experience. Words, he wrote in 1817,

> ... express generalities that can be made *so* clear—they have neither the play of colors, nor the untranslatable meanings of the eye, nor any one of the thousand indescribable things that form the whole reality of the living fuel—
>
> (*CN*, 3: 4350)[14]

Strictly speaking, then, experience is beyond description. According to this passage, the opposition between experience and language shares the exclusivity of that between subject and object, or between noumenon and phenomenon. No aspect of subjective consciousness can be encapsulated in words; yet at the same time, experience is the source of all expression – a creativity which can never be grasped through its products.

The absoluteness of this opposition, as Coleridge presents it, seems to explain his occasional suggestion that experience might occur without involving, or being connected with, any object or representation. If such experience were possible, it would be analogous to that self-consciousness which – he elsewhere argues – only the deity can possess: the unrepresentable origin of representations would be experienced in itself, with no distinction between subject and object.[15] An early suggestion of the possibility of such a 'pure' experience of identity occurs in the discussion of 'identifying the Percipient and the Perceived' which – as noted in Chapter 3 – also highlights his interest in the feelings accompanying the process of reflection. 'I think of the Wall—', Coleridge writes,

> ... it is before me, a distinct Image—here. I necessarily think of the *Idea* & the Thinking I as two distinct & opposite Things. Now <let me> think of *myself*—of the thinking Being—the Idea becomes dim whatever it be—so dim that I know not what it is—but the Feeling is deep & steady—and this I call *I*...identifying the Percipient & the Perceived—.
>
> (*CN*, 1: 921)

Coleridge rarely suggests so directly that such a pure experience – the collapsing of object and subject into each other – is possible.[16]

In Schelling, as we have seen, this identity was merely described as an assumption underlying all knowledge, never as a mode of experience; and Coleridge does not explain how the act of knowing could ever become its own object.[17] His descriptions of the activity of thinking, however, persistently imply the possibility of such self-knowledge, and indeed the conviction that thought is closely related to the 'infinite I AM' – a phrase in which Coleridge specifically identifies the deity with the quality of self-knowing, or of the unity of subject and object, which also characterizes Schelling's 'Absolute'.[18] According to Wlecke, this association of human and divine in terms of productive self-consciousness arises necessarily from the structure of the Coleridgean sublime. In the sublime moment, he writes,

> ... consciousness becomes vividly aware of itself as an indefinitely dynamic agent, as possessing an intentionality in pursuit of an intended object which infinitely recedes from adequate comprehension. Sublime consciousness for Coleridge reveals itself to be, in the last analysis, sublime self-consciousness, and those ideas he designates as sublime are in fact ideas that throw the mind back toward an awareness of its own indefinite activity.[19]

The source of the 'intuition of absolute existence' at the heart of the sublime, Wlecke argues, must therefore be located in the subject. The subject 'cannot constitute itself as an individuated object of thought', and hence consciousness 'intuits its own activity as an absolute'.[20] Coleridge's descriptions of the experience of thinking tend to confirm this view, not only suggesting that an effort of thought is what engenders sublime emotion, but also that the qualities of energy, productivity, and indefinableness involved in thinking made it for him both an instance and a symbol of the noumenal productivity underlying phenomena.[21] As we have seen, Coleridge repeatedly associates thinking (in its opposition to thoughts) with such terms as 'Life', 'Force', and 'Feeling', suggesting that we can only refer to subjective experience by such 'general terms' evoking a capacity for sensation and production. What evades our description is 'the whole reality of the living fuel' – an expression in which he again attempts, and fails, to describe what precedes or underlies experience or representations. His early claim that rather than being explicable in terms of physical causes, life could only be defined as 'I myself I' similarly evokes a pure identity of subject and object existing as human consciousness.[22] This 'mere *apparition*' or 'naked Spirit', he implies, is unintelligible. Nothing can be said about it except that it occurs in and as ourselves, containing the possibility of any representations. In these and many other contexts, Coleridge celebrates the moment of pure experience – experience in itself. It was an essential stage in our intellectual development, he wrote in 1810, '*γνωσαι συν επιστημη, ως δυναμεις νοουμενας, ημαυτων τας αληθεστατας ενεργειας*' (*CN*, 3: 3941) – that is, 'to know with sure knowledge as noumenal powers our own truest energies'.[23]

Such a conception of self-knowledge, however, is doubly paradoxical, not only implying that human beings can experience that pure self-consciousness which Coleridge elsewhere describes as uniquely characteristic of God, but also describing the 'noumenal' powers underlying human consciousness and creativity as having that capacity for being intuited whose very absence is used by Kant to define the word 'noumenon'.[24] Coleridge's attempts to evoke such a pure experience of identity, indeed, persistently demonstrate the quality of paradox which he elsewhere describes as resulting from any attempt to comprehend or express ideas of Reason. The truth affirmed by the Reason, he writes in *Aids to Reflection*, 'in its own proper form ... is inconceivable'. It can only be expressed by understanding in the form of an antinomy representing 'a truth beyond conception and inexpressible', such as 'Before Abraham *was*, I *am*', or 'God is a Circle, the centre of which is every where, and circumference nowhere' (*AR*, 233).[25] Though these specific examples derive variously from the Bible and from medieval theology, the theory that an 'idea' (that is, a product of 'Reason') 'can come forth out of the moulds of the understanding only in the disguise of two contradictory conceptions' (*AR*, 233) owes much to Kant's doctrine of the antinomies of pure reason, according to which the application of space and time or the categories to things that are not experienced gives rise to mutually contradictory propositions each of which can be proved.[26] This Kantian theory, however, itself recalls the 'affirmative and negative theology' particularly associated with the medieval Neoplatonist Erigena, the chief function of which was to emphasize the inexpressible nature of the deity.[27] As Bett observes, in Erigena's system, 'the same predicate may rightly be affirmed and denied of God'. He may, for example, be described as *essentia* (the essence of all things); but because *essentia* involves the notion of a contrary (namely *nihil*), and because God, as the Absolute, is the reconciliation of contraries, he is not strictly *essentia* but *super-essentia*. Similarly, Bett adds,

> ... He is more-than-good, and more-than-goodness ... more than eternal, and more-than-eternity ... But, as Erigena sees, every one of these attempts to express the nature of God by *super-* and ὑπερ- is really a negation. To say that God is superessential is not to say what He is, but what He is not ... God is indeed beyond all words, and all thought, for He surpasses all intellect, and is better known by not knowing, and is more truly denied in all things than affirmed.[28]

Coleridge's attempts to evoke that consciousness which precedes all expression or objectification similarly highlight the extent to which it lies 'beyond all words, and all thought', and the contradictions which result from any attempt to describe it.[29] The terms by which he refers to this experience, indeed, themselves fall into two categories: on the one hand those denoting a subjectivity which has merely not attained to any distinct image or conception – into this class falls the term 'feeling', as well as the 'I myself I' of his early attempt to equate 'life' with self-consciousness – and on the other hand those denoting the incomprehensible origin of knowledge or experience – into this class fall such terms as 'life', 'spirit', and 'being'. As his repeated attempts to combine these two sets of terms and ideas reveal, it is impossible to refer to something which is both subject and object without using such apparently incompatible expressions.[30] 'Fancy' was the name he often gave to the source of language's perpetual reification of the insights of imagination or reason.[31] This 'image-forming or rather re-forming power', he wrote in 1811,

> ... may not inaptly be compared to the Gorgon Head, which *looked* death into every thing—and this not by accident, but from the nature of the faculty itself, the province of which is to give consciousness to the Subject by presenting to it its conceptions *objectively* but the Soul differences itself from any other Soul for the purposes of symbolical knowledge by *form* or body only—but all form as body, i.e. as shape, & not as forma efformans, is dead—Life may be *inferred*, even as intelligence is from black

marks on white paper—but the black marks themselves *are truly 'the dead letter'*.

(*CN*, 3: 4066)[32]

This passage reveals clearly how any attempt to escape from dualism is thwarted by the very act of verbalization. Firstly, Coleridge isolates 'fancy' as the cause of this dualistic tendency – that is, of the impossibility of conceiving of any consciousness which does not depend on the existence of a subject and an object. Even the idea of the soul depends on this distinction – is the concept of that which receives impressions, rather than of that priority to impressions which he evokes in the terms 'feeling', 'life', and so on. To the extent that we seek to objectify it, he suggests, each soul possesses the characteristics of its individual 'contents' – is entirely a *thing in relation* to phenomena. By referring to it, we always imply the existence of something we cannot refer to – a noumenal productivity to which he characteristically gives the name 'Life'.[33] Since all objective knowledge belongs to the realm of understanding or fancy, however, even this conception can never express what it seeks to refer to, but can only gesture towards an unnameable 'other'.

Though sensing the possibility of a pure experience prior to all representations and the concept of a subject, therefore, Coleridge also recognized the impossibility of incorporating this intuition into a systematic philosophy. Every attempt at description, he suggested, would necessarily result in misrepresentation – a view which not only enabled him to avoid explaining the precise relationships between human and divine consciousness or creativity (always a theologically dangerous issue), but also provided a justification for his pursuit of the sublime emotions which resulted from continually attempting to 'go beyond' whatever could be stated or understood.[34] Yet though no fixed or stable description of these relationships was possible, Coleridge increasingly made use of symbolic conceptions invoking relationships which they could not explain. His view of thinking as itself a form of noumenal origin, indeed, is clearly reflected in his conception of 'Reason' as both human and divine. By understanding or fancy, he argues, we are limited to dualistic conceptions of the universe; yet through our Reason, which grounds the operation of the faculties concerned with phenomena, we can intuit that unity of self and other which is only perfectly achieved in the 'self-comprehending Being' of God.[35]

A note which he added to *The Statesman's Manual* in 1827 contains the clearest expression of his distinction between finite and infinite reason. The term 'Reason', he writes,

> ...may or rather must be used in two different yet correlative senses, which are nevertheless in some measure reunited by a third. In its highest sense, and which is the ground and source of the rest, reason is being, the Supreme Being contemplated objectively, and in abstraction from the personality...
>
> The second sense comes when we speak of ourselves as possessing reason; and this we can no otherwise define than as the capability with which God has endowed man of beholding, or being conscious of, the divine light. But this very capability is itself that light, not as the divine light, but as the life or indwelling of the living Word, which is our light...
>
> (*LS* 68n)[36]

The system of ideas expressed in this passage enables us to understand Coleridge's seemingly eccentric statement that Reason 'without being either the SENSE, the UNDERSTANDING or the IMAGINATION contains all three within itself, even as the mind contains its thoughts, and is present in and through them all' (*LS*, 69–70). Since in its highest sense Reason is the supreme being, Reason is also the condition of knowledge – that identity of subject and object which is implied by phenomena as their ground.[37] In describing the relationship between finite and infinite Reason, however, Coleridge does not distinguish between the assumption of self-consciousness which both he and Schelling claim is indispensable to any act of reflection, and that 'absolute identity' in which (according to Schelling) all conscious and unconscious production originates.[38] Insofar as human reason is an 'indwelling' of the deity, he implies, the assumption of self-consciousness involved in reasoning is far from accidental, itself implying the presence of the divine Reason in ourselves.[39] At the same time, however, this 'indwelling of the living Word' (or *logos*) is described as facilitating the intuition of ultimate being which Coleridge most often associates with 'Reason'. This passage, indeed, demonstrates clearly how Coleridge's combination of Kantian, Schellingian, and biblical language and ideas makes these diverse religious and philosophical conceptions almost as interchangeable as the terms by which he refers to them. However well-defined each of these conceptions of

'Reason' or *logos* may be, indeed, such passages can leave little doubt that – as Perkins notes – Coleridge's *logos* primarily represents an idealized mediation 'not only between idealism and atomistic materialism, but between all oppositions which had been misinterpreted as contradictions, or as mutually exclusive'.[40]

In a letter to Humphry Davy of 1809 describing the insights achieved in one of his lectures, indeed, Coleridge not only evokes a similarly heterogeneous conception of finite and infinite Reason, but implicitly connects it with the more dynamically-conceived analogies between human and divine creativity which characterize his earlier writing. The lecture, he writes,

> ... furnished to my Understanding & Conscience proofs more convincing, than the dim Analogies of natural organization to human Mechanism, both of the Supreme Reason as superessential to the World of the Senses; of an analogous Mind in Man not resulting from it's perishable Machine, nor even from the general Spirit of Life, it's inclosed steam or perfluent water-force; and of the moral connection between the finite and the infinite Reason, and the aweful majesty of the former as both the Revelation and the exponent Voice of the Latter, immortal Time-piece [of] an eternal Sun.
> (*CL*, 3: 172)[41]

Though Reason is not to be equated with any natural force or phenomenon, therefore, Coleridge in 1809 preserves the physical emphasis of his earlier 'one Life' conception sufficiently to describe the 'Supreme Reason' as a noumenal force underlying the natural energies which more perceptibly animate the physical world. As noted above, the dynamic analogies through which his earlier works connect the feeling of thinking with the creativity of God become less widespread after 1818. Even his later attempts to resolve the dichotomy of human and divine through a heterodox combination of Trinitarianism and triadic logic, however, implicitly preserve the emphasis on a noumenal productivity underlying phenomena which originates in Coleridge's attempts to objectify the process of his own reflection.

That this pursuit of an ever-elusive priority to phenomena consists primarily in an attempt to give verbal and logical expression to that indescribable 'force' or '*je-ne-scai-quoi*' which Hume described as accompanying the mind's own motions – motions which, paradoxically, themselves arise from a similar effort of expression[42] – is evident not only from Coleridge's repeated emphasis on the impossibility of expressing the 'feeling' or 'living fuel' of intellectual activity, but also from his description of these very failures of language as the best means of communicating an intuition of the infinite. These celebrations of paradox and obscurity, however, highlight an interest in the power of language to dramatize the process of thinking which is also prominent in Coleridge's discussions of prose style more generally. As I will show in the second part of this chapter, these discussions focus not only on the theme of liminality or the limits of language, but also on the necessity of habituating ourselves to the effort involved in a precise logical articulation of ideas, in order to awaken that sensation of thinking which was at once Coleridge's chief source of liberation from everyday dissatisfactions, and his principal model for the energetic creativity underlying phenomena. The importance of such a strenuous engagement with the structures of language, both in order to produce such sensations, and as a means of involving his readers in analogous mental processes (while also evoking the power of his own thought), I argue, is among the principal reasons why the works which Coleridge published after 1802 are predominantly in prose, despite his substantial body of later verse. Spontaneous expressions of emotion, that is, are largely replaced in his later work by effortful attempts to articulate those ideas which most resist expression, and which thus engender the most liberating feelings of his own creative power and indefinable transcendence.

2. THE LETTER AND THE SPIRIT: COLERIDGE AND THE METAPHYSICS OF PROSE

As several critics have noted, Coleridge often claimed that the value of a text was at least partly dependent on the degree to which it tested the reader, firstly because of the intrinsic value of intellectual exercise, and secondly because what was easily understood would not be remembered, and hence could achieve no valuable communication.[43] His own prose style, he claimed, was modelled on the syntactic structures of the ancient Greek and Latin literatures, and on the styles of those English Renaissance writers who imitated the same classical ideals.[44] He contrasted this style with that of popular English writers in his own period, who he claimed were influenced chiefly by the writings of modern French authors.[45]

Classical languages, he argued, are intrinsically complex in their syntax: one cannot use them (at least, cannot write in them) without composing sentences which are long, and in which the individual clauses are subordinated to an overarching structure.[46] Modern languages, on the other hand, tend naturally towards conciseness: they discourage the complexity and subordination of the Greek or Latin sentence.[47] Because of these differences, Coleridge argues, classical languages demand a greater degree of thought from their writers and readers than do modern languages. If one were equally well acquainted with Greek and English, he implies, one would always be more intellectually exercised by writing in Greek; and by the same token, a text written in standard English would always (to the same purely bilingual individual) be more easily understood.[48] He cannot say that modern languages are always less complex, because his own style is claimed to be an imitation of the greater natural complexity of classical languages. The varying degrees of syntactical complexity in the Greek and Latin literatures, however, are hardly ever mentioned by Coleridge.[49] Rather, he describes the classical languages as ideals, attributing to them a degree of difficulty, thoughtfulness, and syntactic richness which has rarely been achieved in English. There is a similar problem in his notion of what constitutes 'good' English: according to his description of them, classical languages seem virtually to entail their correct usage. There is no bad Greek: it is always on a relatively high intellectual plane. English, however, can only be used well when it is used unnaturally, or when we distort the structures towards which it naturally tends.[50]

Before discussing the ways in which these views relate to Coleridge's wider philosophy, it is important to note that most of them can be found in Monboddo's *Of the Origin and Progress of Language*, published in six volumes from 1773–92. Monboddo also finds an intrinsic excellence in ancient Greek, combined with a gradual degeneration of European languages in all later periods. The greater inflectedness of Greek, he argues, makes it naturally more continuous and periodic than modern languages – a superiority which Latin shares, though in certain respects falling short of the Greek excellence.[51] Because it must be apprehended 'altogether or not at all', the meaning of a Greek sentence 'comes upon the mind more close and embodied, as it were, and consequently more forcibly than when broken down, and frittered into small pieces' (*Monboddo*, 4:60–1). The force of this style is increased by the fact 'that it keeps the sense suspended, perhaps for some considerable time ... for by the suspense it makes a greater impression than it would otherwise do' (*Monboddo*, 6: 231). According to Monboddo, the northern languages – and especially English – tend towards the opposite of this Greek ideal, being composed 'almost altogether of hard inflexible words, monosyllables for the greater part ... unskilfully tacked together by ill-favoured particles constantly recurring' (*Monboddo*, 2: 422). The style natural to these languages, moreover, 'has a bad effect upon the readers or hearers; for it weakens their comprehension, by accustoming them to take in the sense only in small parcels, and broken down as it were into pap to feed children' (*Monboddo*, 4: 239–40). In these languages also, however, good writing is possible, and it is to be achieved principally by imitation of Greek models, thus following the example of the best Roman authors, such as Cicero, whose style was formed 'by translating from Demosthenes, Plato, and Xenophon' (*Monboddo*, 6: 174–5). Like Coleridge, Monboddo finds the best English stylists 'about the time of the restoration', naming Hooker and especially Milton as examples of those who most successfully imitated 'the great and genuine classics' (*Monboddo*, 3: 247).[52] The Romans, however, have also provided bad examples for modern writers: Seneca, Sallust, and especially Tacitus are criticized for their 'unconnected', epigrammatic composition, though – Monboddo says – the style derived from it in contemporary English writing is even worse (*Monboddo*, 4: 133).[53] English needs a periodic style to combat its tendency towards fragmentation and uniformity. Hence through imitation of the 'broken, disjointed composition' of Tacitus, English falls below even his mean example (*Monboddo*, 4: 132–4). In contemporary writers, however, we find not only these disadvantages, but also the affectations of 'wit' and 'point' derived from the reading of French authors.[54] French style, Monboddo says, has 'debauched the taste of many of our writers, and made them reject the grave, sober, and sensible style of the great ancient masters' (*Monboddo*, 3: 398).[55] The modern debauchery of French and English style, moreover, is essentially connected with the levity of its content, which is 'atheistical', consisting of 'random incoherent thoughts thrown out upon the subject of morals or politics, without any real knowledge of human nature, and the various steps of its progression' (*Monboddo*, 3: 398–9).

All these, and many more of Monboddo's ideas, can also be found in Coleridge's reflections on prose style – a coincidence which few, if any, critics have noted.[56] Yet Coleridge does not repeat all of Monboddo's views on prose, and rather than taking over the latter's theories and preferences uncritically, seems to select those which can be used to justify a style that interests him for quite different reasons. Whereas Monboddo is primarily concerned with the aesthetic qualities of prose, though also with its efficiency as a communicative vehicle, Coleridge is principally interested in the power of prose to awaken in its readers a sense of the sublime, or – in the process of its composition – to awaken the writer's own conviction of a world beyond the fragmentary scene of empirical consciousness.[57] In many places, however, Coleridge's discussions of prose also seem to involve an opportunistic attack on those he sees as his political and philosophical enemies. It may be, for example, that the short sentences he criticizes are to some extent the natural vehicle of empiricist and democratic opinions; yet his association of short sentences with fragmentary ideas, together with his particular antipathy for French writers, seems too directly to support his rejection of 'modern' or empiricist philosophy for the former to be taken entirely at face value.[58]

Hence these opinions serve important functions in Coleridge's writing which they do not serve in Monboddo. Rather than being academic, Coleridge's interest in prose is in many cases rhetorical, combining a critique of empiricist ideas with a rejection of the language used to express them, and suggesting that fragmentation and an absence of informing thought is the dominant character of modern consciousness in France and Britain.[59] In several passages, indeed, he goes further than this, claiming that the French revolution, French literary style, and French philosophy all manifest the same dissipation of order and intellectual command.[60] His celebration of classical languages is part of the same rhetorical system. The present decayed condition of language, he suggests, is merely the consummation of a downward spiral in which the quality of thought is equally involved, and which can be characterized as a gradual suppression of internal by external values. In several places Coleridge associates this trend with the increasing commercialism and devaluation of scholarship after the revolution of 1688, which – he claims – caused literature to be addressed to 'the common miscellaneous public' rather than to the intellectual elite he calls the 'clerisy'.[61] At other times, however, he argued that the decay of style was by no means a novelty. 'Observe', he is reported as saying, 'the superior truth of language, in Greek, to Theocritus inclusively; in

Latin, to the Augustan age exclusively; in Italian, to Tasso exclusively; and in English, to Taylor and Barrow inclusively.'[62]

Yet there is a serious argument behind this rhetoric: namely that human beings must think if they are not to become victims of their environment, that we do not really exist as individuals except insofar as we struggle to transcend received opinion, and that this struggle for transcendence demands that we wrestle not only with the prevailing materialist philosophy, but also with the short and simple forms of language which encourage its acceptance, entering our consciousness without the countervailing criticism which a heightened awareness of language must engender. Both modern language and modern thought are Coleridge's enemies, and their effects are combined in that philosophy which speaks blandly of atoms or corpuscles, or in general of a material world existing independent of the senses.

What Coleridge attacks in modern prose-writing, therefore, is not so much its simplicity or clarity as its dearth of original thought, its tendency to reproduce without the intervention of a critical intelligence. Language, he suggests, can become so standardized that its users need scarcely think in order to sustain the cycle of production and consumption – a state of language which naturally encourages intellectual passivity, one of whose consequences was the prevailing materialist philosophy. In chapter two of *Biographia*, he describes the mechanization of language in the same way as, more commonly, he describes the mechanization of philosophy. 'I have', he says,

> ... attempted to illustrate the present state of our language, in its relation to literature, by a press-room of larger and smaller stereotype pieces, which, in the present anglo-gallican fashion of unconnected, epigrammatic periods, it requires but an ordinary portion of ingenuity to vary indefinitely, and yet still produce something, which, if *not* sense, will be so like it, as to do as well. (*BL*, 1: 39).

What is needed to correct this situation, he argues, is a thoughtfulness that will re-enliven the forms of language by its new demands, and in so doing disrupt the dogmatic stasis into which most readers have sunk. Only by a continual reshaping of language to fit its communicative intention can intellect preserve itself from such idolatrous passivity.[63] Originality or transcendence of received opinion is essentially the same as the vitality of intellect and of language. In the absence of such productive energy, language is no longer a vehicle enlivened by its user, but part of the tyranny of the sensible.

It is implicit in this argument that the specific opinions we communicate do not themelves determine the value of our thinking. Coleridge *does* suggest that profound reflection will not sustain a blandly materialist philosophy; but rather than recommending a dogmatic idealism, he celebrates a critical activity involving the transcendence of any dogma. According to Christensen, Coleridge's opposition to simplicity in prose implies a recommendation of obscurity, chiefly for the sake of those 'deferrals' (of meaning, knowledge, or understanding) which it facilitates.[64] The simple style which Coleridge denigrates, however, is specifically that of 'witty' epigram, or as he puts it, 'short-winded asthmatic sentences, as easy to be understood as impossible to be remembered, in which the merest common-place acquires a momentary poignancy, a petty titillating sting, from affected point and wilful antithesis' (*Friend*, 1: 26).[65] What he recommends, on the other hand, is a pursuit of clarity with regard to truths which necessarily resist clear expression. As noted earlier in this chapter, Coleridge coincided with Hegel in arguing that the very generality of language—its status as a universal property – prevented it from expressing the reality of our experience. His sense of the struggle between intention and expression is particularly clear in a notebook entry of 1817. 'It is the instinct of the Letter to bring into subjection to itself the Spirit—', Coleridge writes. 'The latter cannot dispute—nor can it be disputed for, but with a certainty of defeat' (*CN*, 3: 4350). By its relation to language, experience itself becomes sublime, and we are most conscious of that sublime reality when our intensest effort to express it comes to nothing. Intellectual effort, the struggle with language, is the source of Coleridge's intuition of transcendent being; yet at the same time it is itself the clearest part of the inexpressible, the 'other' of language that is revealed to us, and in a sense created, only by our striving to express it.[66]

For Coleridge, therefore, good writing can only result from an effort to reach beyond the limitations of language – an effort which itself gives rise to a feeling of the sublime. His conception of what is valuable in prose writing arises chiefly from the experience of striving to express experiential reality, and it is the same struggle with language that produces the long suspensions and cumulative paragraphs for which he is well-known.[67] According to Maskell, however, what Coleridge values in his own prose is mere 'connectedness' – a quality of language only of marginal importance to the thought which it expresses. His emphasis on thought as the basis of good prose, Maskell suggests, can be reduced to an obsession with 'logical consequence'.[68] Certainly Coleridge stresses the importance of formal correctness. Part of what distinguished seventeenth-century writers from the moderns, he said, was 'a superiority in the logical connection of the sentences, in the correct use of conjunctions, and other exponents of the connecting acts in the mind' (*C17thC*, 413). In a lecture of 1818, moreover, he spoke of 'the importance of accuracy of style as being near akin to veracity and truthful habits of mind' (*Lects 1808–19*, 2: 238).[69] Logical thinking, he implies, is indispensable to truthfulness; inaccuracy in our use of language leads to errors in belief and the communication of falsehoods.[70] As Hamilton points out, it is implicit in Coleridge's theory of desynonymy that 'discrimination in the use of language' itself involves 'a progressively more astute apprehension of the world'.[71] The effort of verbalization is a response to pre-existent intuitions, yet only by subjecting those intuitions to the demands of logic contained in a precise use of language can we arrive at knowledge, including a knowledge of the limits of our understanding. Coleridge's emphasis on formal correctness, therefore, does not imply an interest in logical thinking for its own sake. Rather, the pursuit of verbal precision serves to distinguish truth from falsehood, and the knowable from the unknowable, at once clarifying our knowledge of that which can be put into words, and enabling us to recognize those things which are beyond language.[72] Only by struggling with the forms of logical prose, he suggests, will we experience that confrontation with the infinite which is the basis of religious conviction.

The value he finds in this effort is also the source of Coleridge's recommendation of organic structure in prose. This ideal is not merely a matter of the subordination of several clauses to a single intention, of the creation of larger 'wholes' than are commonly to be found in modern popular literature. The 'unity' which Coleridge values is produced by 'the unity of the subject, and the perpetual growth and evolution of the thoughts, one generating, and explaining, and justifying, the place of another' (*Lects 1808–19*, 2: 234).[73] As L. M. Grow points out, this 'organic' form of unity is also evident in Coleridge's own writing:

> In keeping with the criterion that the entity which is to be unified organically must contain *in potentia* in its seed the full set of

> characteristics which the final product will exhibit, Coleridge's sentences nearly always begin with a statement which contains his core meaning, and then is developed towards the full growth of that meaning in the course of the succeeding phrases and clauses.[74]

According to Mays, Coleridge preferred the 'emergent and exploratory' style of writing found particularly in Donne and Taylor, to the 'architectural' one of Milton and Hooker.[75] Yet rather than contrasting these two aspects of seventeenth-century prose, Coleridge in fact describes its 'architecture' as depending on the evolutionary quality of its thought. The perfection of classical unity, he argued, consisted precisely in that continuous development which he discovered in both Milton and Taylor. Spontaneity and progressiveness were not opposed to structured discourse, but its most essential constituents. Only through 'the perpetual growth and evolution of the thoughts' could prose achieve that ideal condition in which, as in the Greek governments, there could be no separation of the parts from the whole.[76]

According to Coleridge, such a style could itself communicate at least part of the feeling by which it was engendered, which was at once a feeling of effort or struggle, and of those sublime realities to which no struggle could give adequate expression.[77] The obscurity which is necessitated by our effort to say the unsayable, Coleridge argues, can itself become an image of the sublime – not only of the will and conviction which shape language into these new forms, not just of the author's private transcendence, but also of the divine realities, those 'ideas of reason' which Kant described as the source of philosophy's systematic or explicative impulse, but whose significance for Coleridge was (as we have seen) far greater.[78] Commenting on his own style in *The Statesman's Manual*, Coleridge wrote:

> In reviewing the foregoing pages, I am apprehensive that they may be thought to resemble the overflow of an earnest mind rather than an orderly premeditated composition. Yet this imperfection of form will not be altogether uncompensated, if it should be the means of presenting with greater liveliness the feelings and impressions under which they were written. Still less shall I regret this defect if it should induce some future traveller engaged in the like journey to take the same station and to look through the same medium at the one main object which amid all my discursions I have still held in view.
>
> (*LS*, 43)

Passionate writing, he argued in *The Courier*, was indispensable to the achievement of *The Friend*'s objectives, namely 'to refer the opinions of men to their proper principles, and the passions of men to their proper objects' (*EOT*, 2: 78).[79] The redirection of feeling he wished to achieve, moreover, was explicitly from phenomenal to noumenal realities. 'The disproportion of human passions to their ordinary objects', he wrote, was 'among the strongest internal evidences of our future destination, and the attempt to restore them to their rightful claimants, the most imperious duty and the noblest task of genius' (*Friend*, 1: 35).[80]

Literary style, it seems, was central to Coleridge's aim of improving the age in which he lived. It was 'the hope of doing ... real good', he claimed, that prevented him from reducing his style to the level of popular fragmentariness.[81] On the one hand he seeks to encourage his readers to think on their own account, to escape from the automatism or conventionality which – he argues – reproduces itself, and indeed subsists, chiefly through inaccuracy in our use of language; on the other, to encourage that sense of the sublime or ineffable which results from the experience of composition or meditation itself. The epiphanies of his own writing, however, are conceived as acting more directly in the encouragement of religious conviction: sensing Coleridge's excitement, the reader is supposed to be urged on in the pursuit of an analogous transcendence. Yet the very aversion of the public to the 'effort of Thought' required by his Ciceronian periods,[82] and which was the condition of communicating any real instruction in taste or philosophy, seemed largely to prevent his satisfaction. Neither simplification nor abstruseness could, it appears, produce a taste for abstruseness; and in recommending such an involuted style he was 'like a Physician who prescribes exercise with the dumb bells to a Patient paralytic in both arms' (*CL*, 3: 253).

3. THE SUBLIME EXPERIENCE: COLERIDGE AND HIS CRITICS

Despite the theories reviewed in the previous section, many critics have complained of Coleridge's obscurity. In his own period, indeed, this was the commonest criticism of his writing. Hazlitt, John Foster, and the *British Critic*'s reviewer of *Biographia* are among those who emphasize its inaccessibleness. Carlyle's description of his conversation is certainly no less harsh, though De Quincey takes a more sympathetic view of its complexity.[83] Paradoxically, however, the reactions even of his more negative critics often seem strikingly to resemble the sense of the sublime which Coleridge explicitly sought to engender. As noted in Chapter 4, in the essay 'Virtue and Knowledge' in *The Friend*, Coleridge recommends

> ... the habituation of the intellect to clear, distinct, and adequate conceptions concerning all things that are the possible objects of clear conception, and thus to reserve the deep feelings which belong, as by a natural right to those obscure ideas that are necessary to the moral perfection of the human being ... for objects, which their very sublimity renders indefinite, no less than their indefiniteness renders them sublime: namely, to the Ideas of Being, Form, Life, the Reason, the Law of Conscience, Freedom, Immortality, God!
>
> (*Friend*, 1: 106)

According to *The Friend*, therefore, we should try to write clearly about everything, but on discovering that we cannot form 'clear, distinct, and adequate conceptions' of certain things, we should not assume that they are non-existent or imaginary. Certain textual obscurities, Coleridge suggests, should be taken as evidence of the limitations of human intellect in respect of their referents; and it is chiefly the terms listed here – at least some of which correspond to those which Kant, in the first *Critique*, uses to refer to ideas of reason – that he wishes to be thus exempted from the demand for clarity.[84] Coleridge's use of the word 'sublimity' in this passage, however, raises important questions about the causation of the sublime experience. The feeling of sublimity – the sense of comprehension failing in the face of something inconceivably vast and magnificent – is supposed to be justified by a corresponding reality of vastness and intellectual limitation.[85] Yet Coleridge's admission that the sensational aspect of sublimity is no less important than the conceptual – that the deepest truths are defined by feeling as much as vice versa – inevitably puts in question the existence of those 'objects' which would give meaning to our perplexity.[86]

A closely analogous conception of the relationship between feelings and ideas occurs in Kant's *Critique of Judgement*, though here the context of sublime feeling is not writing, but landscapes and other objects of distinctly aesthetic experience. No object of nature, Kant says, can be called sublime:

> All that we can say is that the object lends itself to the presentation of a sublimity discoverable in the mind. For the sublime, in the strict sense of the word, cannot be contained in any sensuous form, but rather concerns ideas of reason, which, although no adequate presentation of them is possible, may be excited and called into the mind by that very inadequacy itself which does admit of sensuous presentation.
>
> (*CJ*, 92)

In the case of the 'mathematical' sublime, this 'inadequacy' concerns the inability of comprehension to keep pace with apprehension in the assessment of magnitude. On entering St. Peter's or surveying the Pyramids, Kant suggests, we find that 'the representations of sensuous intuition in the case of the parts first apprehended begin to disappear from the imagination as this advances to the apprehension of yet others', so that 'as much ... is lost at one end as is gained at the other, and for comprehension we get a maximum which the imagination cannot exceed' (*CJ*, 99). The feeling which results from this process, however, is not only one of frustration but also one of pleasure; and its pleasurable aspect is due to the idea of infinite greatness arising from the failure of our understanding.[87] According to Kant, that is, our inability to comprehend huge natural objects in a single intuition produces a concept of the infinite which depends upon 'a faculty of mind transcending every standard of sense', namely the reason (*CJ*, 102–3). An analogous form of negation is central to the 'dynamical' sublime, in which the recognition of our inability to resist the 'might' of natural forces from which we are in fact secure 'reveals a faculty of estimating ourselves as independent of nature', and enables the mind to recognize 'the ... sublimity of the sphere of its own being' (*CJ*, 109–12).

In the *Critique of Judgement*, such ideas of the transcendent power of reason or the mind are merely the basis of the sublime as an aesthetic experience: though, according to Kant, our observation of mountains leads us to entertain the idea of 'a supersensible substrate (underlying both nature and our faculty of thought) which is great beyond every standard of sense' (*CJ*, 104), no claims are made as to the existence of such a substrate. In other words, Kant retains the same neutrality with regard to the noumenon as in the first two

Critiques: though the ideas of freedom, immortality, and God 'all proceed from the principle of morality', and though they have an important 'regulative' function in philosophy, such objects are intrinsically beyond all knowledge, including the knowledge of their existence.[88] According to Coleridge, however, it is of the greatest importance that our feelings be directed towards these ideas. Though his description of them as 'necessary to the moral perfection of the human being' reflects Kant's assertion of their moral importance, he also expresses a spiritual investment in such noumena of the kind which Kant specifically avoided. Moreover, the feeling of the sublime described by Coleridge occurs in the process of reflection or intellectual inquiry (and implicitly in that of reading his own text) rather than resulting from the observation of huge objects or uncontrollable forces in nature, and the ideas associated with it are intended to be the principal focus of his readers' attention, rather than merely underlying their experience of the sublime.[89]

Since these ideas are beyond our comprehension, however, the value of contemplating them can only be religious or mystical, and hence was not appreciated by Coleridge's empiricist opponents. The philosopher James Mackintosh – in whom more than in any other individual Coleridge sought to encapsulate the vices of sensualism and materialistic idolatry[90] – offers some notable examples of the outrage which such mysticism was liable to provoke in empiricists. His *Discourse on the Study of the Law of Nature and Nations* recommends precisely the popular and empirically-based form of philosophy which Coleridge most emphatically rejected, and claims that the obscurities of idealist thinkers are wholly gratuitous. Through the influence of Locke and others, he says, people have been enabled

> … to discuss with precision, and to explain with clearness, the principles of the science of human nature, which are in themselves on a level with the capacity of every man of good sense, and which only appeared to be abstruse from the unprofitable subtleties with which they were loaded, and the barbarous jargon in which they were expressed. … That philosophy on which are founded the principles of our duty, if it has not become more certain (for morality admits no discoveries) is at least less 'harsh and crabbed,' less obscure and haughty in its language, less forbidding and disgusting in its appearance, than in the days of our ancestors.[91]

What begins as a claim for the simplicity of the matters under discussion thus becomes a celebration of simplicity for its own sake, even if it facilitates no increase in knowledge or understanding. Mackintosh's argument is merely that, as far as philosophy is concerned, anything not immediately comprehensible 'to all men of common sense' is nonsense – that nothing is true which is not obvious – and hence his attitude is no less prejudiced than that of Coleridge, who assumes a noumenal reality. Metaphysics, he writes,

> ... is, in truth, nothing more than the employment of good sense, in observing our own thoughts, feelings, and actions ... and those who wrap it up in a technical and mysterious jargon, always give us strong reason to suspect that they are not philosophers but impostors.[92]

With regard to Coleridge's prose-style in particular, however, several contemporary critics seem unconsciously to repeat in their expressions of perplexity the patterns of sublime feeling described by Kant. In his review of *The Friend*, for example, the critic John Foster comments:

> ... there is something that every where compels [the reader] to give the author credit for thinking with great acuteness, even when he is labouring in vain to refine his own conceptions into any state that can place him in real communication with the author's mind.[93]

By the manner in which it evades the reader's grasp, that is, Coleridge's prose arouses the conviction of an intellectual activity greater than any he can comprehend.[94] The vastness or intensity of Coleridge's thinking effectively replaces the idea of a 'supersensible substrate' which Kant describes as resulting from our inability to comprehend huge objects in a single intuition.[95]

More commonly, however, it is the physical context in which Kant locates the sublime's combination of pleasure and displeasure, rather than the structure of this response itself, that is reflected in descriptions of Coleridge's writing. The *British Critic*'s reviewer of *Biographia* and *Sibylline Leaves*, for example, remarks that

> To follow his flights requires very commonly a painful effort of attention, and when we have gained the heights to which he

> carries us, instead of any objects opening upon our view to repay us for our labour, we commonly find ourselves enveloped in mistiness and clouds.[96]

Like the subject of Kant's 'mathematical' sublime, this critic cannot comprehend the totality of which he is aware. Yet whereas, in the case of the visual experiences described by Kant, we nevertheless 'apprehend' a limited physical totality, in the *British Critic*'s image the totality exceeds any perceptible limits, and stretches into an infinite obscurity. Coleridge, in other words, carries us to great heights where we cannot follow him, and hence we can have no final knowledge of his limitations.[97] Yet despite this implication, the critic attaches no pleasurable feelings to the failure of his understanding. Something great is indubitably there, but he is merely frustrated by its invisibility.

Hazlitt, on the other hand, though scarcely expressing a sense of awe in the face of intellectual majesty, perceives very clearly the relation between the sublimity described in *The Friend* and Coleridge's prose style. 'In his weary quest of truth', he writes,

> ...he reminds us of the mendicant pilgrims that travellers meet in the Desert, with their faces always turned towards Mecca, but who contrive never to reach the shrine of the Prophet.[98]

Hazlitt's comment reminds us of the importance of language in Coleridge's pursuit of truth. For what he pursues is in fact the verbalization of an intuition which is always beyond the grasp of language – an intuition which consists primarily in the effort of thought or expression itself, or in the sensation of 'force' which Hume describes as accompanying it. Coleridge cannot reach his destination, firstly because what he principally seeks to express is the effort underlying all expression, and secondly because the specificity of individual experience always resists encapsulation in the generalities of language. The reactions of his critics suggest that he often succeeded in producing a sense of the sublime, and perhaps in promoting deeper thought than that conventionally appealed to by empiricists; yet the effect of his writing is primarily to draw attention to itself, and to the effort involved in producing it, rather than to the sublime ideas which it explicitly invokes. Just as the imaginary sublimation of the physical in his early poems primarily expresses Coleridge's own desire to rise above the limitations of the quotidian,[99] indeed, so the pursuit of impossible expressive aims in his later prose serves principally to engender the liberating sensations of energy and elevation which underlie his evocations of human and divine self-consciousness.

Notes

INTRODUCTION

1. This is the definition given in the first (1932) edition. The 1989 edition revises it to 'human mind (formerly also soul)', hinting at the more limited and mechanistic conceptions of 'psychology' to which we are nowadays accustomed.
2. As Judson S. Lyon points out ('Romantic Psychology and the Inner Senses: Coleridge', *PMLA*, 81 [1966] 247) 'Coleridge is the best illustration of [the] Romantic fascination with psychology and with notions of inner senses', though his rejection of 'the mechanistic implications of associationism' has close parallels in many other Romantic poets, and especially in Blake.
3. See especially Wordsworth's description of how his poems in *Lyrical Ballads* were intended to illustrate not only 'the manner in which we associate ideas in a state of excitement', but also the effects of rural surroundings on consciousness and language (*WProse*, 1: 123–5). Coleridge's later argument that 'The best part of human language ... is derived from reflection on the acts of the mind itself' (*BL*, 2: 54) highlights the contrastingly introspective and idealist emphasis which is already prominent in poems such as 'The Eolian Harp'.
4. See Harold Bloom, *Blake's Apocalypse: A Study in Poetic Argument* (Garden City, NY: Doubleday, 1963), 283, and Jon Mee, *Dangerous Enthusiasm: William Blake and the Culture of Radicalism in the 1790s* (Oxford: Clarendon, 1992), 1.
5. See *The Poetical Works of John Keats*, ed. H. W. Garrod (Oxford: Clarendon, 1939), 257–60 for the best-known example of Keats's self-subverting focus on the fading illusions of 'fancy', and Nicholas Roe (ed.), *Keats and History* (Cambridge: CUP, 1995), 7–12 on the social and political awareness implicit in Keats's imaginative quests for transcendence.
6. See *WProse*, 1: 123–5, and William Wordsworth: *The Prelude, 1799, 1805, 1850*, ed. Jonathan Wordsworth, M. H. Abrams, Stephen Gill (New York: Norton, 1979), 43–63.
7. On the extent to which such subjectivist tendencies in Romanticism more generally seem to reflect the influence of Rousseau see especially Thomas McFarland, *Romanticism and the Heritage of Rousseau* (Oxford: Clarendon, 1995), 50–2.
8. These aims in Coleridge, indeed, have obvious features in common with the pursuit of unity between self and other (as distinct from a Byronic *transcendence* of the other) which Mellor describes as characterizing the 'feminine sublime' of writers such as Ann Radcliffe. See Anne K. Mellor, *Romanticism and Gender* (London: Routledge, 1993), 91–6.

9. This is, indeed, so widespread a perception as to be implied in most of the *OED*'s definitions of 'Romantic'. Though qualifying this principle with specific instances, Webb similarly describes the 'typically Romantic poem' as pointing 'away from contemporary realities' towards 'seductive ... visions' of the ideal (Timothy Webb, *Shelley: A Voice Not Understood* [Manchester: Manchester UP, 1977], 82).
10. See Mellor, *Romanticism and Gender*, 89–106. Even the identification with sublime landscapes which Mellor describes as distinctively masculine, for example, is often prominent in Radcliffe's writing. See, for example, Ann Radcliffe, *A Sicilian Romance*, ed. Alison Milbank (Oxford: OUP, 1995), 104–5.
11. This theoretical position is most prominent in *A Defence of Poetry* (see especially *Shelley's Poetry and Prose*, eds. Donald H. Reiman and Sharon B. Powers [New York: Norton, 1977], 502–8), though as Webb points out (*Shelley*, 115), *Prometheus Unbound*, like *The Revolt of Islam*, is 'an attempt to deliver Shelley's contemporaries from despair and ... directs itself to the French Revolution and its meaning'.
12. As McFarland notes, Byron 'believed in very little' except freedom, and thus eschews the emphasis on 'the need for internal order' which, as Webb points out, was central to Shelley's view of the relationship between the individual and society. See Thomas McFarland, *Paradoxes of Freedom: The Romantic Mystique of A Transcendence* (Oxford: Clarendon, 1996), 46, and Webb, *Shelley*, 121.
13. See Webb, *Shelley*, 111, and McFarland, *Paradoxes of Freedom*, 37.
14. See especially Morton D. Paley, 'The Last Man: Apocalypse Without Millennium', in Audrey A. Fisch, Anne K. Mellor, and Esther M. Schor (eds), *The Other Mary Shelley* (Oxford: OUP, 1993), 107–23.
15. On the particular importance of such topics in Coleridge's later poems see Morton D. Paley, *Coleridge's Later Poetry* (Oxford: Clarendon, 1996), 37–61.
16. See especially *Friend*, 1: 106 and *CN*, 3: 3755.
17. On the sense of incomprehensible power or vastness produced by objects incompletely viewed or understood see especially Edmund Burke, *A Philosophical Enquiry into the Origin of Our Ideas of the Sublime and Beautiful*, ed. James T. Boulton (London: RKP, 1958), 58–64, and *CJ*, 99–105.
18. See especially *BL*, 1: 254–60.
19. As Coleridge points out, however, emotions are often both rational and involuntary at the same time, as in the case of that 'terror' which consists in 'apprehension of Danger' (see *CN*, 3: 4046).
20. See especially *CPR*, 267–8; also *Kant's Latin Writings: Translations, Commentaries, and Notes*, trans. Lewis White Beck (New York: Lang, 1986), 159, and Howard Caygill, *A Kant Dictionary* (Oxford: Blackwell, 1995), 264–5.
21. See especially *STI*, 230.
22. See my discussion of these points in Chapter 5, section 2.
23. See *CJ*, 105–7, Immanuel Kant, *Critique of Practical Reason*, trans. Lewis White Beck (Chicago: Chicago UP, 1949), 61–2, and Caygill, *A Kant Dictionary*, 197, 356–7.

24. As I show in Chapter 4 below, indeed, even Coleridge's attempts to distinguish poetry and philosophy often highlight their similarities as much as their differences (see, for example, *BL*, 2: 15–16 and 2: 25–6). For earlier passages emphasizing the interdependence of poetry and philosophy see *German Aesthetic and Literary Criticism: The Romantic Ironists and Goethe*, ed. Kathleen Wheeler (Cambridge: CUP, 1984) 46, and *STI*, 231.
25. See *CN*, 2: 2372 for an especially vivid example of the simultaneous description and exemplification of these patterns.
26. See, for example, *LS*, 22 and *BL*, 1: 291.
27. David Hume, *Enquiries Concerning Human Understanding and Concerning the Principles of Morals*, ed. L. A. Selby-Bigge (Oxford: OUP, 1975), 77–8n. See also David Hume, *A Treatise of Human Nature*, ed. L. A. Selby-Bigge (Oxford: OUP, 1978), 105–6, and the discussion of these passages in Adela Pinch, *Strange Fits of Passion: Epistemologies of Emotion, Hume to Austen* (Stanford, CA: Stanford UP, 1996), 35–6.
28. The terms by which Coleridge habitually refers to the origin of consciousness, indeed, bear a striking similarity to those which Hume uses to describe the empiricist's notion of the underlying cause of events. See, for example, *CN*, 1: 1077.
29. Hume, *Treatise*, 106.
30. Pinch, *Strange Fits of Passion*, 36.
31. See especially Pinch, *Strange Fits of Passion*, 11–13 on how the Romantic emphasis on individual emotion highlights the contemporary questions of to what extent intention can be deduced from any text or combination of texts, and whether the concept of a feeling which precedes or resists expression is not inherently problematic.
32. See Paley, *Coleridge's Later Poetry*, 36 and Hill, *The Lords of Limit: Essays on Literature and Ideas* (London: Deutsch, 1984), 12 on the 'transfiguring of weakness into strength' repeatedly evoked by Coleridge's later poems.
33. See, for example, *Friend*, 1: 517–18, and Laurence S. Lockridge, *Coleridge the Moralist* (Ithaca, NY: Cornell UP, 1977), 39–40.
34. This point is probably clearest in Schelling and Coleridge (see especially *STI*, 230 and *BL*, 2: 16–17), though Shelley also emphasizes the quality of spontaneity or 'necessity' which, according to Schelling, makes poetry a uniquely paradoxical combination of 'conscious' and 'unconscious' production. See *Shelley's Poetry and Prose*, 506–7.
35. Analogies between Emerson and Coleridge are discussed briefly in Frank Lentricchia, 'Coleridge and Emerson: Prophets of Silence, Prophets of Language', *JAAC*, 32 (1973) 43–5. On Nietzsche's indebtedness to Emerson see especially George J. Stack, *Nietzsche and Emerson: An Elective Affinity* (Athens, OH: Ohio UP, 1992), 1–70. On Stevens's debts to Coleridge see B. J. Leggett, 'Why It Must Be Abstract: Stevens, Coleridge, and I. A. Richards', *SR*, 22 (1983) 500–15. Coleridge, of course, differs from deconstructive thinkers in postulating a transcendent reality; yet as Kathleen Wheeler notes (*Romanticism, Pragmatism and Deconstruction* [Oxford: Blackwell,

1993], 63–6), his prose works are 'often mistaken as dogmatic idealism rather than the exercises in imaginative questioning and the "projects of thought" that they were designed to be', and in addition to emphasizing 'a self-criticism and detachment figured in the organic idea of self-propelling energy', use various 'strategies... which we have come to associate with deconstruction' to disrupt the usual passivity of the reading process.

36. Though Perkins describes Coleridge as eschewing the pessimism of Schopenhauer (see Mary Anne Perkins, *Coleridge's Philosophy: The Logos as Unifying Principle* [Oxford: Clarendon, 1995], 270), the increasing emphasis in his later writings on the 'unfathomable hell within' revealed in his dreams suggests a close analogy with Schopenhauer's notion of the destructive reality underlying civilized illusion.

CHAPTER 1 ON POETRY AND PHILOSOPHY: ROMANTIC FEELING AND THEORY IN COLERIDGE AND SCHELLING

1. See *Letters of John Keats, 1814–1821*, ed. H. E. Rollins, 2 vols (Cambridge, MA: Harvard UP, 1958), 1: 194. As Wheeler notes (*Romanticism, Pragmatism, and Deconstruction*, 70–1), Ludwig Tieck's suspicion 'that for the greater number of English readers [*Biographia Literaria*] is too weighty and profound' is 'only a little less apt today than it was in 1825'.
2. See T. S. Eliot, *The Use of Poetry and the Use of Criticism: Studies in the Relation of Criticism to Poetry in England* (London: Faber, 1933), 67, and Mellor, *Romanticism and Gender*, 89–90.
3. See Kathleen Wheeler, *The Creative Mind in Coleridge's Poetry* (London: Heinemann, 1981).
4. See, for example, Pinch, *Strange Fits of Passion*, 11 on 'the postromantic assumptions about feeling for which romanticism is held to be embarrassingly responsible', including 'the assumption... that feelings are fundamentally private and prelinguistic but knowable only in their representations'.
5. The multiplication of theoretical complexities in recent studies of Romanticism is noted in Mellor, *Romanticism and Gender*, 13. Recent studies focusing almost exclusively on Coleridge's philosophy include Perkins, *Coleridge's Philosophy*, and James W. Clayton, 'Coleridge and the Logos: The Trinitarian Unity of Consciousness and Culture', *Journal* of *Religion*, 70 (1990) 213–40.
6. *BL*, 2: 16–17.
7. On the puzzles in 'The Ancient Mariner' and the stimulus they give to active readership or interpretation see especially Wheeler, *The Creative Mind in Coleridge's Poetry*, 42–64.
8. To extend the comparison further, the psychological archetypes evoked in 'Christabel' are no less clearly aspects of an internal reality of 'feeling' whose forms and logic are presented with particular

directness in the 'outward forms' of characters and imagery. See especially Anthony Harding, 'Mythopoesis: The Unity of Christabel', *Coleridge's Imagination: Essays in Memory of Pete Laver*, ed. Richard Gravil, Lucy Newlyn, and Nicholas Roe (Cambridge: CUP, 1985), 207–17 on this point.

9. See *CPW*, 1: 101–2, esp. ll. 34–64.
10. See, for example, *CPW*, 1: 180 and 1: 240–1.
11. See especially lines 1–44 of 'Religious Musings' (*CPW*, 1: 108–11), where Coleridge describes how through faith the soul 'soars' towards unity with God. His probable sources for this image in Hartley and Priestley are discussed in Chapter 5, section 1.
12. See *BL*, 1: 304 and *STI*, 230–1.
13. See *BL*, 2: 16 and *CPW*, 1: 240–1.
14. See *STI*, 218.
15. For Schelling's use of the term 'imagination' (*Einbildungskraft*) to describe the origin both of the 'primordial intuition' (i.e. sense perception) and of artistic creativity, see *STI*, 230. As I argue in Chapter 5, section 2, this passage seems to be the principal source of Coleridge's discussion in *BL*, 1: 304.
16. For the phrase 'genial coincidence' – used by Coleridge to explain the similarities between his own thought and that of the early Schelling – see *BL*, 1: 160. This 'coincidence', however, cannot remove the problem of Coleridge's unacknowledged translations in *Biographia*.
17. The tendency of poetic imagination to create organic wholes or to combine opposites into unity is the chief practical effect which Coleridge attributes to it in chapters 10, 13 and 14 of *Biographia*, and in chapter 13 this is clearly implied to be the chief evidence of its unity with the power of perception (see *BL*, 1: 168–70, 1: 304 and 2: 15–18).
18. See Chapter 4, section 3 on this point.
19. See especially Perkins, *Coleridge's Philosophy*, 154.
20. On 'trichotomy' see ibid., 116n. On Coleridge's conception of 'an "ideal realism" in which the ideal is never opposed to the real, and in which ideas are their own evidence and *constitutive* of reality', see ibid., 8.
21. On the difficulty of achieving this reconciliation see especially *STI*, 229.
22. See especially *CL*, 1: 349 on Coleridge's need to believe in 'something *one & indivisible*'; also the analogous passage (dating from 1823) in *CN*, 4: 4968. Nigel Leask (*The Politics of Imagination in Coleridge's Critical Thought* [Basingstoke: Macmillan, 1988], 23) notes that the quest for such an underlying unity 'is perhaps above all others the unifying principle of Coleridge's multifarious writings'.
23. See *BL*, 1: 285 and *STI*, 17. The tendency towards stabilizing this dialectic is already prominent in Coleridge's discussion of the 'infinite I AM' in *BL*, 1: 304. See also Nicholas Reid, 'Coleridge and Schelling: The Missing Transcendental Deduction', *SR*, 33 (1994), 457, 471–2 on Coleridge's later attempt to escape from the dialectic of

subject and object which governs Schelling's *System* by defining it as belonging to 'the world of the (finite) Understanding' as distinct from the underlying 'dynamic reality' of Reason or the Trinity.

24. On how the continuity of consciousness stands in, at the end of Schelling's system, for that 'absolute identity of subject and object', which has been postulated but is incapable of demonstration, see especially Chapter 5, section 2.
25. On the 'Pythagorean tetractys' as a symbol of being involving 'the interdependence of polarity and trichotomy', see Perkins, *Coleridge's Philosophy*, 62, 116. For references to this idea, and to the associated figure of the 'pentad', see *CM*, 3: 416, 3: 449–51, 3: 453–4, *CN*, 4: 4829, and *AR*, 179–82.
26. This view is implicit in Perkins's indication of the very generality of the unifying capacity of 'logos', which as she points out, Coleridge intended to mediate 'not only between idealism and atomistic materialism ... but between all oppositions which had been misinterpreted as contradictions, or as mutually exclusive' (Perkins, *Coleridge's Philosophy*, 21–2).
27. S. T. Coleridge, Notebook 54 (British Library, Add. MS 47549), fo. 16v.
28. On how the 'infinite I AM' is added to the dual conception of imagination or productive intuition which Coleridge derived from Schelling see especially Chapter 5, section 2.
29. For the phrase 'Trinitarian Resolution' see Thomas McFarland, *Coleridge and the Pantheist Tradition* (Oxford: Clarendon, 1969), 191–255. On the 'Logosophia' or projected 'Magnum Opus', see ibid., 194.
30. See especially *CL*, 5: 98. This aspect of Coleridge's thought is discussed more fully in Chapter 4, section 3.
31. See McFarland, *Coleridge and the Pantheist Tradition*, 192–5, and Perkins, *Coleridge's Philosophy*, 267–76 and *passim*.
32. See *CN*, 3: 3558 and n.
33. See especially *STI*, 229–30.
34. Quoted in T. F. O'Meara, *Romantic Idealism and Roman Catholicism* (Notre Dame, IN: Notre Dame UP, 1982), 89. On Schelling's increasing 'need to place God beyond reason', see also Gabriel Marcel, *Coleridge et Schelling* (Paris: Aubier-Montaigne, 1971), 151–2.
35. On Coleridge's ubiquitous concept of 'Continuity ... and Individuation' see, for example, *CL*, 4: 769 and *CN* 4: 4814.
36. *Friend*, 1: 519. A similar passage in *AR*, 236 is perhaps even more suggestive of the phases of Coleridge's career which I have delineated: 'In Wonder', he writes, 'all Philosophy began: in Wonder it ends: and Admiration fills up the interspace. But the first Wonder is the Offspring of Ignorance: the last is the parent of Adoration. The First is the birth-throe of our knowledge: the Last is its euthanasy [*sic*] and apotheosis.'
37. For the fullest discussion of Coleridge's struggle with this problem see McFarland, *Coleridge and the Pantheist Tradition*, 107–90.

38. On the importance of locating God beyond the phenomenal realm in order to account for His productive power or conform to Christian principles, and the countervailing need to locate him *within* nature in order to conceive his products as a unified whole, see especially David Vallins, 'Production and Existence: Coleridge's Unification of Nature', *JHI*, 56: 1 (1995) 106–24.
39. See 'Tintern Abbey, ll. 95–6, *WPW*, 1: 262.
40. See especially *Friend*, 1: 106. This point is discussed more fully in Chapter 6, section 2.
41. Leask (*The Politics of Imagination*, 20) argues, with Everest and Fruman, that Wakefield's *Spirit of Christianity* (1794) 'was the major source' for 'Religious Musings', yet Coleridge's own citation of Hartley in a much-discussed note to the poem (*CPW*, 1: 10), together with the close resemblances of its ideas to many of Priestley's (see Chapter 5, section 1) suggest alternative sources for several important passages of the poem, and especially for its first 63 lines.
42. See Chapter 5 on these points.
43. See especially *CPW*, 1: 110, ll. 29–44.
44. Critics' responses to Coleridge's claim that the poem originated in a dream are usually ambivalent. Watson and Wheeler, for example, both emphasize the deliberateness of its depiction of imagination and the creative process, yet also acknowledge what Wheeler calls 'the intuited unity and truth to aesthetic experience' which 'has preserved it as a compelling enigma'. See Watson, *Coleridge the Poet* (London: Routledge, 1966), 117–30, and Wheeler, *The Creative Mind*, 17–41.
45. See *CPW*, 1: 296. The sexual symbolism of the description of the river in lines 17–24 in particular seems hard to deny, though surprisingly little discussed by critics. For examples of Coleridge's modesty or even prudishness, as revealed by his habit of using Greek words or transliterations to refer to sexual topics, see *CN*, 4: 4537 and *CM*, 3: 681.
46. See *CPW*, 1: 298.
47. A similar interpretation is developed in Wheeler, *The Creative Mind*, 30–5.
48. Coleridge's expressions of this alienation are particularly associated with his criticism of empiricists (or 'dogmatists', as Fichte and Schelling called them). See especially *BL*, 1: 262 and *CN*, 4: 4605.
49. See *Friend* 1: 419. *BL*, 1: 31–2n notes that Gerard, Condillac, Kant, and Fuseli were among those who had made similar distinctions. Probably the most important precursor of Coleridge's conception of 'genius', however, is Schelling's in *STI*, 219–24, discussed later in this chapter.
50. See *BL*, 1: 80–2 and *STI*, 228. Among the oppositions which imagination, in chapter 14 of *Biographia*, is said to overcome is that between 'the sense of novelty and freshness' and 'old and familiar objects' (*BL*, 2: 16–17).
51. Though Perkins's claims as to the diachronic unity of Coleridge's thought are perhaps overstated, her analyses of his thought after

1820 demonstrate this obsessiveness with particular clarity. See Perkins, *Coleridge's Philosophy*, 6–7, 10, and *passim*.

52. The 'deep well' is a phrase which Lowes borrows from Henry James to refer to that 'subliminal' area of the mind in which 'Images and impressions converge and blend', and 'the fragments which sink incessantly below the surface fuse and assimilate and coalesce' – an idea closely resembling the creative processes described both by Coleridge in the preface to 'Kubla Khan', and by Schelling in the *System*. See J. L. Lowes, *The Road to Xanadu: A Study in the Ways of the Imagination* (London: Constable, 1927; 1930), 59–60, and *STI*, 223.
53. See *BL*, 1: 262.
54. Schelling's comparison of the artist with the man of destiny coincides interestingly with Coleridge's distinction between 'Commanding Genius', which (as the editors of *BL* note) 'shows itself in the world of practical affairs', and 'Absolute Genius', which 'manifests itself in the world of the arts and the intellect' (see *BL*, 1: 31–2 and n.).
55. Unless the universal critical consensus that the poem was written in 1797–8 is incorrect, Coleridge could not have had Schelling's theories in mind when writing it, since he learned German at least a year later, and first encountered Schelling's works after 1800, when the *System* itself was published. On 'genial coincidence' see *BL*, 1: 160.
56. On the significance of the stylistic and formal eccentricities of 'The Ancient Mariner', and especially the effects of the marginal glosses added in 1817, see especially Wheeler, *The Creative Mind*, 42–64. For a translation of the quotation from Burnet see *The Annotated Ancient Mariner*, ed. Martin Gardner (London: Blond, 1965), 36.
57. See especially *BL*, 2: 16–17.
58. On how the removal of feeling by 'abstruse research' described in 'Dejection' contrasts with Coleridge's numerous evocations of the emotional elevation engendered by philosophizing, see especially Chapter 4, section 1.
59. See *CJ*, 104–9.

CHAPTER 2 FEELING INTO THOUGHT

1. This view of Coleridge's career stems largely from his own description of his philosophical conversion in *BL*, 1: 140–67. See also, for example, Rosemary Ashton, *The Life of Samuel Taylor Coleridge* (Oxford: Blackwell, 1996), 195–6.
2. *PLects*, 348 brings home the absurdity, stating that 'the successors of Hobbes' in fact attributed consciousness to matter itself, that is, 'intelligent fluids that etch and re-etch engravings on the brain for themselves to look at'.
3. Hartley's system is the most extreme example of an attempt to explain our ideas as effects of sensory impressions. Several passages in Hume's *Treatise*, however, express a position closely resembling Hartley's, and imply the possibility of a detailed physiological

explanation which Hume himself did not provide. Hume's description of ideas as the 'copies' which the mind takes of its impressions, and his claim that the difference between impressions and ideas 'consists in the degrees of force and liveliness with which they strike upon the mind', together with his distinction between impressions of sensation and of reflexion – the latter, such as 'desire and aversion, hope and fear', being effects of the pleasurableness or painfulness of our ideas – all seem to have influenced Hartley. See Hume, *Treatise*, 1, 7–8.

4. See Jerome Christensen, *Coleridge's Blessed Machine of Language* (Ithaca, NY: Cornell UP, 1981), 39 on this point.
5. Joseph Priestley discusses this point, and other eighteenth-century attempts to describe something intermediate between body and mind, in his *Disquisitions Relating to Matter and Spirit* (London, 1777; Birmingham, 1782), 103–9, and *Hartley's Theory of the Human Mind* (London, 1775), xix–xx, in both contexts commenting unfavourably on the idea. A passage in Berkeley's *Siris*, however, indicates that Hartley's theory was by no means original. 'The Platonists', Berkeley writes, 'held their intellect resided in soul, and soul in an aethereal vehicle. And that as the soul was a middle nature reconciling intellect with aether; so aether was another middle nature, which reconciled and connected the soul with grosser bodies' (George Berkeley, *Siris* [Dublin, 1744; London, 1744], 78).
6. See *CL*, 1: 137–8.
7. Christensen, *Coleridge's Blessed Machine of Language*, 63. As I argue in Chapter 5, however, Coleridge's description of himself as a 'Necessitarian' probably refers primarily to his belief in the automatic growth of human happiness – a doctrine which others, especially Priestley, expounded without reference to Hartley's physiology.
8. See *CL*, 1: 294–5.
9. See *CL*, 1: 478–9 and 1: 481–2.
10. The clearest evidence of this enthusiasm is a letter of 1794 to his brother George, where Locke is referred to, with Hartley, as among those 'who have written most wisely on the Nature of Man' (*CL*, 1: 126). By July 1801, however, Coleridge's view had changed so dramatically that he could write to Southey: 'Locke, Hume, & Hobbes ... stink worse than Feather or Assafetida' (*CL*, 2: 746).
11. *CL*, 2: 691. Coleridge uses the term 'connate' to mean 'born *at the same time with*', and 'innate' to mean 'born *in*' (ibid.).
12. *CL*, 2: 697. On the sources of Coleridge's theories in this passage see James McKusick, *Coleridge's Philosophy of Language* (New Haven, CT: Yale UP, 1986), 45–6, 66, and H. J. Jackson, 'Coleridge, Etymology and Etymologic', *JHI*, 44 (1983) 80.
13. See *CL*, 2: 696.
14. For 'medullary Substance', see, for example, *OM*, 1: 22. According to the *OED*, the term 'medullary', referring to the '"marrow" or inmost nature of something', was in use from the mid-seventeenth century.
15. See *CL*, 1: 137, and Christensen, *Coleridge's Blessed Machine of Language*, 63–4.

16. See especially Richard Haven, 'Coleridge, Hartley, and the Mystics', *JHI*, 20 (1959) 486 on Hartley's failure to account for intellectual, as distinct from automatic or instinctual, processes.
17. Coleridge's response to Hartley is in some respects anticipated by Godwin, who comments that Hartley's view of motion '"as in all instances the antecedent, and thought never anything more than a consequent" ... is contrary to everything we know of the system of the universe, in which each event appears to be alternately both the one and the other, nothing terminating in itself, but everything leading on to an endless chain of consequences' (William Godwin, *An Enquiry Concerning Political Justice and its Influence on Modern Morals and Happiness*, ed. I. Kramnick [Harmondsworth: Penguin, 1976], 363).
18. As Lockridge points out, essentially the same problem is highlighted by Coleridge's description of Descartes' mere 'grammatical Antithesis of the Terms, Action and Passion, substituted for a real definition of the Things themselves'. 'The body-soul dichotomy', Lockridge comments, 'has produced a dangerous divorce of physiology from psychology, whereas the truth of human passions is found in the "Kennel of my Psycho-somatic Ology", where the mental and the physical intermingle.' See Laurence Lockridge, *Coleridge the Moralist* (Ithaca, NY: Cornell UP, 1977), 80 and *SWF*, 2: 1420 and 2: 1444.
19. See *OM* 1: 65, and *BL*, 1: 108–9; also *BL* 1: 96 and 1: 110–12 on the absurd consequences arising from Hartley's reduction of association to 'the one law of time' (i.e. of the original coincidence of impressions).
20. See also L. M. Grow, 'The Prose Style of Samuel Taylor Coleridge' (PhD Dissertation, University of Southern California, 1971), 33 on this point.
21. See especially *BL*, 1: 254–60 on this point.
22. E. H. Coleridge (ed.), *Letters of Samuel Taylor Coleridge*, 2 vols (London: Heinemann, 1895), 1: 428 (the emphasis on 'you' is mine). The misquotation is repeated in, for example, I. A. Richards, *Coleridge on Imagination* (London: Kegan Paul, Trench, Trubner, 1934), 168.
23. The emphasis on 'for' is mine.
24. This view is also suggested by a letter to John Thelwall of 1796, where Coleridge remarks that his philosophical opinions 'are blended with, or deduced from, my feelings' (*CL*, 1: 279).
25. Wordsworth's actual words are 'the real language of men in a state of vivid sensation'. See *WProse*, 1: 118.
26. Though Hartley claims that the will, the intellect and the affections are 'all deducible from the external Impressions made upon the Senses', the physiological details of his system never explain how the 'vibrations' resulting from these sensations can be identified with 'intellectual Affections and Passions' (see *OM*, 1: 80–1).
27. The alternative reading, 'head', is included by Griggs as printed here.
28. *OM*, 1: 66.

29. See especially Anthony Harding, *Coleridge and the Idea of Love* (Cambridge: CUP, 1974), 33, and Deirdre Coleman, *Coleridge and 'The Friend (1809–10)* (Oxford: OUP, 1988), 58–9 on this point.
30. Henry More, *Enthusiasmus Triumphatus* (1656), in *A Collection of Several Philosophical Writings* (London, 1662) ii: 18. (*Enthusiasmus Triumphatus, or, a Brief Discourse on the Nature, Causes, Kinds, and Cure of Enthusiasm* is the second work in the single-volume *Collection*.) For references to More in Coleridge see, for example, *BL*, 2: 44 and *CN*, 1: 1000I, 1: 1069.
31. Ibid., ii: 12.
32. See also *LS*, 15 on this point.
33. The *OED*'s earliest example of 'Genius' meaning 'Native intellectual power of an exalted type' dates from 1749. More's work, however, was first published in 1656, and the context of 'Genius' here in any case directs us rather to the sense of 'natural character, inherent constitution and tendency' (used especially of diseases), of which the *OED* has examples dating from 1675 to 1747.
34. See *CL*, 2: 961 (quoted in section 1 of this chapter) for an example of Coleridge's use of the term 'soul' to denote inward feeling.
35. See *EOT*, 1: 220.
36. Robert Leighton, *Expository Works*, ed. P. Doddridge, 2 vols (Edinburgh, 1748), 1: 213 (quoted in *CM*, 3: 512).
37. See *CM*, 3: 512.
38. On the importance of this conception of 'life' in Coleridge's metaphysics see especially Vallins, 'Production and Existence', 119–24.
39. Coleridge's association of linguistic 'command' with the French was not accidental, but arose from a complex system of analogies between literary style, politics, and philosophy, according to which the French were absorbed in outward stimulation to the exclusion of all inward light. See my discussion of this point in Chapter 6, section 2.
40. On '*natura naturata*' and '*forma formata*' – phrases denoting the Spinozistic concept of 'passive' as distinct from 'active' nature – and the analogies which Coleridge constructs between this concept and the products of thinking, see, for example, *Lects 1808–19*, 2: 148, and S. T. Coleridge, *Logic*, ed. J. R. de J. Jackson (Princeton, NJ: Princeton UP, 1981), 231–2.
41. See Frank Lentricchia, 'Coleridge and Emerson: Prophets of Silence, Prophets of Language', *JAAC*, 32 (1973), 44 on Emerson's analogous theory that 'The poet turns ... to metaphoric strategy because "man is an analogist, and studies relations in all objects. He is placed in the center of beings and a ray of relation passes from every other being to him." Thus, Emerson sees metaphor ... not as a creation of order or unity among disparate objects, but as an acknowledgement, a way of revealing the order or unity or "relation" that is already there as an inherent quality of being.'
42. See *Friend*, 1: 20, and Christensen, *Coleridge's Blessed Machine of Language*, 208.
43. See especially *Friend*, 1: 106, and 1: 519 on this point.

44. *OM*, 1: 385. See also the analogous discussion of the bodily influence on consciousness in Thomas Reid, *Essays on the Intellectual Powers of Man* (Edinburgh, 1785), 427.
45. On the difficulty of explaining how the subjective can 'supervene to the objective' see especially *BL*, 1: 255–6.
46. See *CN*, 2: 2638: 'The dependence of ideas ... on states of bodily or mental *Feeling* ... strongly exemplified in the first moments of awaking from a Dream ... a nervous man, or one of perturbed or morbid functions of the lower bowels, can often carry on the Dream in his waking Thoughts/and often in its increasing faintness & irrecollectibility has time to *watch* & compare—.'
47. See *CL*, 1: 279.
48. MS note in Jeremy Taylor, *ΣΥΜΒΟΛΟΝ ΘΕΟΛΟΓΙΚΟΝ: or A Collection of Polemicall Discourses* (London, 1674; British Library, Ashley 5174), 297.
49. See, however, *CN*, 1: 188: 'Dreams sometimes useful by ... giving to the well-grounded *fears* & *hopes* of the understanding the *feelings* of vivid sense.'
50. *CL*, 4: 641. Most of the ideas in this passage seem to derive from a discussion of dreams in Darwin's *Botanic Garden*, which explains our tendency to be 'deceived' in our dreams partly by the fact that 'in sleep there is a total suspension of our voluntary power ... Hence, as the trains of ideas are passing in our imaginations in dreams, we cannot compare them with our previous knowledge of things, as we do in our waking hours; for this is a voluntary exertion, and thus we cannot perceive their incongruity' (Erasmus Darwin, *The Botanic Garden*, 2 vols [London, 1789–91]; reprinted in 1 vol. [Menston, Yorks.: Scolar Press, 1973], 2: 47). Coburn (*CN*, 1: 188) suggests that Coleridge and Darwin probably discussed the topic of dreams when they met in 1796.
51. *CN*, 3: 4046. The last four words are translated by Coburn as 'physical or material terror'.
52. A notebook entry of 1804, however, suggests that he noticed a direct relationship between his physical condition and the form of his waking thoughts: 'Images in sickly profusion by & in which I talk in certain diseased States of my Stomach ...' (*CN*, 1: 1822). See also his ironic suggestion in a letter of 1803 that 'All our faulty Laws, Regulations, [and] national mismanagements ... have originated in the false Trains of Ideas introduced by diseased Sensations from the Stomach into the Brains of our Senators, Priests, & Merchants' (*CL*, 2: 987).
53. MS note in Taylor, *ΣΥΜΒΟΛΟΝ ΘΕΟΛΟΓΙΚΟΝ* (British Library, Ashley 5174), 297. The word 'soul' is supplied from Derwent Coleridge's edition of this note, in *NED*, 1: 299. Coleridge is responding to Taylor's words: 'St. Ambrose saith, That *Death is a haven of rest*.'
54. The ideal condition of sleep described in *CN*, 1: 191 extends this explanation of dreams to involve a direct intuition of God: 'In the paradisiacal World Sleep was voluntary & holy—a spiritual before

God, in which the mind elevated by contemplation retired into pure intellect suspending all commerce with sensible objects & perceiving the present deity—.'

55. MS note in Taylor, *ΣΥΜΒΟΛΟΝ ΘΕΟΛΟΓΙΚΟΝ* (British Library, Ashley 5174), 297–8. A similar dream of death, and similar effects of the body on his dreams, are connected with Swedenborg's descriptions of hell in *CN*, 4: 4689 and *CL*, 6: 607, dating from 1820 and 1826 respectively.
56. See especially *CN*, 3: 3474.
57. See *CN*, 4: 4820 and Emanuel Swedenborg, *Heaven and Hell; also, the Intermediate State, or World of Spirits; a Relation of Things Heard and Seen* [trans. J. Clowes] (London: Swedenborg Society, 1850), 270.
58. *BL*, 2: 234–5. See also Coleridge's reference, in *CM*, 2: 559, to 'a state below Time ... which is the direst Evil, that Man can ... eschew or suffer', and which he contrasts with 'a state above Time' which 'is the greatest Good that Man can seek or possess' (quoted in Paley, *Coleridge's Later Poetry*, 50).

CHAPTER 3 THE FEELING OF KNOWLEDGE: INSIGHT AND DELUSION IN COLERIDGE

1. See, for example, *CL*, 2: 709: 'My opinion is this—that deep Thinking is attainable only by a man of deep Feeling, and that all Truth is a species of Revelation.'
2. On the compensatory nature of Coleridge's philosophical optimism see especially John Colmer, 'Coleridge and the Life of Hope', *SR*, 2 (1972) 332.
3. See *Lects 1808–19*, 1: 219.
4. For Coleridge's principal discussions of the varieties of intellectual pleasure see *PLects*, 141 and *CN*, 3: 3558.
5. On Coleridge's view of faith as 'a special form of active knowledge ... gained by active exercise of "the free will, our only absolute *self*"', see James Engell, 'Coleridge and German Idealism: First Postulates, final Causes', Richard Gravil and Molly Lefebure (eds), *The Coleridge Connection: Essays for Thomas McFarland* (London: Macmillan, 1990), 158.
6. See More, *A Collection of Several Philosophical Writings*, ii: 18.
7. Richard Baxter, *Preservatives Against Melancholy and Overmuch Sorrow: Or the Cure of Both by Faith and Physick* (London, 1713), 20.
8. My use of the term 'sublimation' is suggested by Weiskel, who uses it to connect the movement of transcendence involved in the sublime both with the Freudian sense of the term (i.e. a transition from physical satisfactions to emotional ones) and with 'the usual sense of the word in chemistry, i.e., the direct passage from a solid to a gaseous state'. See Thomas Weiskel, *The Romantic Sublime: Studies in the Structure and Psychology of Transcendence* (Baltimore, MD: Johns Hopkins UP, 1976), 31.

9. And as they have done, indeed. See especially Beverly Fields, *Reality's Dark Dream: Dejection in Coleridge* (Kent, OH: Kent State UP, 1967), 101–18.
10. Coburn, indeed, suggests that Coleridge's defence of minds such as Boehme's 'was aroused more by sympathetic psychological understanding than by any agreement in mystical opinions' (*Inquiring Spirit: A New Presentation of Coleridge From His Published and Unpublished Writings*, ed. Kathleen Coburn [London: Routledge, 1951], 16). See also *AR*, 393–4, where Coleridge describes how a mystic whose gifts have been 'developed and displayed by all the arts of Education and favorable Fortune' will recognize that 'the delightful Dream' recorded by authors such as Boehme 'is a Dream of Truth'.
11. See *BL*, 1: 152.
12. Ibid.
13. The quotation is from Wordsworth, *The Excursion*, I, 79 (*WPW*, 5: 10). Coleridge's characterization of the 'enthusiast' in *CN*, 3: 3847 closely resembles this description of Boehme. However, see also *Say*, 1: 51–2, where he quotes Wordsworth not to evoke visionary insight, but rather to illustrate the tendency towards mystical delusion to which, he says, 'men of ardent Minds' are liable.
14. Shaftesbury, whose discussion of 'enthusiasm' bears important resemblances to Coleridge's analysis of Boehme, nevertheless admits the difficulty of making this distinction. Enthusiasm, he says, 'is a matter of nice Judgment, and the hardest thing in the world to know fully and distinctly.... Nor can Divine Inspiration, by its outward Marks, be easily distinguish'd from it. For Inspiration is a real feeling of the Divine Presence, and Enthusiasm a false one' (Shaftesbury, *A Letter Concerning Enthusiasm* [London, 1708], 80–1).
15. My emphasis.
16. On Coleridge's theory of desynonymy see especially Paul Hamilton, *Coleridge's Poetics* (Oxford: Blackwell, 1983), 62–88.
17. For a clarification of Coleridge's use of the expression '*finds me*' in this passage, see *SWF*, 2: 1121–2, where he writes that throughout the Bible he has '<found> words for my inmost Thoughts, Songs for my Joy, Utterances for my hidden Griefs, pleadings for my Shame and my feebleness', and adds: 'In short *whatever finds me* ... bears witness for itself that it had proceeded from a Holy Spirit ...' What he seems to mean by this expression, therefore, is that an apparent coincidence between his feelings and the words of the Bible suggests to him that the Bible is in fact the word of God – a circuitous (if not uncommon) mode of making feeling the basis of belief.
18. See also *CM*, 1: 270: 'Fanaticism is the *fever* of *superstition*. Enthusiasm, on the contrary, implies an undue (or when used in a good sense, an unusual) vividness of ideas, as opposed to perceptions, or of the obscure inward feelings.'
19. *TT*, 1: 333–4, indeed, locates fanaticism not in any disposition or state of mind, but in an appeal to the emotions unmediated by any engagement of the intellect: 'Every attempt in a sermon to cause emotion, except as the consequence of an impression made on the Reason or the

Understanding or the Will', Coleridge is reported as saying, 'I hold to be fanatical and sectarian.'

20. As the editors of *BL* point out, the image of the crowd *'circum fana'* ('around the temple') also occurs in *CM*, 1: 270 and 1: 496, while that of swarming bees can also be found in *CN*, 2: 2434 and *Friend*, 1: 508.
21. See also *BL*, 1: 31, however, where Coleridge writes that 'The sanity of the mind is between superstition with fanaticism on the one hand; and enthusiasm with indifference and a diseased slowness to action on the other.' Enthusiasm, he implies, consists in having such vivid ideas, and possessing so great a power of 'combining and modifying' them, that 'the feelings and affections blend more easily and intimately with these ideal creations, than with the objects of the senses,' and the mind has little interest in any external occurrences until 'by means of meditation they have passed into *thoughts*'.
22. *LS*, 23. See also *CM*, 1: 818, where Coleridge attributes this remark to Seneca.
23. This view is clearest in *CM*, 1: 818: 'Bunyan was a man of too much Genius to be a Fanatic. No two qualities more contrary than Genius and Fanaticism/Enthusiasm indeed ... is almost a Synonime of Genius – the moral *Life* in the intellectual *Light*, the Will in the Reason: and without it, says Seneca, nothing truly great was ever atchieved by Man.' See also, however, *CN*, 3: 3847, where Coleridge gives a description of enthusiasm which exactly duplicates the ambiguity of his discussion of mysticism in *Biographia* and his marginalia on Boehme.
24. This distinction may have been suggested by Cudworth's statement that in geometry as in religion 'mere speculation and dry mathematical reason' are not always sufficient to enforce belief, yet that there is 'a certain higher and diviner power in the soul' – the power of faith – whose insight is secure and unquestionable. See Ralph Cudworth, *The True Intellectual System of the Universe*, ed. J. Harrison (3 vols, London: Thomas Tegg, 1845), 1: xlv.
25. Marginal note in Taylor, *ΣΥΜΒΟΛΟΝ ΘΕΟΛΟΓΙΚΟΝ* (British Library, Ashley 5174), verso of last leaf.
26. *CN*, 1: 1815 refers to 'the warm coloring of one who feels the Truth'. See also *CN*, 2: 2196, where he suggests that truth may be 'eclipsed' by 'passions heterogeneous to it', and expresses the fear that 'in acquiring the *passion* of proselytism' he might 'lose the *sense* of conviction'.
27. *LS*, 175.
28. This view is supported by Coleridge's description of Wordsworth's critics in *BL*, 1: 71: 'Not able to deny that the author possessed both genius and a powerful intellect, they felt *very positive*, but were not *quite certain*, that he might not be in the right, and they themselves in the wrong; an unquiet state of mind, which seeks alleviation by quarrelling with the occasion of it.' Similarly in the case of fanatics, 'The absence of all foundation within their own minds for that, which they yet believe both true and indispensable for their safety

and happiness, cannot but produce an uneasy state of feeling, an involuntary sense of fear from which nature has no means of rescuing herself but by anger' (*BL*, 1: 31).

29. S.T. Coleridge and R. Southey, *Omniana, or Horae Otiosiores*, ed. Robert Gittings (Fontwell: Centaur, 1969), 329.
30. *Friend*, 1: 35.
31. *Friend*, 1: 106. The last three 'obscure ideas' listed here are precisely those which Kant describes as 'the proper object' of metaphysical inquiry (*CPR*, 325n.), and whose moral importance he emphasizes in the *Critique of Practical Reason* (see Immanuel Kant, *Critique of Practical Reason*, trans. Lewis White Beck [Chicago: University of Chicago Press, 1949], 234–6).
32. See *EOT*, 2: 78; also *BL*, 2: 143, and *Lects 1795*, 52.
33. Coleridge's reference in *EOT*, 2: 77–8 to 'that man, who on circumstances which vitally affect the weal and woe of the whole human race in time and for eternity, can reason in as cold-blooded a tone, as if he were demonstrating a problem in geometry' particularly recalls his view of Hume, who according to Coleridge 'devoted his life to the undermining of the Christian religion, and expended his last breath in the blasphemous regret that he had not survived it' (*LS*, 22).

CHAPTER 4 THOUGHT INTO FEELING

1. These topics are discussed with considerable frequency in, for example, Ashton, *The Life of Samuel Taylor Coleridge*, and Norman Fruman, *Coleridge: The Damaged Archangel* (London: Allen & Unwin, 1971).
2. See especially *Friend*, 1: 519 on the 'emotion tranquil from its very intensity' with which he contemplates the infinite and indefinable powers underlying nature and the human mind.
3. See especially *Say*, 1: 76–7 on how the phenomenal self, or 'the phantom by which the individual misrepresents the unity of his personal being ... borrows from [external] objects a sort of unnatural outwardness' and 'becomes as it were a thing'. *Say*, 1: 77–8 associates such objectification of the self with the materialistic 'idolatry' which Coleridge elsewhere criticizes so severely (see, for example, *Friend*, 1: 106). See also *SWF*, 1: 530 on 'the philosophy of Death'.
4. See especially Jacques Derrida, *Writing and Difference*, trans. Alan Bass (Baltimore, MD: Johns Hopkins UP, 1978), 196–231.
5. See especially Edward Kessler, *Coleridge's Metaphors of Being* (Princeton, NJ: Princeton UP, 1979), 27, 30, and my discussion of Coleridge's view of the objective or phenomenal self in section 1 of this chapter.
6. See especially McFarland, *Paradoxes of Freedom*, 61–3 on this point.
7. See *CJ*, 105. The context of Kant's discussion is the sublimity of mountain landscapes, yet his description of how they produce a feeling of imagination's inability to grasp ideas of reason has obvious relevance to Coleridge's quest for metaphysical knowledge.
8. See also the analogous passage in *CPW*, 1: 366–7.

9. See, for example, J. V. Baker, *The Sacred River* (Baton Rouge, LA: Louisiana State UP, 1957), 183–4, and J. H. Muirhead, *Coleridge as Philosopher* (London: Allen & Unwin, 1930), 44.
10. See also J. A. Appleyard, *Coleridge's Philosophy of Literature: The Development of a Concept of Poetry* (Cambridge, MA: Harvard UP, 1965), 9 on this point.
11. See especially Beverly Fields, *Reality's Dark Dream*, 101–18.
12. Lockridge, *Coleridge the Moralist*, 68.
13. On 'transcendence' and 'facticity' – the two components of 'bad faith' – see Jean-Paul Sartre, *Being and Nothingness*, trans. Hazel E. Barnes (London: Methuen, 1957), 47–67.
14. Lockridge, *Coleridge The Moralist*, 39–40. See also Kessler, *Coleridge's Metaphors of Being*, 137 on Coleridge's view that 'whenever he stopped believing in his own power he became an object and his self-evolution ceased, for "all that is truly human must proceed from within"', and ibid., 27 on the considerable moral importance he attached to escaping such objectification.
15. See Jean-Pierre Mileur, *Vision and Revision: Coleridge's Art of Immanence* (Berkeley: University of California Press, 1982), 88.
16. On these points see especially *CN*, 2: 3026, 3: 4007 and 3: 4066.
17. See also *LS*, 90, where Coleridge writes that all creation longs to retire 'into that image, which is its substantial form and true life, from the vanity of Self, which then only *is* when *for itself* it hath ceased to be'.
18. See especially *Lects 1808–19*, 2: 148. Shakespeare, Coleridge says, 'shaped his characters out of the Nature within—but we cannot so safely say, out of *his own* Nature, as an *individual person*.—No! this latter is itself but a *natura naturata*—an effect, a product, not a *power*'. On Spinoza's distinction between *natura naturans* and *natura naturata* see Chapter 6, section 1. On the analogous concepts of 'forma formans' and 'forma formata' see, for example, Coleridge, *Logic*, 231–2.
19. See Mileur, *Vision and Revision*, 88.
20. See especially *CN*, 2: 3026: 'All our thoughts all that we abstract from our consciousness & so form the Phaenomenon Self is a Shadow, its whole Substance is the dim yet powerful sense that it is but a Shadow, and ought to belong to a Substance.' *Say*, 1: 76–7 similarly emphasizes the materialistic implications of any objectification of the self.
21. Colmer notes a similar pattern in a letter to Humphry Davy of 1800 which 'dramatizes the very process by which [Coleridge] universalizes his personal experiences... In a few lines, he passes from complaints of "tumbling on through sands and swamps of Evil, & bodily grievance" to detached analysis of universal relevance' (John Colmer, 'Coleridge and the Life of Hope', 332, quoting *CL*, 1: 648–9). See also *CL*, 1: 558 where Coleridge describes the relief to be found in enthusiastically 'believing the progressiveness of all nature, during the present melancholy state of Humanity'.
22. See also the sonnet 'Composed on a Journey Homeward; the Author Having Received Intelligence of the Birth of a Son' (*CPW*, 1: 153–4), where Coleridge seeks, by reflecting on the eternity of life and the

possibility of our pre-existence, to pre-empt the grief which would result from discovering that his son was dead.

23. Coburn remarks that '*Hope* was perhaps the most important word in Coleridge's vocabulary', appearing in the *Concordance* to his poems over 300 times (Coburn, *The Self Conscious Imagination*, 45n.).
24. See Raimonda Modiano, *Coleridge and the Concept of Nature* (London: Macmillan, 1985), 22; also *CN*, 1: 1675n.
25. *CL*, 1: 482. See also Colmer, 'Coleridge and the Life of Hope', 332 on 'the importance Coleridge attributed to hope in the development of the whole personality and the crucial place it occupied in his political theory'. According to the 'Allegoric Vision' at the beginning of the second *Lay Sermon*, Colmer notes, 'absence of hope inevitably produces superstition and blind worship of materialism' (ibid., 341).
26. As Coleman notes, in a letter to Francis Jeffrey of December 1808 Coleridge stated of the prospective *Friend* that it was 'impossible to succeed in such a work unless at the commencement of it there be a quickening and throb in the pulse of Hope'. Similarly, 'Writing of the first two numbers of *The Friend*, Charles Lloyd commented that Coleridge's mind was one which "except in inspired moods, can do nothing".' See *CL*, 3: 156 and Coleman, *Coleridge and 'The Friend'*, 18n., 50.
27. See especially *CPW*, 1: 366–7 and *BL*, 1: 17.
28. Dorothy Emmet, 'Coleridge on the Growth of the Mind', *Bulletin of the John Rylands Library*, 34 (1952) 287.
29. See *CL*, 1: 623 (the identity of the addressee is uncertain).
30. As Paley points out (*Coleridge's Later Poetry*, 25), Coleridge's later verse rarely makes the 'prophetic' claims of his greatest early poems, but rather establishes a new role for its author 'as a poet of personal sentiment, intimate friendship, and meditative reflection'.
31. See *CPW*, 1: 447, 1: 366–7, 1: 429–31; also the valuable discussion of these poems in Paley, *Coleridge's Later Poetry*, 41–61.
32. See Paley, *Coleridge's Later Poetry*, 36, and Hill, *The Lords of Limit*, 12 on this point.
33. The concentration of Coleridge's notebook entries on Swedenborg's *De Coelo et Inferno* in the period after 1818, together with the similarity of their content to that of his marginalia in the same work, suggest that the latter date from a similar period (see, for example, *CN*, 4: 4689, 4: 5360).
34. See Coleridge's marginalia in Emanuel Swedenborg, *De Coelo et Eius Mirabilibus, et de Inferno, ex Auditis et Visis* (British Library, C.126 k.4), 233; also Emanuel Swedenborg, *Heaven and Hell*, 287–91. A similarly intense longing for redemption from spiritual and bodily evils, and a similar commitment to religious devotion as the means to that release, is evident in *CM*, 3: 746–7.
35. Though the 'soul-stifling shame' associated with his addiction and resulting nightmares is evident as early as 'The Pains of Sleep' (included in a letter to Southey in 1803 [see *CL*, 2: 982–4]), Coleridge's preoccupation with the 'hell' to be expected after death, rather than merely in this life, is far more prominent in his writings

after 1820. See, for example, *CN*, 4: 4689, *CM*, 3: 747, and his marginalia on Taylor, *ΣΥΜΒΟΛΟΝ ΘΕΟΛΟΓΙΚΟΝ* (British Library, Ashley 5174), 297. (An adjoining passage of these marginalia carries the date '1824': see ibid., 301.) On the evidence for Coleridge's development of a unique philosophical system combining Trinitarian thought with elements of Schelling's idealism 'from September 1818 onwards', see especially Reid, 'Coleridge and Schelling', 452.

36. Coleridge's reference, in the note on Swedenborg quoted above, to 'opiates, which [the addict] loathes while he takes, yet still takes, goaded on by pain, and more than pain, and by the dread of both' particularly recalls the 'unfathomable hell' of his nightmares evoked in 'The Pains of Sleep'. See his marginalia on Swedenborg, *De Coelo et Inferno* (see British Library, C.126 k.4), 233, and *CPW*, 1: 389). His late critique of Wordsworth's mysticism in 'Tintern Abbey' (echoing his own self-criticism in 'The Eolian Harp') highlights the increasing orthodoxy of Coleridge's faith (see *Say*, 1: 51–2 and *CPW*, 1: 102).
37. On Coleridge's consistent fascination with such theories of progress, see Chapter 5.
38. See, for example, *Friend*, 1: 108, 2: 7, *CN*, 1: 868, and *EOT*, 2: 78. As Harding notes (*Coleridge and the Idea of Love*, 23) 'The notion that truth is invisible to all but the man of sincere feeling was ... to become axiomatic with Coleridge.'
39. See also *CN*, 1: 1623, from which this passage of *The Friend* is clearly derived. For the 'bad spirits in hell' see *Paradise Lost*, 2: 555–69, Milton, *Poetical Works*, ed. Douglas Bush (Oxford: OUP, 1966), 244.
40. On the probable source of much of this passage in Fichte, see G. N. G. Orsini, *Coleridge and German Idealism: A Study in the History of Philosophy with Unpublished Materials from Coleridge's Manuscripts* (Carbondale: Southern Illinois UP, 1969), 182–3. However, see also Hume's analogous description (*Treatise*, 106) of how 'In thinking of our past thoughts we not only delineate out the objects, of which we were thinking, but also conceive the action of the mind in meditation, that certain *je-ne-scai-quoi*, of which 'tis impossible to give any definition or description, but which every one sufficiently understands.'
41. For Coleridge's use of the phrase 'a naked Spirit' to evoke the dependence of all aspects of reality on the self see *CL*, 1: 295.
42. The deletion of 'pleasures' is Coleridge's.
43. See *AR*, 49.
44. See *CL*, 2: 916.
45. A similar process to Coleridge's 'fermentation' is described by Erasmus Darwin as characterizing the 'pleasurable insanity' of religious fanaticism. 'When the sensorial power of volition excites agreeable ideas, and the pleasure thus produced excites more volition in its turn', he writes, 'a constant flow of agreeable voluntary ideas succeeds; which when thus exerted in the extreme constitutes insanity' (Erasmus Darwin, *Zoonomia*, 2 vols [London, 1794–6], 1: 434).
46. See *OED*.

47. For the source of this analogy see Plato, *The Republic*, trans. F. M. Cornford (Oxford: Clarendon, 1941), 215.
48. Griggs provisionally dates this letter to 1820 (see *CL*, 5: 97n.).
49. This valorization is perhaps expressed most clearly in the etymology by which Coleridge connects the words 'think' (*denken, reor*) and 'thing' (*ding, res*). 'Thought', he writes, 'is the participle past of Thing' (*CN*, 3: 3587): hence it cannot be understood, but is rather the eternal antecedent of the image.
50. See also Immanuel Kant, *Groundwork of the Metaphysic of Morals*, trans. H. J. Paton (New York: Harper & Row, 1964), 88–9 for Kant's most famous statement of the 'universal imperative of duty'.
51. See Kant, *Groundwork of the Metaphysic of Morals*, 83, 89.
52. See especially *LS*, 43, where Coleridge writes that any 'imperfection of form' in his essay 'will not be altogether uncompensated, if it should be the means of presenting with greater liveliness the feelings and impressions under which [it was] written', and thus bring its readers closer to his own intellectual and religious viewpoint, and *Friend*, 1: 15–16, where he expresses the aim of persuading his readers to pursue the same intellectual pleasures as himself, and by means of the same insights.
53. As the editors of *CM* point out, Bernard Mandeville (1670–1733) 'argued with Hobbes that the origin of virtue is to be found in selfish and savage instincts' (see *CM*, 2: 636n.).
54. John Locke, *An Essay Concerning Human Understanding*, ed. P. H. Nidditch (Oxford: Clarendon, 1975), 6.
55. See also *Friend* 1: 104–5, 2: 71, and the analogous passage in *Say*, 1: 21–2. Coleridge is apparently referring to the passage from Ephesians, 3: 14–19 which he quotes in the same paragraph. *AR*, 223–4, however, attributes an almost identical expression to Hooker, who, Coleridge says, used it in the definition of 'reason': 'Reason (says our great HOOKER) is a direct Aspect of Truth, an inward Beholding, having a similar relation to the Intelligible or Spiritual, as SENSE has to the Material or Phenomenal.'
56. Marshall Suther, *The Dark Night of Samuel Taylor Coleridge* (New York: Columbia UP, 1960), 27.
57. On the ancient contempt for 'book-knowledge', see also *Logic*, 31–2.
58. See especially *CN*, 3: 4350 and 3: 4066; also *CM*, 1: 299, where Baxter's description of how he was once almost crushed by books falling from a shelf produces the ironic response from Coleridge: '*μεγα βιβλιον μεγα κακον*' ('a great book is a great evil'). See also Coburn, *Experience into Thought: Perspectives in the Coleridge Notebooks* (Toronto: University of Toronto Press, 1979), 13 on this point.
59. See *Friend*, 1: 491–2 on Bacon's '*idola intellectus*'. For Coleridge, the paradigmatic instance of intellectual idolatry is materialism, which combines intellectual stasis with absorption in the world of sense and a rejection of religious truth. See especially *Friend*, 1: 517–8 and *Say*, 1: 76–8 on these points.

60. For the source of this quotation, see *A Complete Collection of the Historical, Political, and Miscellaneous Works of John Milton*, ed. Thomas Birch, 2 vols (London: A. Millar, 1738), 1: 154. The passage which Coleridge quotes is immediately preceded in Milton by the statement that 'our Faith and Knowledge thrives by Exercise, as well as our Limbs and Complexion' (ibid.). The idea of truth as a process of intellectual exploration and advance is thus paradoxically linked to the recommendation of a certain religious orthodoxy – a combination whose purpose in this work (subtitled *A Speech for the Liberty of Unlicens'd Printing*) is clear, yet which also emphasizes Coleridge's desire both for progress and for belief in a spiritual destination whose form is to some extent defined in advance.
61. G. W. F. Hegel, *Phenomenology of Spirit* (1807), trans. A.V. Miller (Oxford: OUP, 1977), 27. The insertions in square brackets are Miller's.
62. See Kessler, *Coleridge's Metaphors of Being*, 24. Coleridge's enthusiasm for the 'stream' image is particularly clear in *Friend*, 1: 472–3, where he discusses Plato's views on the relation between active discovery and received or communicable knowledge. 'We see', he writes, 'that to open anew a well of springing water, not to cleanse the stagnant tank, or fill, bucket by bucket, the leadern cistern; that the EDUCATION of the intellect, by awakening the principle and *method* of self-development, was his proposed object, not any specific information that can be *conveyed into it* from without ...'.
63. On the composition of Coleridge's 'Preliminary Treatise on Method' for the *Encyclopedia* and its differences from the 'Essays on the Principles of Method' in *The Friend* see A. D. Snyder (ed.), *Coleridge's Treatise on Method* (London, 1934), vii–xxvii.
64. See *Friend*, 1: 453.
65. See also *Friend*, 1: 466, where Coleridge decribes how in the formation of botanical classifications 'some *antecedent* must have been contributed by the mind itself; some *purpose* must be in view; or some question at least must have been proposed to nature, grounded, as all questions are, upon *some* idea of the answer'. This principle appears to derive from Bacon's 'initiative' or '*prudens quaestio* ... which he affirms to be the prior *half* of the knowledge sought' (*Friend*, 1: 489).
66. It is so defined by opposition to 'talent', or 'the comparative facility of acquiring, arranging, and applying the stock furnished by others and already existing in books or other conservatories of intellect' (*Friend*, 1: 419).
67. See *Friend*, 1: 519. As Kessler notes (*Coleridge's Metaphors of Being*, 24), Coleridge also regarded the qualities of continuity and flow as characteristic of his own thinking – a view echoed by Hazlitt. See *The Complete Works of Willam Hazlitt*, ed. P. P. Howe, 21 vols (London: Dent, 1930–4), 11: 32; also J. C. C. Mays, 'Coleridge on Prose' (Oxford DPhil Thesis, 1966), 77–8 on the frequency with which Coleridge's contemporaries 'were led to characterize his conversation in terms of a great fountain, stream or river, by adjectives like "outpouring" and "flow".'

68. This paradox and its ultimate resolution are also noted by Kessler. 'The forward-moving stream', he writes, 'is finally the controlling metaphor for Coleridge, whether it momentarily achieves the sublime marriage of motion and rest in a waterfall, or acquires the hypnotic power of an eddy' (Kessler, *Coleridge's Metaphors of Being*, 24).
69. On this point see also *CN*, 1: 1077: 'A Thought and Thoughts are quite different words from Thought – as a Fancy from Fancy, a Work from Work, a Life from Life, a Force & Forces from Force, a Feeling, a Writing, &c.'
70. Similar distinctions appear in notes taken by J. Tomalin at two lectures given by Coleridge in November 1811, in the *Morning Chronicle*'s report of his lecture of 25 November, and in a contemporary notebook of Coleridge's. See *Lects 1808–19*, 1: 217, 219, 230, 245, 254–5.
71. See also, however, *Lects 1808–19*, 1: 217 (Coleridge's notes for a lecture of 1811), which states that 'The ⟨proper & immediate⟩ Object of Science is the acquirement or communication of Truth.'
72. This sentence is a quotation, with minor alterations, from no. 5 of the periodical *Friend* (see *Friend*, 2: 73). It also appears, again with minor changes, in *The Statesman's Manual* (see *LS*, 25).
73. This definition of poetry also occurs in notes taken at three lectures given by Coleridge in November 1811, in the *Morning Chronicle*'s report of the lecture given on 25 November, and in a contemporary notebook of Coleridge's. See *Lects 1808–19*, 1: 205, 218, 221, 230–1, 245, 255; also *CN*, 3: 4111, 4112.
74. See *CN*, 2: 2372, quoted in Chapter 2, section 3.
75. That the opposition between spontaneous and voluntary corresponds to the distinction between passion and control is put in question by Coleridge's reference in *BL*, 2: 64 to 'that spontaneous effort which strives to hold in check the workings of passion'. Both here and in the above extract from his lecture notes, however, Coleridge seems to be concerned with the dependence of poetic form upon essentially unconscious forces. Poetry may not be structured by the feeling we intend to express; yet the necessity of a certain form is determined by intuition rather than reflection. See also *Lects 1808–19*, 2: 218, where Coleridge notes 'how by excitement of the Associative Power Passion itself imitates Order, and the *order* resulting produces a pleasurable *Passion* (whence Metre) and thus elevates the Mind by making its feelings the Objects of its reflection'.
76. As Roy Park comments with regard to Coleridge's plans for *The Recluse* outlined in *CL*, 4: 574–5 ('Coleridge: Philosopher and Theologian as Literary Critic', *UTQ* 38 [1968]: 31), 'there can be no question [but] that poetry, whose concern with truths Coleridge had denied in order to oppose it to science, is still concerned with one kind of truths, with supersensible and non-natural ones'.
77. See also *BL*, 2: 14. The reader of a 'just' poem, Coleridge writes, 'should be carried forward, not merely or chiefly by the mechanical impulse of curiosity, or by a restless desire to arrive at the final

solution; but by the pleasureable [*sic*] activity of mind excited by the attractions of the journey itself'. According to this description, poetry ought to involve exactly the order of objectives – first truth, and thence pleasure – which Coleridge elsewhere assigns to philosophy (see *BL*, 2: 12, quoted earlier in this section).

78. On this point see Bishop C. Hunt, Jr., 'Coleridge and the Endeavour of Philosophy', *PMLA*, 91 (1976) 833: 'Many of Coleridge's statements, and Wordsworth's also, on the need for good poetry to approach the condition of prose, may just as well be read in reverse order.' It is perhaps worth noting, with Hunt, Coleridge's statement in *BL*, 2: 25–6 that 'No man was ever yet a great poet, without being at the same time a profound philosopher.'
79. This attitude is taken so far, indeed, that Aristotle even asks whether a man can be called happy while he is alive. See *Aristotle's Ethics*, trans. J. A. Ackrill (London: Faber, 1973), 54–5.
80. For Aristotle's chief statement of this principle, see ibid., 49–50.
81. See ibid., 172–7.
82. See, for example, *CM*, 2: 641, where he particularly criticizes Fichte's statement that the pleasures of thinking 'occasion the same *kind* of gratification as Apple-pie & Custard'.
83. The words in square brackets are supplied by Coburn from other contemporary manuscripts. See also *PLects*, 152–3, where Coleridge vigorously denies that the 'particular state of being which we experience from an approving conscience' and the 'different state of being which we possess during the gratification of any appetite' are merely different forms of pleasure.
84. Coleridge's use of *eudaimonia* as a synonym for pleasure interestingly conflicts not only with Aristotle's use of the term, but also with his own distinction between pleasure and 'well-being' in *Friend*, 1: 39.
85. See also *PLects*, 140–1, and *CN*, 3: 3931, 3558n. on this point.
86. Hamilton, *Coleridge's Poetics*, 73.
87. See *CN*, 3: 3312: 'By Synonymes I mean words ... really equivalent, both in ... material meaning & in the feelings or notions associated with them .... and by Homoeonymes those words, falsely thought or carelessly used as Synonymes—To *make* real Synonymes into Homoeonymes, is the privilege of Genius, whether poetic or philosophic.' This passage is discussed in Hamilton, *Coleridge's Poetics*, 73. See ibid., 62–88 for a fuller discussion of Coleridge's theory of desynonymy.
88. In *PLects*, 141 and *CN* 3: 3558, for example, Coleridge clearly implies that the existence of a variety of terms in Greek and Latin for ideas not usually distinguished in English proves the existence of an unacknowledged variety in phenomena. The terms 'pleasure', 'happiness' and 'gladness' are then appropriated to the different meanings he attributes to the Latin and Greek terms.
89. See *SWF*, 1: 375.
90. See *SWF*, 1: 363.
91. This superiority is also discussed in *PLects*, 207.

CHAPTER 5 POWER AND PROGRESS: COLERIDGE'S METAPHORS OF THOUGHT

1. The first of these groups of theories, which borrows from eighteenth-century empiricist thinkers, belongs entirely to the 1790s, though it was not until 1801 that Coleridge overtly rejected associationism (see *CL*, 2: 706). Schelling's influence is at its peak in the philosophical chapters of *Biographia*, though as early as 1818 Coleridge disavowed many of the ideas he had adopted from Schelling (see, for example, *CM*, 1: 138). Theories describing man as the highest stage of natural evolution, on the other hand, can be found in writings dating from 1816 – the probable year of composition of the *Theory of Life* (see *SWF*, 1: 481) – until the last years of his life (see, for example, *C&S*, 179).
2. See, for example, *CL*, 1: 192.
3. For contrasting views on Hartley see, for example, *CL*, 1: 126 and 2: 706; on Priestley, *CL*, 1: 140 and 192; and on Godwin, *CL*, 1: 115 and 199.
4. See, for example, Dorothy Emmet, 'Coleridge on the Growth of the Mind', 280, and J. A. Appleyard, *Coleridge's Philosophy of Literature*, 9.
5. See especially McFarland, *Paradoxes of Freedom*, 35–7 on Coleridge's and Wordsworth's increasing separation of freedom 'from revolutionary aspiration'.
6. See *CL*, 1: 137.
7. See, for example, *CL*, 1: 145 and 147, where Coleridge both expresses his support for 'Necessitarian' views and describes himself as 'a Unitarian Christian and an Advocate for the Automatism of Man' – the latter phrase clearly implying allegiance to both Hartley and Priestley, and an absence of distinction between their doctrines. On Coleridge's view of Priestley as 'the author of the modern Unitarianism' see Basil Willey, *Samuel Taylor Coleridge* (London: Chatto, 1972), 31, and *TT*, 1: 488.
8. Priestley's enthusiasm for Hartley is noted in Clarke Garrett, *Respectable Folly: Millenarians and the French Revolution in France and England* (Baltimore, MD: Johns Hopkins UP, 1975), 128. In *The Present State of Europe Compared with Antient Prophesies* (London, 1794), 35, Priestley describes Hartley's *Observations* as 'that most excellent work, to which I am indebted ... for the whole moral conformation of my mind'. His particular enthusiasm for Hartley's vision of humankind's continuous progression towards happiness and union with the deity is expressed in *The Doctrine of Philosophical Necessity Illustrated* (London, 1777), 127–9.
9. Joseph Priestley, *Hartley's Theory of the Human Mind, on the Principle of the Association of Ideas* (London, 1775), xx.
10. This was apparently the impression created by the passage on first publication. 'I little imagined', Priestley later wrote, 'that such a paragraph as this could have given the alarm that I presently found

it had done. My *doubts* were instantly converted into a *full persuasion*, and the cry against me as an *unbeliever*, and a *favourer of atheism*, was exceedingly general and loud ...' (Joseph Priestley, *Disquisitions Relating to Matter and Spirit* [London, 1777; Birmingham, 1782], viii). Yet though he describes these accusations as 'gross defamation', Priestley admits that his further consideration of the subject 'terminated in a full conviction, that the doubt I had expressed [as to the essential differentness of body and mind] was well founded' (ibid.).

11. Priestley, *Doctrine*, viii.
12. Priestley, *Doctrine*, viii–ix.
13. Ibid., viii, xii–xiii. As Haven points out, in part 2 of the *Observations* Hartley similarly argues that 'As we come to associate greater pleasure with God than with anything else connected with ourselves', we will arrive at 'an intire Annihilation of ourselves, and an absolute Acquiescence and Complacence in the Will of God'. (See Richard Haven, 'Coleridge, Hartley, and the Mystics', *JHI*, 20 [1959] 483, and *OM*, 2: 22, 2: 313.) Whereas the increasing happiness and piety which Hartley describes are entirely products of association, however, Priestley envisages our happiness as resulting from religious faith, and makes no reference to the mechanical causes which, in Hartley, render the concept of human 'will', and hence that of piety, extremely problematic.
14. Priestley, *Doctrine*, xii–xiii.
15. Priestley, *An Essay on the First Principles of Government* (London, 1768), 2–3.
16. Most of this passage also appears in the Introductory Address of 'Conciones ad Populum' (see *Lects 1795*, 40). See also *Lects 1795*, 235–6, where Coleridge connects these ideas directly with Neoplatonism, describing how imagination 'stimulates [us] to the attainment of real excellence by the contemplation of splendid Possibilities ... and fixing our eye on the glittering Summits that rise one above the other in Alpine endlessness still urges us up the ascent of Being'. An additional source for this passage, however, is suggested by the editors of *Lects 1795*, who point out that its content and phrasing recall parts of Akenside's *Pleasures of Imagination* (see *Lects 1795*, 235–6n., and *The Poetical Works of Mark Akenside*, ed. Robin Dix [Madison, NJ: AUP, 1996], 96–8, 121).
17. Priestley, *Doctrine*, xiv.
18. Ibid., viii–ix, xiii.
19. See especially *Lects 1795*, 12, where Coleridge praises those who have 'made their duty a necessary part of their self-interest, by the long-continued cultivation of that moral taste which derives our most exquisite pleasures from the contemplation of possible perfection, and proportionate pain from the perception of existing depravation'.
20. See Priestley, *Doctrine*, ix.
21. See *WPW*, 4: 281–4.
22. In 1797 the line 'All self-annihilated ...', to which this note was attached, was line 44 rather than 43 (see S. T. Coleridge, *Poems*

[2nd edn, Bristol and London, 1797], 122). As Fairchild points out, however, 'After 1797, the note to line 44 ... was carefully omitted, and thenceforward Coleridge never disclosed the fact that he had once prized Hartley as a non-enthusiastic demonstrator of the beatific vision' (H. N. Fairchild, 'Hartley, Pistorius, and Coleridge', *PMLA*, 62 [1947] 1021).

23. See Fairchild, 'Hartley, Pistorius, and Coleridge', 1017–18, and *BL*, 1: 121–2. On the 'Neoplatonic' content of Hartley's system see also Ian Wylie, 'How the Natural Philosophers Defeated the Whore of Babylon in the Thought of S.T. Coleridge', *Review of English Studies*, New Series, 35 (1984) 497.
24. Coleridge does, however, emphatically celebrate Hartley's associationism near the end of 'Religious Musings', though not in connection with the process by which humankind moves towards union with the deity. See 'Religious Musings', ll. 368–70, *CPW*, 1: 123.
25. Inge, *The Philosophy of Plotinus*, 2 vols (London: Longman, 1923), 2: 20. In *TT*, 1: 461 Coleridge praises Origen as 'almost the only very great scholar and genius combined amongst the early Fathers'.
26. See Philip Merlan, *From Platonism to Neoplatonism* (The Hague: Nijhoff, 1953), 114; Inge, *The Philosophy of Plotinus*, 1: 161, 1: 254; *CPW*, 1: 120–3 (esp. 1: 122n.).
27. See *CL*, 1: 158.
28. See Herbert Piper, 'The Pantheistic Sources of Coleridge's Early Poetry', *JHI*, 20 (1959) 47, and Wylie, 'How the Natural Philosophers Defeated ...', 497–8.
29. According to Wylie, Priestley's essays on Hartley not only express his theory of 'the progression of mankind from an original state of innocence and ignorance to full knowledge', but also conclude 'that the millennium [will be] the final stage in the ascent of man' (Wylie, 'How the Natural Philosophers Defeated ...', 498). In the passage Wylie cites as evidence for these points, however, Priestley says nothing explicitly of the millennium (see *Hartley's Theory of the Human Mind*, 365–7), and Priestley's millenarian reflections are rather to be found in his *Institutes of Natural and Revealed Religion* and *The Present State of Europe Compared with Antient Prophesies*, in neither of which are they closely connected with the theories of 'necessity' discussed above.
30. On the prevalence of millenarianism in the 1790s see Mark Philp, *Godwin's Political Justice* (London: Duckworth, 1986), 96–7.
31. See *CL*, 1: 154, and Leonard W. Deen, 'Coleridge and the Sources of Pantisocracy: Godwin, the Bible, and Hartley', *Boston University Studies in English*, 5 (1961) 232–45.
32. See especially Godwin, *An Enquiry Concerning Political Justice and its Influence on Modern Morals and Happiness* (Harmondsworth: Penguin, 1976), 547–54 and 725–35. That these aspects of Godwin influenced the early Coleridge, however, is particularly evident from *CL*, 1: 163, which states the 'leading idea' of pantisocracy to have been the abolition of property as a means to 'remove the *selfish* Principle from ourselves, and prevent it in our children'.

33. Godwin, *Enquiry*, 127–8.
34. Ibid., 97.
35. Priestley, *Essay*, 3–4.
36. Godwin, *Enquiry*, 146.
37. Locke, *Essay*, 104.
38. See also Cornwell, *Coleridge, Poet and Revolutionary*, 40 on this point.
39. See Locke, *Essay*, 242–3.
40. See, for example, Philp, *Godwin's Political Justice*, 84, and Godwin, *Enquiry*, 136–7, 146.
41. On the ending of Coleridge's enthusiasm for Godwin and pantisocracy see especially *CL*, 1: 158, 1: 199.
42. See, for example, J. G. Fichte, *Science of Knowledge*, trans. Peter Heath and John Lachs (Cambridge: CUP, 1982), ix, 9–11, and *STI*, 37.
43. *STI*, 231.
44. See especially *STI*, 2, where Schelling describes philosophy as 'a progressive history of self-consciousness', and states that his *System* will depict 'a *graduated sequence* of intuitions, whereby the self raises itself to the highest power of consciousness'.
45. The Absolute – otherwise referred to as 'the absolute synthesis', 'absolute identity' or 'the absolutely identical principle' – is the theoretical unity of all that is necessarily opposed in consciousness. In its role of unifying subjective and objective, conscious and unconscious, the free and the determined, however, the Absolute also represents the common source of all production, an original identity about which nothing can be said (see *STI*, 208 on these points). Because duality is the condition of all consciousness, the Absolute 'can never attain thereto'; moreover, it 'can never be an object of knowledge, being an object only that is eternally presupposed in action, that is, an object of belief' (*STI*, 208–9).
46. See, for example, *CN*, 3: 3558 and *PLects*, 141, 207.
47. Bolman notes, for example, that in his *Ideen zu einer Philosophie der Natur* (1803), Schelling was 'content to analyze an absolute idealism in terms which borrow from Spinoza, from the Renaissance tradition of Nicolaus Cusanus and Giordano Bruno, as well as from Plato and Leibniz' (F. W. J. Schelling, *The Ages of the World: A Fragment, from Writings Left in Manuscript*, trans. F. de Wolfe Bolman, Jr [New York: Columbia UP, 1942], 17). According to Coleridge, however, Schelling's debt was more specific than this. 'You will find,' he wrote to J. H. Green, '... the entire principia philosophiae Schellingianae in the fragments collected by Fr. Patricius from the Pagan and Christian Neo-platonists, Proclus, Hermias, Simplicius, Damascius, Synesius, & others ... as Oracles of Zoroaster – the inconsistencies of which betray the variety of the Forgers, yet strangely co-exist in the works of Schelling, Baader & Oken' (*CL*, 4: 874).
48. See, for example, *Friend*, 1: 112–13, *LS*, 192–4, and *BL*, 1: 303. For Coleridge's brief marginalia on *Siris* see *CM*, 1: 409–10.
49. Berkeley, *Siris*, 145.
50. Berkeley, *Siris*, 141–2.
51. See Godwin, *Enquiry*, 127–8.

52. See especially Philp, *Godwin's Political Justice*, 84, and Godwin, *Enquiry*, 136–7, 146.
53. As explained above, the Absolute is a purely theoretical unity and hence can never attain to consciousness. The notion of such a development, however, is indispensable to Schelling's transcendence of dualism, albeit that the terms 'intelligence' and 'nature' are used alternately to describe that which achieves self-consciousness in human reflection. See, for example, *STI*, 6.
54. Godwin, *Enquiry*, 160.
55. Berkeley, *Siris*, 146.
56. *OM*, 2: 438–9, quoted in Priestley, *Doctrine*, 129. Priestley's quotation ends at this point, leaving the conditional ('It *would* be') hanging rather confusingly in the air. He also omits the words 'to say', thus detaching the conditional from the second half of the sentence, and implying that our difficulties *will* all end in unbounded knowledge. In Hartley, however, this passage is immediately followed by the words: 'But alas! this is chiefly Speculation …' (*OM*, 2: 439).
57. See, for example, *STI*, 49–50: 'Philosophy as such is … nothing else but the free imitation, the free recapitulation of the original series of acts into which the one act of self-consciousness evolves.' Hence 'Philosophy is … a history of self-consciousness, having various epochs, and by means of it [the] one absolute synthesis is successively put together.'
58. See especially *STI*, 229–30 on these points.
59. See *BL*, 1: lxxxv, xcv–vi, and Norman Fruman, *Coleridge: The Damaged Archangel*, 187–8 on this point.
60. *STI*, 230.
61. See *STI*, 230n. and *BL*, 1: 304. The editors of *BL* suggest that the tripartite divisions of imagination made by several earlier thinkers, especially Kant and Tetens, may also be important sources for Coleridge (see *BL*, 1: lxxxv–vi), yet the correspondence of Coleridge's dualistic conception with the two forms of imagination described by Schelling in *STI*, 230 is particularly close. See Inge, *The Philosophy of Plotinus*, 1: 162, however, on Plotinus's analogous theory that 'The Soul that understands Nature is continuous and homogeneous with the Soul that creates it'. Margaret Sherwood (*Coleridge's Imaginative Conception of the Imagination* [Wellesley, MA: Hathaway House, 1937], 14) points out Coleridge's debt to the same theory, while Beer (*Coleridge's Poetic Intelligence*, 29) suggests that Plotinus may have been a direct source for Coleridge's concept of imagination.
62. A point made also by Marcel. 'The truth,' he writes, 'is that [Coleridge] believed himself capable of reconciling a doctrine of immanence with his theism, though he had nowhere explained how this could be done' (Marcel, *Coleridge et Schelling*, 158–9 [my translation]).
63. For the passage from which Coleridge borrows the first half of this sentence, see *STI*, 6. His use of Schelling's text in this part of *Biographia* is discussed in *BL*, 1: 252–4n.

64. See also Judson S. Lyon, 'Romantic Psychology and the Inner Senses: Coleridge', 256 on how Coleridge 'characteristically grafted onto' Schelling's argument an identification of the Absolute Ego with the personal God of Christianity.
65. *Psalms*, 19: 1, suggested as a source for this passage in *BL*, 1: 256n. See also *CL*, 3: 38 (quoted in Beer, *Coleridge's Poetic Intelligence*, 210) where, in an analogous passage, Coleridge not only equates the laws of nature with the laws of intellect and the influence of the deity, but also implies a pantheistic conception of this relationship, albeit in Latin and with reference to 'Jupiter'.
66. Schelling, *The Ages of the World*, 29. His statement in the *Kritische Fragmente* of 1806 that 'what alone is in experience is just the living, the eternal, or God' suggests this identification particularly clearly. See Schelling, *The Ages of the World*, 25, and F. W. J. Schelling, *Sämmtliche Werke*, ed. K. F. A. Schelling, 14 vols (Stuttgart: Cotta, 1856–61), I, 7: 245. However, see also Schelling, *Of Human Freedom*, 31–2, where he reaffirms the difference between 'Being insofar as it exists' and 'Being insofar as it is the mere basis of existence,' claiming that his own theory 'brings about the most definite distinction between nature and God'.
67. See especially *LS*, 22.
68. Coleridge, Wellek writes, 'could not have formulated the distinction [between reason and understanding] as he did it [*sic*] without Kant, even if his interpretation of the distinction is closer to the meaning' of the seventeenth-century writers to whom Coleridge ascribes it in *The Friend* and *Aids to Reflection*. See Wellek, *Immanuel Kant in England*, 103–5, *Friend*, 1: 154–6, and *AR*, 214–15, 223–4, 253–4.
69. On Kant's theory of the 'regulative' function of ideas of reason, according to which the ideas of 'the soul, the world as an absolute whole, [and] God' demand 'that whatever we know be cast in systematic form, that empirical laws and principles be not a mere aggregate, but be parts of a self-differentiating whole', see *CPR*, 532–4, 556–7, and W. H. Walsh, *Kant's Criticism of Metaphysics* (Edinburgh: Edinburgh UP, 1975), 241–3. See also Lewis White Beck, *A Commentary on Kant's Critique of Practical Reason* (Chicago: Chicago UP, 1960), 259–83, however, on the contrasting role which Kant attaches to ideas of reason in the sphere of morality.
70. According to *Friend*, 1: 517–18 it is only by transcending the 'law of his understanding and fancy' that man can escape a purely sensual and brutish existence. In referring to those who contemplate the powers which distinguish man 'from the animal, and ... the nobler from the animal part of his own being', therefore, Coleridge clearly invokes the distinction between reason and understanding, and excludes empiricists from his discussion.
71. See *Aristotle's Ethics*, 58–9.
72. See, for example, *TT*, 1: 172–4, and *PLects*, 185–91.
73. A. O. Lovejoy, *The Great Chain of Being: A Study of the History of an Idea* (Cambridge, MA: Harvard UP, 1936), 58.

74. Aristotle, *De Animalibus Historia*, book 8, chapter 1, 588b, translated in Lovejoy, *The Great Chain of Being*, 56.
75. See, however, Inge, *The Philosophy of Plotinus*, 1: 161 on Aristotle's theory that 'Every natural thing … in its own way longs for the Divine and desires to share in the Divine life as far as it can. "The Good moves the whole world because it is loved." This is to admit a principle of movement and progress in Nature.'
76. On the Neoplatonists' combination of Platonic and Aristotelian theories see Lovejoy, *The Great Chain of Being*, 61–4.
77. See Beer, *Coleridge's Poetic Intelligence*, 45–6, and Trevor H. Levere, *Poetry Realized in Nature: Samuel Taylor Coleridge and Early Nineteenth-Century Science* (Cambridge: CUP, 1981), 205.
78. See *CN*, 3: 4226n, *TT*, 1: 111 and n, *C&S*, 179, and Levere, *Poetry Realized in Nature*, 202–3.
79. See Inge, *The Philosophy of Plotinus*, 1: 247, and Plotinus, *Enneads*, 564–5.
80. See *CN*, 3: 4226n, and Coleridge's marginalia on Heinrich Steffens, *Beyträge zur innern Naturgeschichte der Erde* (British Library C.43.b.12.[2]), 74.
81. See Priestley, *Doctrine*, xii–xiii.
82. See Perkins, *Coleridge's Philosophy*, 10–11.
83. Coleridge's famous discussion of the varying degrees of 'inner sense' in *BL*, 1: 251 reflects the same values as this distinction. In a passage partly derived from Jenyns's essay 'On the Chain of Universal Being', *CL*, 3: 483 similarly describes the gradual ascent of mind 'till it arrives at a Bacon, a Newton, and then, when unincumbered by matter, extending its illimitable sway through Seraph and Archangel, till we are lost in the GREAT INFINITE!' See Soame Jenyns, *Works*, 4 vols (London, 1790), 3: 184–5, quoted in Lovejoy, *The Great Chain of Being*, 197.
84. *TT*, 1: 435. See also *Friend*, 1: 253: '… with states, as well as individuals, not to be progressive is to be retrograde'.
85. See also Schelling's analogous statement that 'man can only stand above or beneath animals' because only in human beings do the principles of 'darkness' and of 'light' become separated, and in accepting this conflict (rather than striving to re-establish their original unity) we are morally 'below' those creatures in which they never become differentiated (F. W. J. Schelling, *Of Human Freedom*, trans. James Gutman [Chicago: Open Court, 1937], 37–9, 49).
86. Colmer (*C&S*, 169n.) points out an almost identical passage in Coleridge's marginalia on Hooker's *Ecclesiastical Polity* (see *CM*, 2: 1147), though he is unable to find such a remark in Augustine.
87. See *CN*, 1: 256.
88. See, for example, *Aristotle's Ethics*, 58–9.
89. As Modiano observes (*Coleridge and the Concept of Nature*, 169), 'Coleridge could not tolerate a system that purported to explain the genesis of a higher order of being from a lower one. This was a point on which he frequently challenged the views of the *Naturphilosophen*.' See also *CM*, 2: 1000 (cited by Modiano), where Coleridge

notes the far greater difficulty of conceiving 'That the Vis vitae sublimes itself into mind' than that (as Plato suggested) 'Mind reflects itself & has ... its confused echo, in Life', and argues that by adopting the former position, *Naturphilosophie* fails to explain 'the chasm, the difference in kind, between Man and the noblest mere animal'.

90. See Locke, *Essay*, 242–3.
91. For Oken's analogous description (published in 1809) of how animals 'become nobler in rank, the greater the number of the organs which are collectively liberated or severed from' the animal kingdom as a whole, see Lorenz Oken, *Elements of Physiophilosophy*, trans. A. Tulk (London: Ray Society, 1847), 494, quoted in Levere, *Poetry Realized in Nature*, 204.
92. See *CN*, 3: 4226n.
93. See also *AR*, 116.
94. On the 'tendency to individuation' which characterizes all forms of organic life, and by which (at the same time) humanity liberates and detaches itself from nature, see especially *SWF*, 1: 510–11.
95. S. T. Coleridge, *Hints Towards the Formation of a More Comprehensive Theory of Life*, ed. Seth B. Watson (London: John Churchill, 1848), 9. Coleridge's use of the term 'life' in the *Theory of Life*, however, has important precursors in Neoplatonic authors. See especially Inge, *The Philosophy of Plotinus*, 1: 161–2, and Muirhead, *The Platonic Tradition in Anglo-Saxon Philosophy*, 38 on analogous theories in Plotinus and Cudworth.
96. Coleridge, *Theory of Life*, 9.
97. Coleridge suggests this Neoplatonic circle without obviously diverging from Christian orthodoxy. Though the *Theory of Life* concentrates almost entirely on the upward progression of nature, it includes several indirect references to the origin of that system. See, for example, *SWF*, 1: 520 on 'the *omnipresence* of the Supreme Reality', and *SWF*, 1: 550, where Coleridge indicates the particularly direct involvement of nature's 'sovereign Master' in the creation of man, who is the consummation of nature's series.
98. Inge, *The Philosophy of Plotinus*, 1: 161.
99. Ibid., 1: 254. For a further description of Plotinus's cosmology showing its resemblances to Coleridge's evolutionary theory see Sherwood, *Coleridge's Imaginative Conception of the Imagination*, 11.
100. See *SWF*, 1: 556–7. Levere, *Poetry Realized in Nature*, 212, and Joseph Warren Beach, 'Coleridge's Borrowings from the German', *ELH*, 9 (1942) 45–6.
101. George Potter, 'Coleridge and the Idea of Evolution,' *PMLA*, 40 (1925) 393–4. See also Beach, 'Coleridge's Borrowings from the German', 50, and A. D. Snyder, 'Coleridge on Giordano Bruno', *Modern Language Notes*, 42 (1927) 431.
102. Coleridge, *Theory of Life*, 10–11.
103. On this paradox see also Muirhead, *Coleridge as Philosopher*, 128.
104. For further expressions of this paradox see *SWF*, 1: 517 and *PLects*, 357. According to *SWF*, 1: 550–1, man, as at once the consummation

and 'Microcosm' of nature's process, exhibits 'the most perfect detachment with the greatest possible union'.

105. This formula occurs several times in the *Theory of Life*. See, for example, *SWF*, 1: 511, 517.

106. According to Beach ('Coleridge's Borrowings from the German', 45–6), the views that 'Life is definable as a process of progressive "individuation"' and that 'The life in organized beings is a later step in a life-process already manifested in inorganic matter', are derived directly from Schelling and Steffens. Levere also notes Coleridge's debts to these writers, though differing from Beach in stating that Coleridge's description of life as 'the *power* which discloses itself from within as a principle of *unity* in the *many*' (*SWF*, 1: 510) differs 'markedly from Schelling and Steffens', drawing on Neoplatonic sources as well as the hierarchies of *Naturphilosophie* (see Levere, *Poetry Realized in Nature*, 217).

107. See, however, *STI*, 122–39, where Schelling explains organic nature as a product of intelligence's 'endless endeavor towards self-organization' (ibid., 123).

108. See Inge, *The Philosophy of Plotinus*, 1: 127 on Plotinus's analogous view that 'the lower can never generate the higher. In other words, the *explanation* of a thing must always be sought in what is above it in the scales of value and existence, not in what is below.' On a similar theory in Cudworth, see Muirhead, *The Platonic Tradition in Anglo-Saxon Philosophy*, 52.

109. Paradoxically, Coleridge in this passage uses an analogous bi-directional method of explanation to that which he criticized in Schelling's *Einleitung* (see *CN*, 3: 4449). As Modiano comments (*Coleridge and the Concept of Nature*, 169), 'Schelling shows the evolution of intelligence from nature, i.e. of a higher power from a lower one, while at the same time he follows "the method of descent, or emanation", demonstrating that the higher order is prior to and the causative ground of the lower. Such is the case with his derivation of the powers of irritability and reproduction from sensibility. This methodological instability, this "*up* and *down* in one and the same Sphere", was for Coleridge a major drawback in Schelling's system.'

CHAPTER 6 THE LIMITS OF EXPRESSION: LANGUAGE, CONSCIOUSNESS, AND THE SUBLIME

1. See *The Letters of Charles and Mary Lamb*, 1: 56. Precisely what provoked Lamb's comment is unclear, though Coleridge's pantheistic evocation of an 'intellectual breeze' uniting 'soul' and 'God' seems particularly relevant (see *CPW*, 1: 100–2).

2. See Perkins, *Coleridge's Philosophy*, *passim*, and Reid, 'Coleridge and Schelling', 471–7.

3. See, for example, the passage from his marginalia on Swedenborg's *De Coelo et Inferno* (BM c.126 k.4), 233, discussed in Chapter 4, section 1.
4. See especially Reid, 'Coleridge and Schelling', 452 and Perkins, *Coleridge's Philosophy*, 10.
5. See especially *STI*, 229 on this point.
6. On the assumption of self-consciousness see *STI*, 16–17 and *BL*, 1: 285.
7. See, for example, *LS*, 18.
8. 1818 is the date which Reid, following Modiano, attaches to Coleridge's commencement of 'a stable, coherent and systematic philosophy' involving the reconciliation of Schelling's system with 'the dynamic act of the Trinity' (see Reid, 'Coleridge and Schelling', 452, 477).
9. Marcel, *Coleridge et Schelling*, 31 (my translation).
10. See McKusick, *Coleridge's Philosophy of Language*, 49–50 on the 'idealistic premisses' underlying this passage; also *CN*, 1: 923 on the difference between 'thinking' and 'thoughts', and *CN*, 2: 2784 on the etymological connection between 'thing' and 'think'.
11. See *CM*, 2: 627 for an analogous series of oppositions.
12. For further uses of these terms in the senses described here see, for example, *CL*, 1: 294–5 and *CN*, 1: 1561.
13. See *STI*, 229 for an analogous argument in Schelling.
14. Hegel, *Phenomenology of Spirit*, 66 similarly notes how 'the sensuous This ... cannot be reached by language', because one can say of it 'only what is *universal*'.
15. See, for example, *CL*, 2: 1195: 'God is the sole self-comprehending Being, i.e. he has an Idea of himself, and that Idea is consummately adequate, & superlatively real ...'
16. *TT*, 1: 448, indeed, seems directly to deny this possibility: 'Let a young man separate I from Me as far as he possibly can, and remove the Me till it is almost lost in the remote distance. *I am Me* is as bad a fault in intellectuals and morals [*sic*] as it is in grammar—whilst none but one—God—can say, "I Am I" or "That I Am".'
17. See, however, Plotinus, *The Enneads*, trans. Stephen MacKenna (London: Faber, 1956), 431 for an analogous conception of 'perfect self-identity', and the discussion of this passage in Inge, *The Philosophy of Plotinus*, 1: 238.
18. See *BL*, 1: 304.
19. Albert O. Wlecke, *Wordsworth and the Sublime* (Berkeley: University of California Press, 1973), 82.
20. Ibid., 92.
21. On Coleridge's paradoxical attempts to combine the idea of a noumenon with that of a productive energy in terms of which nature can be regarded as a unified whole, see Vallins, 'Production and Existence', *passim*.
22. See *CL*, 1: 295.
23. Coburn (*CN*, 3: 3941n) gives this 'tentative' translation of Coleridge's Greek, in which breathings and accents are omitted.

24. See *CPR*, 268.
25. As Beer points out (*AR*, 233, n.4), the first of these propositions derives from St John's Gospel, 8: 58, while the second is widely used by medieval theologians, though sometimes attributed to Aristotle. See also *Say*, 1: 28 for a further instance of the second proposition.
26. See *CPR*, 384–484, and Bertrand Russell, *A History of Western Philosophy* (London: Allen & Unwin, 1946), 735.
27. On the use of this method in Augustine and its sources in Plotinus and later Neoplatonism see Inge, *The Philosophy of Plotinus*, 2: 111–12, and John J. O'Meara, 'The Neoplatonism of Saint Augustine', in Dominic J. O'Meara (ed.), *Neoplatonism and Christian Thought* (Albany, NY: State University of New York Press, 1982), 39–40. In *CL*, 2: 954, Coleridge writes that he has 'received great delight & instruction from Scotus Erigena', though also describing him as 'the modern founder of the School of Pantheism'.
28. Henry Bett, *Johannes Scotus Erigena* (Cambridge: CUP, 1925), 23–4. With regard to the impossibility of describing the nature of God by '*super*- and *ὑπερ*-', Inge notes that the Plotinian 'One' is similarly insusceptible of description: 'After ascribing to it the highest attributes that we can conceive, we must add, "yet not these, but something better"' (Inge, *The Philosophy of Plotinus*, 2: 113).
29. See also *Say*, 1: 27–8 on the 'negative terms' through which alone we can refer to that truth which 'is not to be measured by words'.
30. See especially *AR*, 233 for Coleridge's theory that the truths affirmed by the reason can only be expressed by understanding in the form of an antinomy representing 'a truth beyond conception and inexpressible', such as 'Before Abraham was, I am', or 'God is a circle, the centre of which is every where, and circumference nowhere'.
31. Kathleen Wheeler (*Sources, Processes and Methods in Coleridge's 'Biographia Literaria'* [Cambridge: CUP, 1980], 144–5) notes that '*Biographia* is the only major published work in which the primary vehicle for the distinction between the discursive and the intuitive is the fancy/imagination distinction', arguing that in Coleridge's later works it was superseded by the distinction between understanding and reason. Though describing understanding as indispensable to thought and perception, Coleridge often deprecates it on the ground of a repetitiveness or conservatism which, as Wheeler points out, he also attributes to fancy (see ibid., 139).
32. On 'forma efformans' or 'forma formans' see, for example, Coleridge, *Logic*, 232.
33. On Coleridge's repeated use of the term 'life' to evoke the idea of a force informing phenomena see especially Vallins, 'Production and Existence', 116–24.
34. See *PLects*, 166: 'The mind always feels itself greater than aught it hath done. It begins in the feeling that it must go beyond it in order to comprehend it....'
35. See *CL*, 2: 1195. On how Coleridge's Reason 'spans the gulf between man and God' see Huw Parry Owen, 'The Theology of Coleridge',

Critical Quarterly, 4 (1962) 63. According to Coleridge, Owen writes, 'The human spirit *is* the divine spirit operating in a finite mode. We come to discern God through Reason because through that same Reason we already participate in him' (ibid.). See also Inge, *The Philosophy of Plotinus*, 1: 215–16 on Plotinus's conception of the 'higher' and 'lower' souls.

36. What the 'third' sense is, by which these two are reunited, Coleridge does not explain: presumably this synthesis is rendered unnecessary by the intrinsic complementarity of the two he does describe. Similar conceptions occur in *LS*, 18 and 113–14, and in *Friend*, 1: 190 and 316n (the latter, perhaps providing the 'third term' omitted in *LS* 68n, explains how Christ 'became the *Light*=Reason, of Mankind'), and in *C&S*, 182.
37. Coleridge's equation of reason with such a grounding identity is made still clearer in the sentence immediately following that quoted above. 'Each individual', he says, 'must bear witness of [Reason] to his own mind, even as he describes life and light: and with the silence of light it describes itself, and dwells in *us* only as far as we dwell in *it*. It cannot in strict language be called a faculty, much less a personal property, of any human mind' (*LS*, 70).
38. On the assumption of self-consciousness, see *STI*, 16–17 and *BL*, 1: 284–5. On Schelling's 'Absolute' see Chapter 5, section 2.
39. See also *LS*, 18 on this point.
40. Perkins, *Coleridge's Philosophy*, 21–2.
41. The word 'of' is supplied by Griggs.
42. See Hume, *Treatise*, 106, and Pinch, *Strange Fits of Passion*, 35–6.
43. For the principal expressions of this view in Coleridge see *Friend*, 1: 20–1, 26, and *CL*, 3: 253–4. The point is discussed in, *inter alia*, Christensen, *Coleridge's Blessed Machine of Language*, 208–11.
44. See especially *CL*, 3: 237 and *Friend*, 1: 20. On the resemblances between Coleridge's style and the seventeenth-century writers on whom he claims it is partly modelled see L. M. Grow, 'The Prose Style of Samuel Taylor Coleridge' (PhD Dissertation, University of Southern California, 1971), 117, 121 and 125.
45. See *Friend*, 1: 20, and *CL*, 3: 234, 3: 254.
46. In Coleridge's view this is especially true of Greek, though he also refers to 'the classical writers' in general as models of a superior style. See *Lects 1808–19*, 2: 93, 2: 233.
47. See especially *PLects*, 290, where Coleridge attributes the independence of the couplets in Johnson's and Dryden's poems to 'the character of the language, marked by a smaller number of cases, and inflexions, and the manifest tendency to lose those which it possessed, compared with the interwoven sentences of the Romans and Greeks, which doubtless permitted them a much more logical position of words, according to the order of thought'. *Lects 1808–19*, 2: 231 extends this distinction, contrasting the organic quality of Greek language and government with the fragmentariness of modern languages and the overriding importance of the 'individual interest' in the 'northern or Gothic nations'.

48. These are the clear implications of Coleridge's reflections on the thoughtlessness of much modern writing when compared with his descriptions of the greater natural connectedness and intrinsic grammatical suspensions of ancient Greek. See *BL*, 1: 39 and *CL*, 3: 234, 3: 237, 3: 254.
49. In the case of Greek, indeed, he never mentions such variations, though a fragment of reported conversation includes Greek in his description of a progressive (or repeated) decay from the earlier perfection of languages (see *TT*, 1: 81). Seneca, however, is mentioned in *Lects 1808–19*, 2: 234 as an example of the opposite of the 'classical' unity which Coleridge finds in Milton, Bacon, Hooker, and Taylor, and the style of Tacitus is mentioned in *Lects 1808–19*, 2: 237 as a Latin parallel to the antithetical and 'pointed' style of Gibbon and Johnson.
50. This view is implicit in Coleridge's praise of Milton and those other English writers who imitated the more 'architectural' structure of the classical languages. It is in relation to *Paradise Lost*, however, and not to Milton's prose writings, that this position is most clearly expressed. 'Milton', Coleridge says, 'attempted to make the English language obey the logic of passion as perfectly as the Greek and Latin. Hence the occasional harshness in the construction' (*Lects 1808–19*, 2: 427).
51. See *Monboddo*, 6: 116–7, 2: 504–5, 3: 388.
52. Though his discussions of style are chiefly concerned with prose, Monboddo stresses the value of *Paradise Lost* as an example of 'periodic' writing (*Monboddo*, 3: 59).
53. Tacitus, indeed, is criticized not only for his fragmentariness, but also for his affectation of 'point and turn' (*Monboddo*, 6: 111), and of 'expressing common things in an uncommon manner' (*Monboddo*, 3: 224) – qualities which Coleridge attacks in post-Restoration writers generally, and especially in Gibbon and Johnson (see *C17thC*, 418–19, and *Lects 1808–19*, 2: 237). For further comments on the faults of Sallust, Seneca, and Tacitus see *Monboddo*, 3: 58, 3: 213, 3: 215–16. Their corrupting influence on modern English writers is discussed in *Monboddo*, 3: 247–8, 3: 402.
54. *Monboddo*, 3: 399. See also *Monboddo*, 3: 247–8, however, where he suggests that these qualities arose from the influence of Tacitus, rather than the French.
55. See also *Monboddo*, 6: 124 on the absence of parenthesis – in Monboddo's view, a very grave omission – in modern French writing and its English derivatives, especially Gibbon.
56. J. C. C. Mays, 'Coleridge on Prose' (D Phil Thesis, Oxford University, 1966), 47–8, however, notes certain similarities between Coleridge's and Monboddo's views on prose, while Woodring (*TT*, 1: 302n.) comments that Coleridge's discussion of the beauties of Greek in *Table Talk* resembles certain of Monboddo's opinions.
57. See *Monboddo*, 2: 241–2, 3: 213, 3: 224; also *Friend*, 1: 106.
58. Coleridge's choice of the French as his particular stylistic whipping-boy, indeed, may also indicate a desire to challenge the claims of his

continuing allegiance to Jacobinism made, for example, by Hazlitt (see Hazlitt, *Works*, 7: 135). The influence of such accusations on his views in *The Friend* is noted in Coleman, *Coleridge and 'The Friend'*, 4.

59. See also William Paley, *The Principles of Moral and Political Philosophy* (London, 1785), iv on the 'sententious apothegmatizing style' of modern writings on morality, which, 'by crowding propositions and paragraphs too fast upon the mind, and by carrying the eye of the reader from subject to subject in too quick a succession, gains not a sufficient hold upon the attention to leave either the memory furnished or the understanding satisfied', and *Monboddo*, 3: 247 on 'the short, smart, unconnected sentences, the *vibrantes sententiolae*, as Petronius calls them' of contemporary English writers.
60. See especially *EOT*, 1: 324 and *PLects*, 190. Here also, however, Coleridge seems in part to echo the opinions of Monboddo described above. The latter's statement that French philosophy puts forward 'a system of nature, without that which is principal in nature, I mean *mind*', and his connection of this with the view that French authors have 'propagated, almost all over Europe, the disbelief of all religion' (*Monboddo*, 3: 398), show a particular proximity to Coleridge's position.
61. *Lects 1808–19*, 2: 236. On the same point see *C17thC*, 418, and *Friend*, 1: 23–4, which predicts that an 'ensnaring meretricious *popularness*' will soon replace all seriousness in literature.
62. *Specimens of the Table Talk of the Late Samuel Taylor Coleridge*, ed. H. N. Coleridge, 2 vols (London: John Murray, 1835), 12 July 1827. The notes from which H. N. Coleridge reconstructed this passage are reprinted in *TT*, 1: 81.
63. On intellectual passivity as a source of materialism and idolatry see, for example, *Friend*, 1: 517–8.
64. See Christensen, *Coleridge's Blessed Machine of Language*, 207–10.
65. See also *Lects 1808–19*, 2: 236–7, where he describes the use of this style in Gibbon, Johnson, and *The Letters of Junius*.
66. See also Margaret Wiley, 'Coleridge and the Wheels of Intellect', *PMLA*, 67 (1952) 102 on Coleridge's conviction that we 'must never relax in the false assumption that any combination of words has finally fixed and encompassed an idea, nor … abandon the quest for closer and closer verbal approximations of ideas, whose only complete incarnation is in action'.
67. See also Sister Maria Osinski, 'A Study of the Structures of Co-ordination in a Representative Sample of the Biographia Literaria' (PhD Dissertation, Catholic University, 1953), 91–2, quoted in Grow, 'The Prose Style of Samuel Taylor Coleridge', 78, on this point.
68. Duke Maskell, *Coleridge's Prose and 'the present state of our language in its relation to literature'* (Retford: Brynmill, 1983), 18.
69. See also *CN*, 3: 4210: 'Intellectual Accuracy is the faithful Friend, and next-door Neighbor of Moral Veracity, so that both are comprized in the one term, Truth.'
70. See *EOT*, 1: 114: 'We think *in* words, and reason *by* words.—The man who, while he is speaking or writing his native language, uses words

inaccurately, and combines them inconsequentially, may be fairly presumed to be a lax and slovenly reasoner.'

71. Hamilton, *Coleridge's Poetics*, 72. R. H. Fogle (*The Idea of Coleridge's Criticism* [Berkeley: University of California Press, 1962], 90–1) similarly notes that 'Unless meaning is preserved by verbal precision, mental accuracy and finally veracity suffer, for the relation of words to the mind is reciprocal: they are created but in turn create.'
72. *CN*, 2: 2075, indeed, presents this principle as a direct justification of prolixity: 'Does not [the] dread of Prolixity in ourselves, & criticism of it in others, tend to make all knowledge superficial as well as desultory—incompatible with the pleasure derived from seeing things as they are, as far as the nature of Language permits it to be exhibited?' Parenthesis also, though Coleridge admitted it was taken to an unnecessary extreme in *The Friend*, he cited as a concomitant of thoughtfulness: 'a book of reasoning without parentheses must be the work either of adeptship or of a *friable* intellect' (*CL*, 4: 685).
73. See also *Coleridge's Miscellaneous Criticism*, ed. T. M. Raysor (London: Constable, 1936), 89, where Coleridge remarks that in Shakespeare 'All is growth, evolution, γένεσις—each line, each word almost, begets the following—and the will of the writer is an interfusion, a continuous agency, no series of separate acts.'
74. Grow, 'The Prose Style of Samuel Taylor Coleridge', 64.
75. Mays, 'Coleridge on Prose', 81.
76. See *Lects 1808–19*, 2: 231.
77. As Coleman points out (*Coleridge and 'The Friend'*, 52), Coleridge argues in *Friend*, 2: 277 that in order for the 'evil' of mental laziness to be rectified, his reader must bring to the work 'that "most difficult and laborious Effort" whereby he reproduces in his own mind those states of consciousness to which the author has referred him'.
78. See *CPR*, 532–4, 556–7, and Walsh, *Kant's Criticism of Metaphysics*, 241–3.
79. This aim is also expressed in *Friend*, 1: 16.
80. See also *Friend*, 1: 106: 'To connect with the objects of our senses the obscure notions and consequent vivid feelings, which are due only to immaterial and permanent things, is profanation relatively to the heart, and superstition in the understanding.'
81. See *CL*, 3: 253–4.
82. The term 'Ciceronian' is not used by Coleridge, but is used by several later critics to describe the style of writing 'in comprehensive periods' depending on 'a complex suspended syntax', and as the opposite of the 'Senecan' or 'pointed' style, which involves 'profuse employment of the Balanced Sentence, in conjunction with antithesis, epigram, and climax'. See George Williamson, *The Senecan Amble: A Study of Prose Form from Bacon to Collier* (London: Faber, 1951), 36, 55–6.
83. Contemporary criticism of Coleridge's prose is discussed later in this chapter. For Carlyle's description see *The Works of Thomas Carlyle*, ed. H. D. Traill, 30 vols (London, 1896–9), 11: 55–7. For De Quincey's view see especially *The Collected Writings of Thomas De Quincey*, ed. David Masson, 14 vols (Edinburgh: A. & C. Black, 1889–90),

2: 152–3, where he suggests that most who heard Coleridge speaking were unable to follow the illustrations of his arguments, and hence assumed there was no connecting thread to his conversation.

84. See *CPR*, 325n.
85. Coleridge's footnote to this passage, however, itself casts doubt on the legitimacy of this assumption. For, he writes, 'the truth of the assertion, that deep feeling has a tendency to combine with obscure ideas, in preference to distinct and clear notions, may be proved by the history of Fanatics and Fanaticism in all ages and countries' (*Friend*, 1: 106).
86. A point made also in Christensen, *Coleridge's Blessed Machine of Language*, 31–2.
87. See *CJ*, 106.
88. See Kant, *Critique of Practical Reason*, 234 and *CPR*, 532–4.
89. See also Wlecke, *Wordsworth and the Sublime*, 78, and Modiano, *Coleridge and the Concept of Nature*, 116 on the analogous forms of the sublime which Coleridge associates with intellectual and visual experiences.
90. See, for example, *TT*, 1: 42, and *CL*, 1: 588, 2: 736.
91. Sir James Mackintosh, *A Discourse on the Study of the Law of Nature and Nations* (London, 1799), 24–5.
92. Ibid., 33–4.
93. *Eclectic Review*, 7 (1811) 921, reproduced in Donald H. Reiman (ed.), *The Romantics Reviewed: Contemporary Reviews of British Romantic Writers*. Part A. *The Lake Poets*, 2 vols (New York: Garland, 1972), 1: 347.
94. A point also made by Hazlitt. 'I firmly believe', he wrote, '[that Coleridge] would make just the same impression on half his audiences, if he purposely repeated absolute nonsense with the same voice and manner and inexhaustible flow of undulating speech' (Hazlitt, *Works*, 12: 35).
95. See *CJ*, 104.
96. *British Critic*, 2nd Series, 8 (1817): 461, reproduced in *The Romantics Reviewed*, Part A, 1: 150. The imagery of clouds occurs frequently in Hazlitt's descriptions of Coleridge's writing (see, for example, Hazlitt, *Works*, 12: 15, 12: 199, and 16: 100), and is also to be found in Carlyle's description of his conversation (see *The Works of Thomas Carlyle*, 11: 57).
97. This critic's reaction, indeed, could even be used to illustrate Burke's thesis that 'It is our ignorance of things that causes all our admiration, and chiefly excites our passions', or in other words that 'A clear idea is ... another name for a little idea'. See Burke, *A Philosophical Enquiry into the Origin of Our Ideas of the Sublime and Beautiful*, ed. J. T. Boulton (London: Routledge, 1958), 61, 63.
98. Hazlitt, *Works*, 16: 100.
99. See 'This Lime-Tree Bower My Prison', ll. 32–43 (*CPW*, 1: 179–80) for perhaps the best example of such 'sublimation' in Coleridge's poetry.

Select Bibliography

MANUSCRIPT SOURCES

Coleridge, S. T. Notebooks 35–55. British Library, Add. MSS. 47, 530–47, 550
——. MS notes in Schelling, F. W. J., *System des transcendentalen Idealismus* (Tubingen, 1800; British Library C.43.b.10)
——. MS notes in Steffens, Heinrich, *Beyträge zur innern Naturgeschichte der Erde* (Freyberg, 1801; British Library C.43.b.12 [2])
——. MS notes in Swedenborg, Emanuel, *De Coelo et Eius Mirabilibus, et de Inferno, ex Auditis et Visis* (London, 1758; British Library C.126.k.4)
——. MS notes in Taylor, Jeremy, *ΣΥΜΒΟΛΟΝ ΘΕΟΛΟΓΙΚΟΝ: or A Collection of Polemicall Discourses* (London, 1674; British Library Ashley 5147)
University of Toronto, Victoria College Library MS 29

PRINTED SOURCES

Akenside, Mark. *Poetical Works*. Ed. Robin Dix. Madison, NJ: AUP, 1996.
Anderson, Wayne C. 'The Dramatization of Thought in Coleridge's Prose', *Prose Studies*, 6 (Dec. 1983), 264–73.
Appleyard, J. A. *Coleridge's Philosophy of Literature: The Development of a Concept of Poetry, 1791–1819*. Cambridge, MA: Harvard UP, 1965.
Aristotle, *Ethics*. Trans. J. L. Ackrill. London: Faber, 1973.
Armour, Richard W. and Howes, Raymond F. (eds). *Coleridge the Talker: A Series of Contemporary Descriptions and Comments, with a Critical Introduction*. Ithaca, NY: Cornell UP, 1940.
Ashton, Rosemary. *The German Idea: Four English Writers and the Reception of German Thought, 1800–1860*. Cambridge: CUP, 1980.
——. *The Life of Samuel Taylor Coleridge*. Oxford: Blackwell, 1996.
Badawi, M. M. *Coleridge: Critic of Shakespeare*. Cambridge: CUP, 1973.
Baker, J. V. *The Sacred River: Coleridge's Theory of the Imagination*. Baton Rouge, LA: Louisiana State UP, 1957.
Barfield, Owen. *What Coleridge Thought*. London: OUP, 1972.
Barth, J. Robert. *Coleridge and Christian Doctrine*. Cambridge, MA: Harvard UP, 1969.
——. *The Symbolic Imagination: Coleridge and the Romantic Tradition*. Princeton, NJ: Princeton UP, 1977.
Bate, Walter Jackson. *Coleridge*. London: Weidenfeld & Nicholson, 1969.

Baxter, Richard. *Preservatives Against Melancholy and Overmuch Sorrow: Or the Cure of Both by Faith and Physick*. London, 1713.
——. *Reliquae Baxterianae: Or Mr. Richard Baxter's Narrative of the Most Memorable Passages of His Life and Times*. Ed. Mathew Sylvester. London, 1696.
Beach, Joseph Warren. 'Coleridge's Borrowings from the German', *ELH*, 9 (1942) 36–58.
Beattie, James. *An Essay on the Nature and Immutability of Truth; in Opposition to Sophistry and Scepticism*. Edinburgh, 1770.
Beck, Lewis White. *A Commentary on Kant's Critique of Practical Reason*. Chicago: University of Chicago Press, 1960.
Beer, John. *Coleridge's Poetic Intelligence*. London: Macmillan, 1977.
——. *Coleridge the Visionary*. London: Chatto, 1959.
——. 'Blake, Coleridge, and Wordsworth: Some Cross-Currents and Parallels, 1789–1805', in Morton D. Paley and Michael Phillips (eds), *William Blake: Essays in Honour of Sir Geoffrey Keynes*. Oxford: Clarendon, 1973.
Benziger, James. 'Organic Unity: Leibniz to Coleridge', *PMLA*, 62 (1951) 24–48.
Berkeley, George. *Siris: A Chain of Philosophical Reflections and Inquiries Concerning the Virtues of Tar Water, and Divers Other Subjects Connected Together and Arising One From Another*. Dublin, 1744; London, 1744.
Bett, Henry. *Johannes Scotus Erigena: A Study in Medieval Philosophy*. Cambridge: CUP, 1925.
Bloom, Harold. *Blake's Apocalypse: A Study in Poetic Argument*. Garden City, NY: Doubleday, 1963.
Boehme, Jacob. *The Works of Jacob Behmen, The Teutonic Theosopher*. Ed. G. Ward and T. Langcake, 4 vols. London, 1764–81.
Boulger, James D. *Coleridge as Religious Thinker*. New Haven, CT: Yale UP, 1961.
Brinkley, R. F. 'Coleridge on Locke', *Studies in Philology*, 46 (1949) 521–43.
Brown, Robert F. *The Later Philosophy of Schelling: The Influence of Boehme on the Works of 1809–1815*. Lewisburg, PA: Bucknell UP, 1977.
Burke, Edmund. *A Philosophical Enquiry into the Origin of our Ideas of the Sublime and Beautiful*. Ed. J. T. Boulton. London: RKP, 1958.
Burnet, James (Lord Monboddo). *Of the Origin and Progress of Language*, 6 vols. Edinburgh, 1773–92.
Butler, Marilyn (ed.). *Burke, Paine, Godwin, and the Revolution Controversy*. Cambridge: CUP, 1984.
——. *Romantics, Rebels and Reactionaries: English Literature and Its Background, 1760–1830*. Oxford: OUP, 1981.
Bygrave, Stephen. *Coleridge and the Self: Romantic Egotism*. London: Macmillan, 1986.
Byron, George Gordon, Lord. *The Complete Poetical Works*. Ed. Jerome J. McGann, 7 vols. Oxford: Clarendon, 1980–93.
Carlyle, Thomas. *The Works of Thomas Carlyle*, Ed. H. D. Traill, 30 vols, London: Chapman & Hall, 1896–9.
Caygill, Howard, *A Kant Dictionary*. Oxford: Blackwell, 1995.

Chayes, Irene H. 'Coleridge, Metempsychosis, and "Almost All the Followers of Fenelon"', *ELH*, 25 (1958) 290–315.

Christensen, Jerome. *Coleridge's Blessed Machine of Language*. Ithaca, NY: Cornell UP, 1981.

Clayton, James W. 'Coleridge and the Logos: The Trinitarian Unity of Consciousness and Culture, *Journal of Religion*, 70 (1990) 213–40.

Coburn, Kathleen. *Experience into Thought: Perspectives in the Coleridge Notebooks*. Toronto: University of Toronto Press, 1979.

——. *The Self Conscious Imagination: A Study of the Coleridge Notebooks in Celebration of the Bi-Centenary of His Birth*. London: OUP, 1974.

Coleman, Deirdre. *Coleridge and 'The Friend' (1809–1810)*. Oxford: Clarendon, 1988.

Coleridge, S. T. *Aids to Reflection*. Ed. John Beer. *Collected Works*, Vol. 9. Princeton, NJ: Princeton UP, 1993.

——. *The Annotated Ancient Mariner*. Ed. Martin Gardner. London: Blond, 1965.

——. *Biographia Literaria*. Eds James Engell and W. Jackson Bate, 2 vols. *Collected Works*, Vol. 7. Princeton, NJ: Princeton UP, 1983.

——. *Coleridge on Logic and Learning*. Ed. Alice D. Snyder. New Haven, CT: Yale UP, 1929.

——. *Coleridge on the Seventeenth Century*. Ed. R. F. Brinkley. Durham, NC: Duke UP, 1955.

——. *Coleridge's Miscellaneous Criticism*. Ed. T. M. Raysor. London: Constable, 1936.

——. *Coleridge's Shakespearean Criticism*. Ed. T. M. Raysor, 2 vols. London: Constable, 1930.

——. *Coleridge's Treatise on Method: As Published in the Encyclopaedia Metropolitana*. Ed. A. D. Snyder. London: Constable, 1934.

——. *Collected Letters of Samuel Taylor Coleridge*. Ed. E. L. Griggs, 6 vols. Oxford: Clarendon, 1956–71.

——. *The Collected Works of Samuel Taylor Coleridge*. Princeton, NJ: Princeton UP, 1969–.

——. *The Complete Poetical Works of Samuel Taylor Coleridge*. Ed. E. H. Coleridge, 2 vols. Oxford: Clarendon, 1912.

——. *Essays on His Times in 'The Morning Post' and 'The Courier'*. Ed. David V. Erdman, 3 vols. *Collected Works*, Vol. 3. Princeton, NJ: Princeton UP, 1978.

——. *The Friend*. Ed. Barbara E. Rooke, 2 vols. *Collected Works*, Vol. 4. Princeton, NJ: Princeton UP, 1969.

——. *Hints Towards the Formation of a More Comprehensive Theory of Life*. Ed. Seth B. Watson. London: John Churchill, 1848.

——. *Inquiring Spirit: A New Presentation of Coleridge from his Published and Unpublished Writings*. Ed. Kathleen Coburn. London: RKP, 1951.

——. *Lay Sermons*. Ed. R. J. White. *Collected Works*, Vol. 6. Princeton, NJ: Princeton UP, 1972.

——. *Lectures 1795 On Politics and Religion*. Eds Lewis Patton and Peter Mann. *Collected Works*, Vol. 1. Princeton, NJ: Princeton UP, 1971.

——. *Lectures 1808–1819 On Literature*. Ed. R. A. Foakes, 2 vols. *Collected Works*. Vol. 5. Princeton, NJ: Princeton UP, 1987.

——. *Letters of S. T. Coleridge*. Ed. E. H. Coleridge, 2 vols. London: Heinemann, 1895.
——. *Logic*. Ed. J. R. de J. Jackson. *Collected Works*, Vol. 13. Princeton, NJ: Princeton UP, 1981.
——. *Marginalia*. Ed. George Whalley. *Collected Works*, Vol. 12. Princeton, NJ: Princeton UP, 1980–.
——. *The Notebooks of Samuel Taylor Coleridge*. Ed. Kathleen Coburn. London: Routledge, 1957–.
——. *Notes on English Divines*. Ed. Derwent Coleridge, 2 vols. London: Moxon, 1853.
——. *Notes Theological, Political, and Miscellaneous*. Ed. Derwent Coleridge. London: Moxon, 1853.
——. (with R. Southey). *Omniana, or Horae Otiosiores*. Ed. Robert Gittings. London: Centaur, 1969.
——. *On the Constitution of the Church and State*. Ed. John Colmer. *Collected Works*, Vol. 10. Princeton, NJ: Princeton UP, 1976.
——. *The Philosophical Lectures of Samuel Taylor Coleridge*. Ed. Kathleen Coburn. London: Pilot, 1949.
——. *Poems ... Second Edition. To Which Are Now Added Poems by Charles Lamb, and Charles Lloyd*. Bristol, 1797.
——. *Shorter Works and Fragments*. Eds H. J. Jackson and J. R. de J. Jackson, 2 vols. *Collected Works*, Vol. 11. Princeton, NJ: Princeton UP, 1995.
——. *Specimens of the Table Talk of the Late Samuel Taylor Coleridge*. Ed. H. N. Coleridge, 2 vols. London: John Murray, 1835.
——. *Table Talk*. Ed. Carl Woodring, 2 vols. *Collected Works*, Vol. 14. Princeton, NJ: Princeton UP, 1990.
——. *The Watchman*. Ed. Lewis Patton. *Collected Works*, Vol. 2. Princeton, NJ: Princeton UP, 1970.
Colmer, John. *Coleridge, Critic of Society*. Oxford: Clarendon, 1959.
——. 'Coleridge and the Life of Hope', *SR*, 2 (1972) 332–41.
Cooper, A. A. (3rd Earl of Shaftesbury). *A Letter Concerning Enthusiasm*. London, 1708.
Copleston, Frederick. *A History of Philosophy*, 9 vols. London: Burns & Oates, 1946–75.
Cornwell, John. *Coleridge, Poet and Revolutionary, 1772–1804: A Critical Biography*. London: Allen Lane, 1973.
Corrigan, Timothy. *Coleridge, Language, and Criticism*. Athens, GA: University of Georgia Press, 1982.
Cudworth, Ralph. *The True Intellectual System of the Universe: Wherein All the Reason and Philosophy of Atheism is Confuted, and its Impossibility Demonstrated*. Ed. J. Harrison, 3 vols. London: Thomas Tegg, 1845.
Darwin, Erasmus. *The Botanic Garden; A Poem, in Two Parts*, 2 vols. London, 1789–91; reprinted in 1 vol., Menston, Yorks.: Scolar Press, 1973.
——. *Zoonomia; Or, The Laws of Organic Life*, 2 vols. London, 1794–6.
Deen, Leonard W. 'Coleridge and the Sources of Pantisocracy: Godwin, the Bible, and Hartley', *Boston University Studies in English*, 5 (Winter, 1961) 232–45.
Dekker, George. *Coleridge and the Literature of Sensibility*. London: Vision Press, 1978.

De Quincey, Thomas. *The Collected Writings of Thomas de Quincey*. Ed. David Masson, 14 vols. Edinburgh: A. & C. Black, 1889–90.

Derrida, Jacques, *Writing and Difference*. Trans. Alan Bass. London: RKP, 1978.

Eliot, T. S. *The Use of Poetry and the Use of Criticism: Studies in the Relation of Criticism to Poetry in England*. London: Faber, 1933.

Emmet, Dorothy. 'Coleridge on the Growth of the Mind', *Bulletin of the John Rylands Library*, 34 (1952) 276–95.

Engell, James. *The Creative Imagination: Enlightenment to Romanticism*. Cambridge, MA: Harvard UP, 1981.

Erdman, David V. 'Coleridge on Coleridge: The Context (and Text) of His Review of *Mr. Coleridge's Second Lay Sermon*', *SR*, 1 (1961) 47–64.

Esposito, Joseph L. *Schelling's Idealism and Philosopy of Nature*. Lewisburg, PA: Bucknell UP, 1977.

Fairchild, H. N. *Religious Trends in English Poetry*, Vol. 3. *1780–1830: Romantic Faith*. New York: Columbia UP, 1949.

——. 'Hartley, Pistorius, and Coleridge', *PMLA*, 62 (1947) 1010–21.

Fichte, J. G. *Science of Knowledge* (1794). Trans. Peter Heath and John Lachs. Cambridge: CUP, 1982.

Fields, Beverly. *Reality's Dark Dream: Dejection in Coleridge*. Kent, OH: Kent State UP, 1967.

Fisch, Audrey A., Mellor, Anne K., and Schor, Esther M. (eds). *The Other Mary Shelley*. Oxford: OUP, 1993.

Fogle, R. H. *The Idea of Coleridge's Criticism*. Berkeley, CA: University of Calfornia Press, 1962.

Ford, Jennifer. *Coleridge on Dreaming: Romanticism, Dreams, and the Medical Imagination*. Cambridge: CUP, 1998.

Fruman, Norman H. *Coleridge: The Damaged Archangel*. London: Allen & Unwin, 1972.

Fulford, T. *Coleridge's Figurative Language*. London: Macmillan, 1991.

Garrett, Clarke. *Respectable Folly: Millenarians and the French Revolution in France and England*. Baltimore, MD: Johns Hopkins UP, 1975.

Godwin, William. *An Enquiry Concerning Political Justice and its Influence on Modern Morals and Happiness*. Ed. I. Kramnick. Harmondsworth: Penguin, 1976.

Gravil, Richard and Lefebure, Molly (eds). *The Coleridge Connection: Essays for Thomas McFarland*. London: Macmillan, 1990.

Gravil, Richard et al. (eds). *Coleridge's Imagination: Essays in Memory of Pete Laver*. Cambridge: CUP, 1985.

Grow, Lynn Merle. 'The Prose Style of Samuel Taylor Coleridge'. PhD Dissertation, University of Southern California, 1971.

Hamilton, Paul. *Coleridge's Poetics*. Oxford: Blackwell, 1983.

Harding, Anthony. *Coleridge and the Idea of Love: Aspects of Relationship in Coleridge's Thought and Writing*. London: CUP, 1974.

——. *Coleridge and the Inspired Word*. Kingston, Ontario: McGill-Queen's UP, 1985.

Hartley, David. *Observations on Man: His Frame, His Duty, and His Expectations*, 2 vols. London, 1749.

Hartman, Geoffrey H. (ed.). *New Perspectives on Coleridge and Wordsworth: Selected Papers from the English Institute*. New York: Columbia UP, 1972.

Haven, Richard. 'Coleridge, Hartley, and the Mystics', *JHI*, 20 (1959) 477–94.

Hazlitt, William. *The Complete Works of William Hazlitt*. Ed. P. P. Howe, 21 vols. London: Dent, 1930–4.

Hegel, G. W. F. *The Difference Between Fichte's and Schelling's System of Philosophy*. Trans. H. S. Harris and Walter Cerf. Albany, NY: State University of New York Press, 1977.

——. *Phenomenology of Spirit*. Trans. A. V. Miller. Oxford: Clarendon, 1977.

Hill, Geoffrey. *The Lords of Limit: Essays on Literature and Ideas*. London: Deutsch, 1984.

Hipple, Walter John, Jr. *The Beautiful, The Sublime, and The Picturesque in Eighteenth-Century British Aesthetic Theory*. Carbondale, Ill.: Southern Illinois UP, 1957.

Holmes, Richard. *Coleridge*. Oxford: OUP, 1982.

Houston, Robert W. 'Coleridge's Psychometaphysics', *Thoth*, 9 (1968) 14–24.

Howard, Claud. *Coleridge's Idealism: A Study of Its Relationship to Kant and to the Cambridge Platonists*. Boston: R. G. Badger, [1924].

Hume, David. *Enquiries Concerning Human Understanding and Concerning the Principles of Morals*. Ed. L. A. Selby-Bigge. Oxford: OUP, 1975.

——. *A Treatise of Human Nature: Being an Attempt to Introduce the Experimental Method of Reasoning into Moral Subjects*. Ed. L. A. Selby-Bigge. Oxford: Clarendon, 1978.

Hunt, Bishop C., Jr. 'Coleridge and the Endeavor of Philosophy', *PMLA*, 91 (1976) 829–39.

Inge, William Ralph. *The Philosophy of Plotinus*, 2 vols. London: Longman, 1918; 1923.

——. *The Platonic Tradition in English Religious Thought*. London: Longman, 1926.

Jackson, H. J. 'Coleridge, Etymology and Etymologic', *JHI*, 44 (1983) 75–88.

——. *Method and Imagination in Coleridge's Criticism*. London: RKP, 1969.

Jasper, David. *Coleridge as Poet and Religious Thinker: Inspiration and Revelation*. London: Macmillan, 1985.

Jenyns, Soame. *The Works of Soame Jenyns*, 4 vols. London, 1790.

Kallich, Martin. *The Association of Ideas and Critical Theory in Eighteenth-Century England: A History of a Psychological Method in English Criticism*. The Hague: Mouton, 1970.

Kant, Immanuel. *The Critique of Judgement*. Trans. J. C. Meredith. Oxford: Clarendon, 1952.

——. *Critique of Practical Reason*. Trans. Lewis White Beck. Chicago: Chicago UP, 1949.

——. *Critique of Pure Reason*. Trans. Norman Kemp Smith. London: Macmillan, 1929; 1933.

——. *Groundwork of the Metaphysic of Morals* (1785). Trans. H. J. Paton. New York: Harper & Row, 1964.

——. *Kant's Latin Writings: Translations, Commentaries, and Notes*. Ed. Lewis White Beck. New York: Lang, 1986.

——. *Observations on the Feeling of the Beautiful and Sublime*. Trans. John T. Goldthwaite. Berkeley, CA: University of California Press, 1960.

Keats, John. *The Letters of John Keats, 1814–1821*. Ed. H. E. Rollins, 2 vols. Cambridge, MA: Harvard UP, 1958.

——. *The Poetical Works of John Keats*. Ed. H. W. Garrod. Oxford: Clarendon, 1939.

Kessler, Edward. *Coleridge's Metaphors of Being*. Princeton, NJ: Princeton UP, 1979.

Lamb, Charles and Mary. *The Letters of Charles and Mary Lamb*. Ed. Edwin W. Marrs, Jr. Ithaca, NY: Cornell UP, 1975–.

Law, William. *An Appeal to All that Doubt, or Disbelieve the Truths of the Gospel, Whether they be Deists, Arians, Socianians, or Nominal Christians. In which, the True Grounds and Reasons of the Whole Christian Faith and Life are Plainly and Fully Demonstrated*. London, 1742.

Leask, Nigel. *The Politics of Imagination in Coleridge's Critical Thought*. London: Macmillan, 1988.

Leggett, B. J. 'Why It Must Be Abstract: Stevens, Coleridge, and I. A. Richards', *SR*, 22 (1983) 489–515.

Leibniz, G. W. *Theodicy: Essays on the Goodness of God, the Freedom of Man, and the Origin of Evil*. Trans E. M. Huggard, ed. Austin Farrer. London: RKP, 1951.

Leighton, Robert. *Expository Works*. Ed. P. Doddridge, 2 vols. Edinburgh, 1748.

Lentricchia, Frank. 'Coleridge and Emerson: Prophets of Silence, Prophets of Language', *JAAC*, 32 (1973) 37–46.

Levere, Trevor H. *Poetry Realized in Nature: Samuel Taylor Coleridge and Early Nineteenth-Century Science*. Cambridge: CUP, 1981.

Locke, John. *An Essay Concerning Human Understanding*. Ed. Peter H. Nidditch. Oxford: Clarendon, 1975.

Lockridge, Laurence S. *Coleridge the Moralist*. Ithaca, NY: Cornell UP, 1977.

Lovejoy, A. O. *The Great Chain of Being: A Study of the History of an Idea*. Cambridge, MA: Harvard UP, 1936.

——. 'Coleridge and Kant's Two Worlds', *ELH*, 7 (1940) 341–62.

Lowes, John Livingston. *The Road to Xanadu: A Study in the Ways of the Imagination*. Boston: Houghton Mifflin, 1927.

Lyon, Judson S. 'Romantic Psychology and the Inner Senses: Coleridge', *PMLA*, 81 (1966) 246–60.

McFarland, Thomas. *Coleridge and the Pantheist Tradition*. Oxford: Clarendon Press, 1969.

——. *Paradoxes of Freedom: The Romantic Mystique of a Transcendence*. Oxford: Clarendon, 1996.

——. *Romanticism and the Heritage of Rousseau*. Oxford: Clarendon, 1995.

McGann, Jerome J. *The Romantic Ideology: A Critical Investigation*. Chicago: University of Chicago Press, 1983.

McKenzie, Gordon. *Organic Unity in Coleridge*. Berkeley, CA: University of California Press, 1939.

Mackintosh, Sir James. *A Discourse on the Study of the Law of Nature and Nations*. London, 1799.

McKusick, James C. *Coleridge's Philosophy of Language*. New Haven, CT: Yale UP, 1986.
Magnuson, Paul. *Coleridge's Nightmare Poetry*. Charlottesville, VA: University Press of Virginia, 1974.
Marcel, Gabriel. *Coleridge et Schelling*. Paris: Aubier-Montaigne, 1971.
Marks, Emerson R. 'Means and Ends in Coleridge's Critical Method', *ELH*, 26 (1959) 387–401.
Maskell, Duke. *Coleridge's Prose and 'the present state of our language in its relation to literature'*. Retford: Brynmill, 1983.
Mays, J. C. C. 'Coleridge on Prose'. DPhil Thesis, Oxford University, 1966.
Mee, Jon. *Dangerous Enthusiasm: William Blake and the Culture of Radicalism in the 1790s*. Oxford: Clarendon, 1992.
Mellor, Anne K. *Romanticism and Gender*. London: Routledge, 1993.
Metzger, Lore. 'Coleridge's Vindication of Spinoza: An Unpublished Note', *JHI*, 21 (1960) 279–93.
Mileur, Jean-Pierre. *Vision and Revision: Coleridge's Art of Immanence*. Berkeley, CA: University of California Press, 1982.
Mill, J. S. *Mill on Bentham and Coleridge*. Ed. F. R. Leavis. London: Chatto, 1950.
Milton, John. *A Complete Collection of the Historical, Political, and Miscellaneous Works of John Milton*. Ed. Thomas Birch, 2 vols. London, 1738.
——. *Poetical Works*. Ed. Douglas Bush. Oxford: OUP, 1966.
Mitchell, W. Fraser. *English Pulpit Oratory from Andrewes to Tillotson: A Study of its Literary Aspects*. London: SPCK, 1932.
Modiano, Raimonda. *Coleridge and the Concept of Nature*. London: Macmillan, 1985.
——. 'Coleridge and the Sublime; A Response to Thomas Weiskel's *The Romantic Sublime*', *Wordsworth Circle*, 9 (1978) 110–20.
Monk, Samuel H. *The Sublime: A Study of Critical Theories in XVIII-Century England*. New York: MLA, 1935.
More, Henry. *A Collection of Several Philosophical Writings*. London, 1662.
Muirhead, J. H. *Coleridge as Philosopher*. London: Allen & Unwin, 1930.
——. *The Platonic Tradition in Anglo-Saxon Philosophy*. London: Allen & Unwin, 1931; 1965.
Oken, Lorenz. *Elements of Physiophilosophy*. Trans. A. Tulk. London: Ray Society, 1847.
O'Meara, Dominic J. (ed.). *Neoplatonism and Christian Thought*. Albany, NY: State University of New York Press, 1982.
O'Meara, Thomas Franklin. *Romantic Idealism and Roman Catholicism: Schelling and the Theologians*. Notre Dame, IN: University of Notre Dame Press, 1982.
Orsini, G. N. G. *Coleridge and German Idealism: A Study in the History of Philosophy with Unpublished Materials from Coleridge's Manuscripts*. Carbondale, IL: Southern Illinois UP, 1969.
——. 'Coleridge and Schlegel Reconsidered', *Comparative Literature*, 16 (1964) 97–118.

Osinski, Sister Maria. 'A Study of the Structures of Co-ordination in a Representative Sample of the *Biographia Literaria*'. PhD Dissertation, Catholic University, 1953.
Owen, Huw Parry. 'The Theology of Coleridge', *Critical Quarterly*, 4 (1962) 59–67.
Paley, Morton D. *Coleridge's Later Poetry*. Oxford: Clarendon, 1996.
Paley, William. *The Principles of Moral and Political Philosophy*. London, 1785.
Park, Roy. 'Coleridge and Kant: Poetic Imagination and Practical Reason', *British Journal of Aesthetics*, 8 (1968) 335–46.
——. 'Coleridge: Philosopher and Theologian as Literary Critic', *UTQ*, 38 (1968) 17–33.
Perkins, Mary Anne. *Coleridge's Philosophy: The Logos as Unifying Principle*. Oxford: Clarendon, 1994.
Philp, Mark. *Godwin's Political Justice*. London: Duckworth, 1986.
Pinch, Adela. *Strange Fits of Passion: Epistemologies of Emotion, Hume to Austen*. Stanford, CA: Stanford UP, 1996.
Piper, H. W. *The Active Universe: Pantheism and the Concept of Imagination in the English Romantic Poets*. London: Athlone, 1962.
——. 'The Pantheistic Sources of Coleridge's Early Poetry', *JHI*, 20 (1959) 47–59.
Pistorius, Herman Andrew. *Notes and Additions to Dr. Hartley's Observations on Man.... To Which is Prefixed a Sketch of the Life and Character of Dr. Hartley*. London, 1791.
Plato. *The Republic*. Trans. F. M. Cornford. Oxford: Clarendon, 1941.
Plotinus. *The Enneads*. Trans. Stephen MacKenna. London: Faber, 1956.
——. *An Essay on the Beautiful*. Trans. Thomas Taylor. London, 1792.
Potter, George R. 'Coleridge and the Idea of Evolution', *PMLA*, 40 (1925) 379–97.
Powell, Grosvenor. 'Coleridge's "Imagination" and the Infinite Regress of Consciousness', *ELH*, 39 (1972) 266–78.
Prickett, S. *Coleridge and Wordsworth: The Poetry of Growth*. London: CUP, 1970.
——. *Romanticism and Religion: The Tradition of Coleridge and Wordsworth in the Victorian Church*. Cambridge: CUP, 1976.
Priestley, Joseph. *An Address to the Inhabitants of Birmingham upon the Necessity of Attending to the Philosophy of the Mind – Previous to their Forming a Just or Complete Theory of Education*. Birmingham, 1791.
——. *Disquisitions Relating to Matter and Spirit. To Which is Added, The History of the Philosophical Doctrine Concerning the Origin of the Soul, and the Nature of Matter; with its Influence on Christianity, especially with Respect to the Doctrine of the Pre-Existence of Christ*. London, 1777; Birmingham, 1782.
——. *The Doctrine of Philosophical Necessity Illustrated; Being an Appendix to the Disquisitions Relating to Matter and Spirit*. London, 1777.
——. *An Essay on the First Principles of Government; and on the Nature of Political, Civil, and Religious Liberty*. London, 1768.
——. *Hartley's Theory of the Human Mind, on the Principle of the Association of Ideas; with Essays Relating to the Subject of it*. London, 1775.

——. *Institutes of Natural and Revealed Religion*, 3 vols. London, 1772–4; 2 vols, Birmingham, 1782.

——. *The Present State of Europe Compared with Antient Prophesies; A Sermon, Preached at the Gravel Pit Meeting in Hackney, February 28, 1794*. London, 1794.

Pym, David. *The Religious Thought of Samuel Taylor Coleridge*. Gerards Cross, Bucks.: Smythe, 1978.

Radcliffe, Ann. *A Sicilian Romance*. Ed. Alison Milbank. Oxford: OUP, 1995.

Rea, John D. 'Coleridge's Intimations of Immortality from Proclus', *MP*, 26 (1928) 201–13.

Reid, Nicholas, 'Coleridge and Schelling: The Missing Transcendental Deduction', *SR*, 33 (1994) 451–79.

Reid, Thomas. *Essays on the Intellectual Powers of Man*. Edinburgh, 1785.

Reiman, Donald H. (ed.). *The Romantics Reviewed: Contemporary Reviews of British Romantic Writers*. Part A. *The Lake Poets*, 2 vols. New York: Garland, 1972.

Richards, I. A. *Coleridge on Imagination*. London: Kegan Paul, Trench, Trubner, 1934.

Roe, Nicholas (ed.). *Keats and History*. Cambridge: CUP, 1995.

Rousseau, Jean-Jacques. *The Confessions*. Trans. J. M. Cohen. Harmondsworth: Penguin, 1954.

Russell, Bertrand. *A History of Western Philosophy*. London: Allen & Unwin, 1946.

Sartre, Jean-Paul. *Being and Nothingness: An Essay on Phenomenological Ontology*. Trans. Hazel E. Barnes. London: Methuen, 1957.

Schelling, F. W. J. *The Ages of the World: A Fragment, from Writings Left in Manuscript*. Trans. Frederick de Wolfe Bolman, Jr. New York, 1942.

——. *Of Human Freedom* (1809). Trans. James Gutmann. Chicago: Open Court, 1937.

——. *Sämmtliche Werke*. Ed. K. F. A. Schelling, 14 vols. Stuttgart: Cotta, 1856–61.

——. *System of Transcendental Idealism (1800)* Trans. Peter Heath. Charlottesville, VA: University Press of Virginia, 1978.

Schrickx, W. 'Coleridge and the Cambridge Platonists', *Review of English Literature*, 7 (1966) 71–91.

Seidel, George J. *Activity and Ground: Fichte, Schelling, and Hegel*. Hildesheim: Olms, 1976.

Shelley, Mary. *The Last Man*. Ed. Morton D. Paley. Oxford: OUP, 1994.

——. *Lodore*. Ed. Lisa Vargo. Peterborough, Ontario: Broadview, 1997.

Shelley, P. B. *Shelley's Poetry and Prose*. Eds Donald H. Reiman and Sharon B. Powers. New York: Norton, 1977.

Sherwood, Margaret. *Coleridge's Imaginative Conception of the Imagination*. Wellesley, MA: Hathaway House, 1937.

Simpson, David (ed.). *German Aesthetic and Literary Criticism: Kant, Fichte, Schelling, Schopenhauer, Hegel*. Cambridge: CUP, 1984.

Spinoza, Benedict de. *Complete Works*. Ed. and trans. Edwin Curley. Princeton, NJ: Princeton UP, 1985–.

Stack, George J. *Nietzsche and Emerson: An Elective Affinity*. Athens, OH: Ohio UP, 1992.

Suther, Marshall. *The Dark Night of Samuel Taylor Coleridge*. New York: Columbia UP, 1960.

Swedenborg, Emanuel. *Heaven and Hell; also, the Intermediate State, or World of Spirits; a Relation of Things Heard and Seen*. Trans. J. Clowes. London: Swedenborg Society, 1850.

Tennyson, A. *The Poems of Tennyson*. Ed. Christopher Ricks. London: Longman, 1969.

Tooke, John Horne. *'Επεα Πτερόεντα, or, The Diversions of Purley*, 2 vols. London, 1786–1805; Menston, Yorks.: Scolar Press, 1968.

Vallins, D. 'Production and Existence: Coleridge's Unification of Nature', *JHI*, 56 (1995) 107–24.

Walsh, W. H. *Kant's Criticism of Metaphysics*. Edinburgh: Edinburgh UP, 1975.

Watson, George. *Coleridge the Poet*. London: Routledge, 1966.

Webb, Timothy. *Shelley: A Voice Not Understood*. Manchester: Manchester UP, 1977.

Weiskel, Thomas. *The Romantic Sublime: Studies in the Structure and Psychology of Transcendence*. Baltimore, MD: Johns Hopkins UP, 1976.

Wellek, René. *Immanuel Kant in England, 1793–1838*. Princeton, NJ: Princeton UP, 1931.

Werkmeister, Lucyle. 'Coleridge and Godwin on the Communication of Truth', *MP*, 55 (1958) 170–7.

Whalley, George. 'The Aristotle–Coleridge Axis', *UTQ*, 42 (1973), 93–109.

——. 'The Bristol Library Borrowings of Southey and Coleridge, 1793–8', *Library*, 4 (1949) 114–31.

Wheeler, Kathleen. *The Creative Mind in Coleridge's Poetry*. London: Heinemann, 1981.

——. (ed.). *German Aesthetic and Literary Criticism: The Romantic Ironists and Goethe*. Cambridge: CUP, 1985.

——. *Romanticism, Pragmatism, and Deconstruction*. Oxford: Blackwell, 1993.

——. *Sources, Processes and Methods in Coleridge's 'Biographia Literaria'*. Cambridge: CUP, 1980.

White, Alan. *Schelling: An Introduction to the System of Freedom*. New Haven, CT: Yale UP, 1983.

Wiley, Margaret L. 'Coleridge and the Wheels of Intellect', *PMLA*, 67 (1952) 101–12.

Willey, Basil. *Nineteenth Century Studies: Coleridge to Matthew Arnold*. London: Chatto, 1949.

Williamson, George. *The Senecan Amble: A Study of Prose Form from Bacon to Collier*. London: Faber, 1951.

Wlecke, Albert O. *Wordsworth and the Sublime*. Berkeley, CA: University of California Press, 1973.

Wood, Barry. 'The Growth of the Soul: Coleridge's Dialectical Method and the Strategy of Emerson's "Nature"', *PMLA*, 91 (1976) 385–97.

Wordsworth, William. *The Poetical Works of William Wordsworth*. Ed. E. De Selincourt and Helen Darbishire, 5 vols. Oxford: Clarendon, 1940–9.

——. *The Prose Works of William Wordsworth*. Ed. W. J. B. Owen and J. Worthington Smyser, 3 vols. Oxford: Clarendon, 1974.

Wylie, Ian. *Young Coleridge and the Philosophers of Nature*. Oxford: Clarendon, 1989.

——. 'How the Natural Philosophers Defeated the Whore of Babylon in the Thought of S. T. Coleridge', *Review of English Studies*, New Series, 35 (1984) 494–507.

Index